796.334.

D1461668

LIVERPOOL CULT HEROES

LEO MOYNIHAN

LIVERPOOL CULT HEROES

LEO MOYNIHAN

First published by Pitch Publishing, 2014

Pitch Publishing
A2 Yeoman Gate
Yeoman Way
Durrington
BN13 3QZ
www.pitchpublishing.co.uk

A CIP catalogue record is available for this book from the
British Library.

ISBN 978-1-90962-651-5

Typesetting and origination by Pitch Publishing

Printed in Great Britain

Contents

To the 96 fans who lost
their lives at Hillsborough
on 15 April 1989

Introduction

The Kop is not the members' enclosure at Ascot, and nor does it regret it.

Arthur Hopcraft, writer

JOEY Jones – that most wonderful of Cult Heroes – tells a funny story. In 1977, Liverpool played FC Zurich in the semi-finals of the European Cup. The second leg (an easy 3–0 win to secure a 6–1 aggregate win) at Anfield ends with Joey swapping his shirt with Swiss international, Rene Botteron. Joey has a few beers and goes home, his Zurich shirt very much still with him and now among his impressive collection.

A few days later, a guy walking along the street approaches Joey and says he's got hold of one of his shirts. 'How did you get that then?' asks Joey.

'My missus is a cleaner at the Holiday Inn and she was clearing up in one of the rooms and found it. One of the Zurich players had left it behind.'

Joey Jones – and his shirt – might not hold a massive amount of sway in European circles but walk among a group of Liverpool fans and ask who ate the frogs legs, who made the Swiss roll and who then munched on 'Gladbach, and you will only get smiles and dreamy tales of Rome and a left-back called Joey Jones.

Cult Heroes don't have to have opponents queuing up to bag their shirts. Some might but mostly they aren't about that. Cult Heroes and the affection they garner isn't as simple as the goals they score or stop. The *Oxford English Dictionary* explains the term by suggesting a Cult

Hero is, 'Greatly admired by a small audience or is influential despite limited commercial success.' It's a basic definition that can't try to explain the sometimes unexplainable reasons a football fan can take to a player, but it does help get to the bottom of why some of the greatest men ever to pull on Liverpool red aren't in the next few hundred pages.

Writing a book on Liverpool that includes the word HERO but doesn't include chapters on Kenny Dalglish, Ian Rush, Steven Gerrard, Roger Hunt or Billy Liddell did cause the odd sleepless hour or so, but here's the thing; those players were universally idolised, they were heroes, they were legends, they were the best. Cult Heroes? No.

In this book I wanted to explore other players who have hugely contributed to the club's rich tapestry of success and history, but who also tickled something extra in those who came to watch them.

Take Jamie Carragher. Anfield, May 2005. The Champions League semi-final. Chelsea are in town and Jose Mourinho is getting as frustrated as his strikers as Liverpool resolutely defend their early one-goal lead. Mourinho steps from his dug-out and chastises Luis Garcia. The Portuguese thinks he's diving.

Now, the run to Istanbul is famous for many amazing goals, blocks and saves but Carragher marching over to the Chelsea manager and reminding him that his old Porto team was the most cynical he'd ever seen, is as memorable for other reasons. Then, when Carragher is finished, he tells the Chelsea manager to 'fuck off'. See, that sort of thing stays with fans as much as the goals and the blocks and the saves.

Some of the players here are greats too. Carragher for one. Alex Raisbeck in the 1900s, Elisha Scott in the 1920s and 1930s, Ian St John, Ray Kennedy, Steve Nicol, John Barnes, Luis Suarez; they all make a great case for making an all-time Liverpool XI. They also offered something more. Something distant but fantastic. Something that is a step away from the great things they did with the ball.

I will have missed some out of course. People have got in touch and asked, 'Is Ronnie Rosenthal in then? Is Titi Camara in? How about Tommy Lawrence? Is Torben Piechnik in?' Now the first three all have a case, but Piechnik? No. People mustn't get confused with a cult and a poor player. None of the guys in this book are that.

Writing about them all – and talking to plenty of them – has been a pleasure. By researching the likes of Albert Stubbins and Elisha Scott, I often felt like Kevin Costner in that wonderfully sentimental baseball movie, *Field of Dreams*. The more I discovered and the more I learnt, the more I was sure those old-timers in their baggy shorts and woollen jumpers had come out of the corn and were kicking a ball about in my garden.

I hope you enjoy reading it as much as I did writing it and yes, I hope you scream at some of the selections and demand to know why your favourite Cult Hero hasn't made the cut.

You'll Never Walk Alone.

Leo Moynihan, September 2014

Foreword

by Gary McAllister

WHEN I first arrived at Liverpool in the summer of 2000, I did so very much thinking of the players who had been at this wonderful club before me. Specifically, the Scottish players. I was ambitious and I wanted to win things at the club but I was also very much aware of what those players from north of the border had achieved over the years.

Ian St John, Kenny Dalglish, Graeme Souness, Alan Hansen; legends in the game and I genuinely didn't want to let them down. I had it at Leeds too. I looked at the greats there; Billy Bremner, Eddie Gray and Peter Lorimer; you want to impress and live up to those standards.

Soon though, you settle and whilst you always want to win trophies and be as successful as you can be, I found I had a huge connection with the supporters at Anfield. There is something about the crowd at Liverpool. Yes, they are a knowledgeable lot, able to support opponents as well as rip them to shreds, and yes they are capable of making their ground so much more than merely a sporting arena; but there is something extra, something special.

Maybe it's because I won things at Liverpool but I do, to this day, feel a very real bond with the fans. I was lucky to celebrate with them. We won a treble and that open top bus in May 2001 was unbelievable. Scary but unbelievable. After that sort of acclaim and mutual appreciation, you can never let go. You have looked into the eyes of those fans and seen what the club means to them. You've worked hard, you've given the team everything and you have won a trophy, or in our case three.

That's great. But then you also see what it means to the people and you are lifted even higher.

You can get good wages as a player, you can look at the medal collection and you can watch re-runs of glorious goals and games, but you can't beat that feeling you get when you see the pure joy on the faces of the men, women and children who have travelled all over the place to watch and support you. It might sound a wee bit romantic and a cliché, but to be able to look back and think of those people, you do smile, and you say to yourself, 'That's why I did it. That was good.'

A club like Liverpool gets under your skin and the place's heart and soul is that connection between player and fan. I got Scousers immediately. Having Robbie Fowler, Stevie Gerrard and Carra in the dressing room helped of course and from the off I enjoyed the company of the locals.

I remember once at Bradford, I had scored a free kick. Right in the top corner. Lovely. About 15 minutes later, we got another and once again I took it, this time missing the post by about a foot. As I strolled away, our travelling fans started to sing, 'You don't know what you're doing.' That made me laugh. That is the sort of humour that connects us Jocks and the Scousers.

It's fantastic to be involved with a book like Leo Moynihan's that celebrates that connection between player and fan. To be considered a hero of any sort at a club as special as Liverpool Football Club is an honour, and to be in a book with Carra and Robbie again brings back a wealth of wonderful memories. Memories I hope you have as much pleasure reliving as I did playing for your football club.

Enjoy the book.

Gary McAllister, September 2014

Acknowledgements

I'D like to thank Paul Camillin at Pitch Publishing. Delivery on this book certainly went into extra-time and penalties, so thank you Paul for your patience. Thanks also to Graham Hales, Duncan Olner, Derek Hammond, Paul Dalling and Alasdair Norrie for all their work on the project.

Thanks especially to the players for all the memories and for those able to talk to me. Thank you John Barnes, Jamie Carragher, Peter Cormack, Luis Garcia, Joey Jones and Steve Nicol. Thank you Gary McAllister for the great chat and for a great foreword. That's right up there with your derby goal and your baldy head mate!

Thanks so much to the following for their constant support and for their help in making this book possible: Frans Adelaar, Michael Aitchison, Tammy Aitchison, Matt Allen, Neil Atkinson, Patrick Barclay, Justyn Barnes, Ian Callaghan, Peter Etherington, Brian Glanville, Marty Flynn, James Lawton, Kira Milmo, Marc Milmo, Peter Marshall, Louis Massarella, Nick Moore, Eli Nathenson, Laura Nathenson, Kevin O'Rourke, Mark Platt, Sam Pilger, Gareth Roberts, Mark Riches, Less Scott, Simon 'Shakey' Shakeshaft, Ian 'Iggy' Shaw, Kevin Taylor, Gavin Whitfield, Janneke Versteeg and Geoff Young.

Thank you to the good people at LFCHistory.net. A valuable site, brilliantly put together.

Finally, thanks to my six-year-old daughter Daisy who now loves, 'Our favourite bird'.

Alex Raisbeck

1898–1909
Appearances: 341
Goals: 19

L ESS than a decade in, but they came. Less than a decade in, and there they were, in their droves. Less than ten years since their club's birth and here were their team – for the first time in their young history – champions of England. The best around. And so they came.

Liverpool had won their last game of the 1900/01 season at West Bromwich Albion to claim the title, and crowds had gathered at Liverpool's Central Station to welcome them home. This act of mass appreciation would of course in the club's rich future become common practice but today, this was new and this was wonderful.

Some squads returning from glorious travels would be greeted by seemingly millions, as they travelled home from far and wide to show off the spoils of war. Track, road and air would be used to transport glorious teams in the future but today, for the first time it was the former and the crowds gathered with a novel glow.

This wasn't 2005. A hundred and four years later the team returning from Istanbul with the European Cup were met by their own Bosphorus river of red as they showed off the famous trophy for the fifth time. This was different, more conservative, more Edwardian in its manner but no matter, hordes of locals made their way to meet the train carrying their men.

The train's engine pulls into the station. A fife and drum band strikes up 'The Conquering Hero', perfect for a team and its individuals who have become more than just footballers at the local club. They have captured an emotion, awoken something in supporters who now see them as just that, conquering heroes.

Steam filled the platform as the engine stopped but then there he was. Amid the train's clouds and the grey Edwardian suits, there was this shock of blonde hair and as he stepped off the train onto Liverpool soil, hats soared toward the station's 65m-arched roof and cheers rang out. This was their captain, their first superstar. This was Alex Raisbeck.

The bond between heroes in red and those who have travelled from Tottenham to Tokyo to watch them would be part of the very essence of the football club for decades to come, but this was arguably the first; the one that set that bond in stone.

Ask many with a long lasting interest in Liverpool to name an all-time XI and Alex Raisbeck will often be the name on the team-sheet that raises an eyebrow. Those picking such teams though aren't being clever for clever's sake. The football hipster is a new breed of football fan that will take pleasure in telling the pub about what they are missing if they aren't watching German football or how the next big thing will actually be the Norwegian first division.

Those who tell you Raisbeck deserves his place in an all-time Anfield XI are not football hipsters. They are looking at the facts and the facts tell you that not many players had an impact on the football club like Raisbeck, a defender who arrived, galvanised, inspired and ultimately deserves to be talked about in the same conversation as Liddell, Dalglish and Gerrard.

Signed from Hibernian in his native Scotland, Raisbeck arrived at Anfield in 1898 and whilst the club had settled into the new choppy waters of Association Football in the first six years since they were formed, they and their fans – themselves trying to get a foothold above their city rivals, Everton – were in need of a push, a player to bring more than amateurish enthusiasm. They needed something special and in Raisbeck they got just that.

Liverpool Football Club was formed in 1892; the product of a good old fashioned boozy row. Everton had been founded in 1878, but the board were soon to fall out with the club president and landlord, John Houlding, a prominent local businessman and brewer.

The 1880s had seen Association Football flourish on Merseyside and in the city of Liverpool. Clubs were popping up everywhere and the Liverpool Cup competition – formed in 1886 – attracted 20 clubs, including Everton.

Football though hadn't always been an easy sell in an area traditionally more taken with both rugby and cricket. In 1878, the city had not one football club, as the upper and middle classes trying to bring the sport from their public schools to the masses, found an unwilling audience in the working class population of Liverpool. John Williams in his brilliant history of Liverpool Football Club writes:

'There were plenty of returning ex-Harrow public schoolboys living in Liverpool who might have been expected to spread Association Football. But because of the stark divisions between rich and poor in the city, sport could not be so easily passed down from local social elites, as had happened elsewhere. And, in any case, the poor in Liverpool's docklands had neither the space nor the good health to play sport.'

Those working people in Liverpool also didn't have the free time afforded to others around the country. The Ten Hours Act passed in 1847 had eventually seen East Lancashire textile workers' hours reduced and they were granted a one o'clock finish on Saturdays from 1874.

From the mid 1870s most men in Birmingham did not even work on Saturdays and playing football and cricket became common practice. In Liverpool, dockworkers wouldn't see free Saturday afternoons until 1890 and by then the Football League was two years old.

The 1880s though had seen the tide turn. 1882 saw over a thousand fans watch an exhibition match on Stanley Park and a year later the local press were carrying results from the newly formed FA Cup competition.

By now Everton had been founded, firstly as St Domingo, a Methodist Church parish that offered locals both cricket and Association Football. This was common practice. Football often stemmed mainly from religious groups and churches. Four of the five Merseyside clubs that would play professional football originated from religious groups.

As mentioned Association Football had been born in the nation's public schools; Victorian institutions hell-bent on ensuring the moral wellbeing of the future ruling classes and beyond. Football was celebrated for its cleansing properties, a way to save both the young and the urban poor from themselves.

The laws of football had been written up and agreed upon in 1862 and embraced by schools such as Eton and Harrow. Effeminate characteristics in boys had to be quashed, individualism outlawed and the sport of football was seen as key in doing this and eradicating supposedly evil sexual desires.

The headmaster at Harrow in 1895 even sewed up the boys' pockets; such was his and society's fear of sexual freedom. Victorian men were constantly advised to 'master the beast'.

It was amid this puritanical backdrop that Liverpool Football Club was formed. Everton were playing their games at Anfield, near Stanley Park and were attracting good crowds for their Football League games.

The stadium was owned by the less God-fearing John Houlding who charged a competitive rent that he felt was fair for a ground described in 1889 by the local press as a 'huge circus, with its two immense galleries, rising tier after tier, and its covered stands, stretching the length of the ground.'

Houlding also owned the Sandon Hotel near the ground, in which the players would change and plenty of his beer would be sold (he also wanted the stuff to be exclusively sold in his stadium). The Methodist board at Everton began to get twitchy about their president's off-field business interests and when Houlding – in his mind fairly – raised the rent, relations broke down and the club eventually broke away, buying a new plot of land on Mere Green in Walton, a spot that would eventually become Goodison Park.

A frustrated Houlding tried to keep one step ahead and register the name of Everton Football Club but was usurped by his old tenants and so this forward-thinking, ambitious man was left with a football stadium but no team to play in it.

As ever, Houlding thought big. Who wants a name that is so localised anyway? Everton wasn't big enough? Why not go the whole hog? Liverpool Football Club and Athletic Grounds Company Limited was created on 3 June 1892 and Houlding along with those who had stayed loyal to him following the split had to go about creating a team that would attract the punters and eventually compete at the highest level.

There would be hoops to jump through though. The fledgling club applied to the Football League for immediate membership but their request was declined. Houlding smelt a rat and was sure the Everton board had wielded their influence on the Football League's committee and blocked the move.

'[Liverpool FC] didn't comply with regulations,' said the League, but with a fine stadium, good financial backing and in an area more than warming to the sport and on the cusp of fanatical support, there was an air of mischief to the decision. No matter, the club and its founding fathers would persevere.

For now the Lancashire League would have to do and so the priority was to get men, good men, to wear the kit and call themselves Liverpool Football Club players. Players. Those hundreds of men who over the years have persevered, stumbled, entertained, broken hearts, bled and excelled all in the name of Liverpool.

Fans would come to love them, scorn at them, painfully will them on and of course envy them. Kenny Dalglish, that master of his craft and arguably the best of them once scored one of those goals where in a whirl of red he has turned a defender inside out before battering the poor ball into the pained rigging.

After the game, he was asked how he did it. 'I just shut my eyes and hit it,' he said.

If only it was that easy and how those fans – who over the years have yearned to just shut their eyes and hit it – have come to look on Dalglish's breed as godlike heroes, wishing away the days until they could next get to the match and see them. For now though, there weren't any and the club had to start casting their net.

Everton had won the league championship in 1891 and so to lure those who had achieved that wasn't going to be easy. The big coup for Houlding and his directors was the skipper Andrew Hannah, a Scottish right-back and it was from north of the border (like so often throughout the club's history) that many of the new players would call home.

On Thursday 1 September, Liverpool FC played a friendly against Rotherham Town and two days later their first competitive game against Higher Walton in the Lancashire League, a game they won 8–0 in front of a couple of hundred curious fans. Ten of the players were Scottish, whilst one – Joe Pearson – was a Scouser. Locals might have wondered just how representative this Liverpool team were, but with the Lancashire League won that season, those intrepid first fans were soon supporting a Football League club.

Attendances had risen dramatically and whilst not as healthy as Everton, the club was competing. Yes there was relegation in 1895, but they bounced straight back and in 1896 appointed their first manager, Tom Watson formerly of Sunderland and regarded as one of the great footballing men around.

Watson was a forward-thinking boss. Tobacco for example should be 'sparingly used' and he set about building a team that came spine-tinglingly close to winning a first title in 1899, only to lose their last winner-takes-all match at league stalwarts Aston Villa.

By now Watson's team had a spine; a strength respected around the country and at its heart was Alex Raisbeck. A Scottish international, a powerhouse and a winner the club and its growing army of fans could pin their hopes on.

Alexander Galloway Raisbeck was born in Stirling in 1878, but more importantly moved to Larkhall in Lanarkshire as a young boy. Important because of the area's prolific cradling of footballing talent that would one day include Jock Stein and Sir Matt Busby.

The Raisbeck family lived opposite a common and it was on that stretch of grass that Raisbeck honed his skills. He and his six brothers were to be found 'chasing the leather', as much as their free time allowed it. They were hours well spent.

Like so many in the area, a life in the mines beckoned for Raisbeck, but he had shown real talent playing for Larkhall Thistle aged just 15. Here he played at outside-right, an explanation for why – although he played at centre-back for most of his career – he was so comfortable on the ball. He was signed by Edinburgh giants Hibernian and on 12 September 1896, made his debut in a 2–2 draw with Abercorn.

Raisbeck shone immediately, impressing those in his own country and of course those south of the border. Having played 29 games (he scored four goals) Raisbeck was loaned out to Stoke City, a club struggling to avoid relegation from Division One at the end of the 1897/98 season. A play-off system was in place back then and thanks largely to Raisbeck's impressive displays, the club from the Potteries survived.

It seemed certain that Stoke would make their move and sign the defender, but instead Raisbeck headed north once more. It is unclear whether Stoke simply refused to pay the money needed to guarantee Raisbeck's services; they were due to meet the Hibernian chairman, but instead failed to turn up.

One man who was with the Hibernian officials that day though was Liverpool's astute manager, Tom Watson. Watson made it his business to know of talent and especially talent that might just be available. Watson made his move, agreed a £350 fee to the Edinburgh side, and convinced Raisbeck that his playing future was with Liverpool.

Liverpool had finished mid-table but they were a club on the up. Everton may have been the big spenders of the time (the Blues paid out a huge £5,787 on new players during the 1898/99 season) but it was their neighbours who under Watson were building something; catching the eye.

Eighteeen thousand fans turned out at Anfield for the first game of the season, a 4–0 thumping of The Wednesday. Raisbeck made his debut, impressed with his strength, guile and never-say-die lung-busting bombasity. The fans were beginning to come and now they were beginning to adore their heroes.

Those 18,000 fans would have left Anfield on that early September evening, proud and hopeful of their team, just as they were of their city; for decades a place that enjoyed worldwide fame as arguably the world's foremost port. John Masefield, a well-travelled and eminent writer of the time and future poet laureate compared the Thames in London to Liverpool's famous river and port:

'It is a wretched river compared to the Mersey, and the ships are not like the Liverpool ships, and the docks barren of beauty… It is a beastly hole after Liverpool; for Liverpool is the town of my heart and I would rather sail a mudflat there than command a clipper ship out of London.'

For centuries, Liverpool had built its reputation as a thriving port, attracting thousands and thousands of immigrants from as close as Wales and as far as China. Yes, this was a city buzzing with trade, poverty and wealth in equal extremes, crime, drunkenness and religious diversity. In 1839, Herman Melville, then merely a cabin boy who had sailed from New York (his novel *Moby Dick* wasn't written until 1851), arrived in Liverpool and was taken by the sheer madness of its port and streets:

'In the evening, especially when the sailors are gathered in great numbers, these streets present a most singular spectacle, the entire population of the vicinity being seemingly turned into them. Hand organs, fiddles and cymbals, plied by strolling musicians, mix with the songs of the seamen, the babble of women and children, and the groaning and whining of beggars… Sailors love this Liverpool; and upon long voyages to distant parts of the globe, will be continually dilating on its charms and attractions, and extolling it above all other seaports in the word.'

It was a reputation that had continued to grow, as had its population, reaching over 700,000 by 1901. In 1880 it was granted city status and of course away from those docks, the pursuit of footballing glory was firmly on the peoples' agenda.

Football as a pastime and an organised spectacle had thrived in cities all over Britain. Liverpool had come relatively late to the party but like so many industrial hubs, the game was becoming bigger and bigger to city folk everywhere.

That wonderful sportswriter, Geoffrey Green summed it up when he wrote: 'Football is the game that grew to its full powers in the cities. Unlike the gentle rhythm of cricket, which is of the soft English countryside, this football is the product of town dwellers. It is full of passion and emotion. It is strident and raucous. It symbolises the hopes and disappointments of the people who are imprisoned within the high walls of brick and mortar.'

Those who called their collection of bricks and mortar Liverpool and who now called themselves fans of the football club with the same name, by now had a fine team and the 1898/99 campaign – although ending in disappointment – underlined the massive strides now taken on and off the pitch. Defeat to Aston Villa on the last day of the season cost them the title. A semi-final defeat at the hands of Sheffield United caused further heartache but the team was now noticed and so was Raisbeck.

Despite his young age, Raisbeck had proved a powerhouse in red (the colour adopted by the club in 1896; they had previously worn Everton's hand-me-down blue and white shirts). A box-to-box man, a defender yes, but a man with incredible stamina and footballing nous able to turn defence into attack in a swashbuckling instant. At 5ft 10in he was tall for the age and used that height brilliantly, rarely losing an aerial challenge.

Built like Gerrard, with the defensive wherewithal of Sami Hyypia and the competitive qualities of Graeme Souness, Raisbeck was the complete player and the fans adored him. He was Gerrard the box-to-box player we fans fell in love within the 2000s but also the Gerrard who has wowed crowds with his defensive discipline in the latter part of his career. He was both Steven Gerrards, all rolled into one and oh, how the fans loved him for it.

The blonde hair and the lush moustache gave Raisbeck that boys-own Edwardian style, but don't be fooled by the position he played. In Raisbeck's day the centre-half was the team's number 10. Sure he also had to stop attacks but he would start them too.

From the days of village versus village games played between 50 plus people chasing a pig's bladder, football had gentrified itself, laws had been drawn up, but going into the 1880s refined passing and tactics were still rarities.

A columnist wrote in the *Scottish Umpire* in 1884 that, 'Take any club that has come to the front and the onward strides will be found to date from the hour when the rough and tumble gave place to swift accurate passing and attending to the leather rather than the degraded desire merely to coup an opponent.'

Cerebral passing was starting to be embraced and soon so was a more considered approach to players' positions. The idea of six forwards (with two centre-forwards often getting in each other's way) was being re-thought and a new 2–3–5 formation meant a new position was born and embraced, that of the centre-back.

Jonathan Wilson in his excellent book, *Inverting The Pyramid* writes, 'The gradual spread of 2–3–5 meant that the centre-half soon became the fulcrum of the team, a figure far removed from the dour stopper he would become. He was a multi-skilled all rounder, defender and attacker, leader and instigator, goal-scorer and destroyer. He was, as the great Austrian football writer Willy Meisel put it, "the most important man on the field".'

At Liverpool, Raisbeck was certainly that and with gifted players around him, honours started to be challenged for. After the disappointment of 1899, Liverpool finished a deflated tenth but then came that push for a first title and the inaugural tag of champions.

Liverpool got off to a flying start and destroyed back-to-back title winners Aston Villa 5–1 at Anfield to cement their ascendency. Raisbeck was 'ever prominent with head and feet', whilst new signing Sam Raybould was providing the goals.

A trip to Goodison Park in the September had warranted only a point but Raisbeck's performance was the standout, especially to the correspondent at the *Liverpool Mercury*. '[Raisbeck was] the prominent figure in every movement whether of attack or defence… Now taking the ball clean from opponents' toes, now urging on his forwards with a well judged pass, now darting to the assistance of his backs and checking many a dangerous rush. Always when danger threatened or opportunity presented itself was the light-haired Scot.'

The return fixture at Anfield in January saw Raisbeck and his opposing skipper, Jimmy Settle discuss abandoning the game at 1–1 due to the torrential rain. The crowd began to sing, 'Play the Game' and so on they went, but it was Everton who prevailed with a late winner.

Three days later Queen Victoria died and whilst there was immediate shock, the *Liverpool Review* noted that, 'The city of Liverpool went about its business pretty much as if little or nothing had happened.'

The death of a monarch couldn't sway the city from an optimism that saw businesses thriving. The docks were planning expansion on a huge scale and whilst Victoria's death saddened many, life was good.

Suddenly though, things were not so good at Anfield. Defeat to Everton was followed by an FA Cup defeat at Notts County and then another league setback at Bolton. Then that same optimism flowed back into the club with the sort of run that would win so many later titles. Eleven games unbeaten saw Liverpool top the table and that last day win at West Bromwich Albion meant the league championship – for the first time – was theirs. As the team returned to the city, there were those fans.

'Long before 11 o'clock last night,' wrote the *Daily Post* on 30 April 1901, 'a large concourse of people assembled on the Central Station.' They had come to cheer, to lift their heroes aloft as way of appreciation for the glory they had bestowed upon this now thriving and proud set of fans.

The rather rotund manager Tom Watson was given the hero treatment although, according to the *Post*'s observer, 'No arms were long enough to grip his girth and no muscle strong enough to lift him up.'

Watson had shown a talent for management as large as that waistline and thanks largely to his skipper, the team had blossomed into the best around.

Captain and talisman, Raisbeck's ability was never in question and his popularity among the fans wouldn't waver but the club's fortunes were about to go on a short, sharp rollercoaster ride that would see Liverpool go from champions, to also-rans, to relegation, to promotion and back up to champions again all in only half a decade.

Relegation was a bitter pill to swallow. A 5–2 hammering at Goodison on April Fool's Day in 1904 was a blow and the joke might have been on the Reds when fellow relegation strugglers Stoke won easily at the same ground just days later to cement Tom Watson's side's fate.

Promotion occurred swiftly and without fuss. Liverpool lost just three games and Raisbeck was once again instrumental in their good form. Second Division sides were dismantled with ease and so an FA Cup tie against Everton caused many Reds to believe that a 'shock' was on the cards. Everton drew at Anfield and were fortunate to win the replay at Goodison where Raisbeck was at his swashbuckling best.

'Never has Raisbeck shown more wondrous football,' wrote an observer in the Liverpool programme. 'He was here, there and everywhere. Now initiating an attack, now breaking up another, and again chasing Sharp when that lithe young man appeared to be all on his own. He dominated the whole field, and was, without question, the one superlative player. I am never inclined to over-elaborate praise, but truly, Alec Raisbeck was a giant among pigmies.'

Watson was confident that his side wouldn't just survive back in the top-flight but could compete and even win it again. He was right. Three heavy defeats wasn't a great start to the season but soon they found their groove and with Raisbeck (albeit without his Edwardian moustache – '[Raisbeck] has joined the bare-faced brigade,' remarked one hack) instrumental as ever, the title was for the second time nestled at Anfield.

As, 'Ubiquitous as a sprite' was how the *Daily Post* described Liverpool's great Scot and once again on arriving back from Bolton on the penultimate weekend of the season (Liverpool had lost but so had their closest rivals, Preston North End) they were greeted by hordes of fans, or as the *Daily Post* observed, 'several hundreds of enthusiasts who cheered the players lustily and escorted them to their wagonette.' And so it was off to the Sandon Hotel in Anfield for a party fit for champions.

Fans will have woken with their own sore heads the following morning but – better than any pill – the thought of Raisbeck dominating opponents and games alike will have soothed their boozed-up brows.

Those same fans were rewarded with a new mass of cinder and soil at the southern end of the ground, on Walton Breck Road. That championship season had seen attendances average 18,000 but the Liverpool board recognised that they could get more in and so that summer the new section of Anfield was built.

Other clubs such as Woolwich Arsenal had their Spion Kops, named after the *Spioenkop*, a hill in South Africa that was the scene of a bloody battle in 1900 that cost the lives of thousands of British men; many of them from the Lancashire regiment. Liverpool's new stand would be called the same, and this one would last and last. On it, Raisbeck was the first hero.

The 1905/06 triumph was to be Raisbeck's last glorious moment in Liverpool red. He remained the team's most vital cog, but the wheel wasn't always turning as it should, most notably though when Raisbeck was injured, or in the case of 1907, missing thanks to a long and serious case of diarrhoea.

'Raisbeck is beyond comparison,' wrote an admiring *Daily Post*. 'Raisbeck has been for years the Liver's lucky star – a great, outstanding personality, not only in his team but in the football firmament… Without Alex Raisbeck Liverpool would have to be born again, so to speak. That the redoubtable half-back may regain health and strength during the recess is the earnest prayer of everyone. It is, however, probably a subject which will cause the executive most serious deliberation.'

In 1909, Liverpool's 'lucky star' twinkled for his last ever time for Liverpool. He had played 341 games for the club, scoring 19 times whilst leading the club to the first of many trophies.

Raisbeck played five further seasons back in his home country for Partick Thistle before managing Hamilton Academical, Bristol City, Halifax, Chester and Bath City before returning to Liverpool in 1939 where he served as a scout until his death in March 1949.

The club were – as the *Daily Post* prophesied – born again and in the early 1920s had another multi-championship-winning team but in 1924, 15 years after Raisbeck left, Victor Hall, a writer for the *Liverpool Echo*, reminisced about the greatness he had witnessed in Raisbeck and the player the fans had skipped to Anfield to see more than any other. A player who Hall remarked – as well as raising supporters' pulses – had, 'Raised Liverpool's prestige.'

'Let us recall his characteristics,' wrote Hall. 'Tall, lithe, sinuous, and yet gifted with muscular and physical development beyond the ordinary. Active to a degree, speed either on the turn or in flight, and with niche, at the addition of resourcefulness and judgment that would have been all sufficient in another player, without those added gifts, methodical in training, painstaking in preparation, genial with his players and considerate with his committee. With a perfect blending of the qualities that to make a really great player!

'Raisbeck was wholeheartedly a destroyer of attacks when it came from the opposing wing. We have said that he was speed in turn and on the run. We might amplify this and say, that we have never seen in England, a speedier half-back, who could tackle a speedy forward, turn with him, and overtake and tackle him again. There may be and may have been others so gifted. We have not seen them. His judgment was sound, his valour outstanding and, naturally for a half-back, his control and placing of the ball was equally confident. During his playing career at Anfield, he had to meet forwards whose names and records were outstanding in the history of the game, and yet of none of them could it be said that they were the superior or master of Raisbeck's defensive play. His temperament rarely failed him, no matter how vigorous the play he had to meet.'

Hall also noted the impact the player had had on those who were now filling the stadium, those who would find their usual spot on the Kop on a Saturday and think of little else whilst not there. The fans.

'When the time eventually arrived to sever his connection with the Anfield club, Raisbeck carried with him many mementoes of happy associations, and the warm regards and esteem of a wide circle of friends who had watched his career develop with real pride and genuine appreciation.

'[Raisbeck] left the club admittedly one of the most brilliant and the most successful clubs in the English League. It is no far flight of fancy to suggest that the individual merit of that "one man" had more than a little to do with this progress.'

Elisha Scott

1912–1934
Appearances: 468
Goals: 0

BOLD Street in Liverpool. The early 1930s. A large, athletic man strolls down the road with a swagger. Tall, confident, his hair perfectly brylcreemed, that middle parting as sharp as the suit that he's wearing. He is at total ease and he has every right to be. This is William 'Dixie' Dean, the best footballer in England, a goalscoring legend at Everton, the scourge of defenders and goalkeepers everywhere.

'Dixie!' comes a cry from over the road. The big man recognises its earthy tone. He has heard that voice on many occasions. Usually it is barracking its own defenders but now it is after him. 'Dixie!' It's Elisha Scott, Liverpool's granite-like goalkeeper from Ulster. Their eyes meet, as they have on so many occasions at Anfield or Goodison Park.

'Dixie!' Dean smiles at his nemesis and call it habit but instead of sending words back, the Everton centre-forward leaps in the air and mimics heading a ball firmly past his friend. Scott though is on to him and without a pause; the keeper hurls himself through the air into the gutter and tips the imaginary bullet around an imaginary post. He gets up and both men go on with their day.

'Dixie' Dean often told this story to enthusiastic crowds. Some think it may be a tall tale but frankly, who cares if it is? It is worthy testament to the sort of rivalry and respect the two greats from either side of Stanley Park enjoyed for one another. What isn't in doubt is that the two men were firm friends as well as rivals.

After a ferociously fought derby at either ground, punters would head to the city's distilleries to either brag or console and those at the Lisbon Pub (today a gay and lesbian bar) in Victoria Street would often be met with the sight of these two giants of the game; Dean on the ale, Scott on his native stout; both in deep discussion about the afternoon's hostilities.

The sight of Scott in town was, by now, not anything new. The keeper had arrived from Northern Ireland in 1912, just days before his 19th birthday. For two decades he had kept goal for the club and in that time he had not only won football matches but also the hearts of the fans that filled the ground to see his entertaining style of shot stopping.

By the time he left in 1934, aged 40 he had played 468 times (a then club record) and helped Liverpool win two league championships, putting in a level of performance between the sticks that was not only way ahead of its time, but earned him admiration from way beyond Liverpool 4.

Over the years, those who wore the goalkeeper's jersey in front of the Kop so often held a special place in its inhabitants' hearts. Even opposition keepers will tell you of their special days in front of Anfield's sprawling mass of enthusiasm. Sure, they may be in for the most industrial kind of banter but as a team's last line of defence and themselves supposed to be slightly different to those around them, they always held the terrace's respect.

After Scott, the likes of Tommy 'The Flying Pig' Lawrence, Ray Clemence, Bruce Grobbelaar, Jerzy Dudek and Pepe Reina have all had strong links to the fans. All could be said to be cult heroes. How can they not be, when their game is to fling themselves, to do what any fan would do to stop a goal against their team?

'In big-time Soccer the goalkeeper is the dickens of a fellow,' wrote Scottish sportswriter R.C. Robertson-Glasgow in 1943. 'Photographs in the newspapers show him to be perpetually in flight. Excelsior. He is a trapeze artist without the trapeze. Compared with him the star of the ballet is a rheumatic elephant.'

At Liverpool, Scott though was the original trapeze artist. Sam Hardy before him had excelled in the late 1900s but in Scott, the Kop forged its first actual relationship with a player. Scott was a player the fans adored, but he was also a man they felt they knew.

Every other week, there he was, not only doing everything in his agile powers to stop the enemy scoring goals, but also a familiar face from a similar background who would talk to them – no make that shout at them – about the game and the players they were watching.

'[Scott] holds conference with them,' remarked the *Liverpool Echo* on the relationship between player and fan. 'He chats and back-chats. They hear his opinion about positions and positional play. He was built in with the Kop.'

Scott was also arguably the greatest goalkeeper to play for Liverpool, but that's a debate to be had elsewhere; what isn't in doubt is that the man from Belfast was indeed built into the Kop.

Scott's original foundations were laid in Belfast. Born at 6 Bismarck (perhaps appropriately considering how many strikers' hearts sank when they faced him) Terrace on 24 August 1893, Scott was the seventh of nine children and was named after his grandfather, a farmer from County Antrim.

Scott's father had also been a farmer, but with agricultural work suffering hardships, William Scott moved his family to the city, where work was plentiful and living just a short goal kick from Windsor Park, so was football.

Scott left school at 13 – he immediately took jobs to pay his way, including that of a debt collector, due largely to his running ability – and was encouraged to play football by his father. Like his peers, Scott had wiled away many days as a schoolboy kicking whatever kind of ball could be fashioned. Tin, paper or actual leather; all were used over the years but it was scoring goals that first grabbed his attention, not stopping them.

In 1909, whilst playing for the Belfast Boys' Brigade, it is said that Scott berated his keeper (in the years ahead, his contemporaries would empathise with the youngster) screaming, 'What is the use of us scoring goals against the other team and you're letting them in? My granny could be a better goalie than you.'

Scott was a no-nonsense kind of young man. Where he grew up in Belfast you had to be. Right on the edge of the city this was tough, working class and increasingly troubled by sectarian violence and in 1912, the year Scott left for Merseyside, the Ulster Volunteers had formed to block the IRA's moves for self-government.

The young Scott cared little for such matters, but had excelled in goal and was soon playing for Broadway United, a local junior club playing in the Irish Junior Football Alliance for whom he won a league and cup double. Aged 17, Scott was scouted when William, his own older brother over from England where he played in goal for Everton, watched his sibling and saw enough to recommend to his employers that the younger Scott was worth investing in.

A life in the English game must have been an exciting option, not that work was scarce in Belfast. The 1900s saw the city's shipyards boom, employing up to 30,000 men, many of them working on the *Titanic*.

Everton had a look at the youngster but decided that he was both too young and too small. William though, putting family before club, talked to Liverpool chairman John McKenna, extolling his sibling's virtues and the manager, Tom Watson, was dispatched to Ireland where – size and age clearly meaning less to the wily boss – he liked what he saw and made his move. There was some dispute about money as Scott was an amateur but registered as a pro. Liverpool wanted the deal done, so rather than a straightforward transfer fee, Broadway United had themselves – according to the player himself – a new and 'very tidy ground and enclosure'.

It was the summer of 1912, just weeks after *Titanic* had set off from Belfast for the first time and now, like the ship that had been built under his young nose, Scott was about to make his own maiden voyage but with ultimately far more buoyant results.

Scott's early days in Liverpool were blighted by a broken wrist sustained at Crewe for the reserves. The injury had occurred from a brave and good save but it was not one that was to cause too many sleepless nights among either the Liverpool hierarchy or the fans and the management were in no hurry to promote a young man who scouts had described as, 'Raw as meat'.

Liverpool had been well served in goal. Sam Hardy was a fine keeper who played for England and now – in Scott's way – was Kenny Campbell, a Scottish international and far from ready to be ousted from his position by this young man from over the Irish Sea.

Scott's wrist had been damaged in November 1912, but being of the hardest stock, by January he was ready to play again and after a busy Christmas period (the club played three games in four days), Scott was given his chance in a game up at Newcastle on the first day of 1913.

'The match was a tough one,' Scott later said. 'I remember going to the ground and gazing at the big crowd. As I was wandering around the ground I wondered what the finish would be. It turned out to be a tough afternoon. I had heaps to do and at the end, finished with a clean sheet.'

Scott was being modest. The young man was brilliant, making several fine saves and the *Liverpool Echo* remarked that the, 'Young custodian was called upon to give a good account of himself'. Glowing praise in these hyperbole-free Edwardian times. One national paper went as far as to say that, 'The lad faced heavy artillery like a veteran.'

Newcastle had certainly seen enough. On the train home to Merseyside, Tom Watson sat with Scott and told him that the Geordie club had offered Liverpool £1,000 for the young man's services. It was a staggering amount of money for a player who had just wiped away First Division mud from his knees for the very first time. Less than two years earlier Blackburn Rovers had paid a world record amount of money when they gave Falkirk £1,800 for Scottish international John Simpson's services, now Newcastle were willing to part with close to that for an unknown rookie.

Scott suggested Liverpool accepted the money, simply because he felt he wouldn't get his chance with a fine keeper like Campbell in his way. Watson knowingly smiled. Scott's time at Liverpool would come and he wasn't going to be accepting anything.

Soon the 'artillery' that Scott had fended off at St James' Park was replaced with the real thing across northern Europe with the onset of the Great War, and Scott was heading home, a blow considering he had displaced Campbell in goal for the last 23 fixtures of the 1914/15 season.

In Belfast, Scott turned out for Linfield before being granted permission by his employers in Liverpool to play for Belfast Celtic – a club he would later so grace as manager – where his form won hearts, minds and trophies. 'The club had been formed with the help of Glasgow Celtic and with the same objectives,' explains Martin Flynn, a member of the Belfast Celtic Society. 'Those were to help the community and of course, to win trophies.' In 1918 Celtic won the Irish Cup for the first time. 'That was absolutely massive,' says Flynn. 'Scott was a hero.' He was also in demand. The war was over and Liverpool sent directors to Belfast to collect some prize assets. He may have been a hero in his home town, but it was time to get back to Liverpool and work on those Scousers.

Liverpool's early foray back into football was unsettled. Tom Watson had died during the war and for Scott, well he was once again second fiddle to Campbell in goal. An enlarged testicle (well, they do say goalkeepers are different) had to be operated on, but in March 1920 at Manchester City's Hyde Park, Scott replaced his rival who was soon heading home to Partick Thistle and so for the next 14 years, it was the brilliant Ulsterman, that the fans hoped to see keeping their goal from harm.

Liverpool finished the 1920/21 season in a decent fourth spot but then came back-to-back titles and unheralded brilliance. The 1921/22 season saw the club take their first title in 16 years, running out winners by a comfortable six points from Tottenham Hotspur. Scott by now was Liverpool's regular keeper and by conceding a then very stingy figure of 36 goals, his role in the team's success was not in question.

Unlike the 1900s there wasn't to be the rollercoaster ride that accompanied league titles and instead the ride just went higher. In October 1922, a huge crowd close to 55,000 saw Liverpool cement their domination with a 5–1 win over Everton ('1–2–3–4–5', the Kop roared).

If that wasn't enough, the following week's fixture at Goodison Park saw the Reds win again, this time by the only goal in a game in which Scott put on a show of both fine goalkeeping and courage.

'Scott injured his right wrist making a difficult save and minutes later he saved again and gave away a corner,' wrote the *Echo*. 'From it, he found three men on top of him and again needed attention.'

Liverpool lost their manager David Ashworth in December 1922, who (apparently for family reasons) took the job at Oldham, despite by now having a team at Anfield that looked more than likely to reclaim the championship.

Without Ashworth (former player Matt McQueen took over the following February) the team continued to prosper. On Boxing Day, Scott was given a benefit game at Anfield (normal league fixtures, but collections were taken for players and despite the fact that he would play another 12 years, Scott was deemed worthy having already been at the club for a decade). According to the press, 'A fine collection was taken.'

It was no surprise that the fans cared enough to delve into their pockets for Scott. He was now a fine, dominating goalkeeper and thought of as among the best around. He missed only three games on the way to the 1922 title and was one of only three ever-presents during the following year's success.

Since the war, crowds at Anfield had been very healthy. Football was now an essential part of people's lives and the efforts of Scott and his team-mates had gone a long way in lifting the gloom that accompanied so many men back from the horrors of war. 'Liverpool have fixed ridiculously cheap rates if judging by the London standards,' wrote the *Liverpool Echo* in 1919. 'The team's ground, you may not know had a huge sum spent on it during the summer months to make good the rot that had set in some parts of the Spion Kop and in the general woodwork of the ground. Liverpool have also put in ten new turnstiles, so great is the crush anticipated to enter the ground.'

The fans had a team of heroes and whilst trophies dried up after the 1923 championship, in Elisha Scott the fans and the Kop (now also with its own shiny roof) had more than a mere shot stopper.

'Lisha, Lisha!' Up went the chant from the terraces every time the keeper headed out onto the field. It is said his was the first ever player specific song and it is no surprise, such was the rapport the man from Belfast had built with like-minded working men who had they not been watching him keep goal for their team, would have been sharing some industrial language over a pint or two in a local pub.

In 1932, such was the Kop's growing mystique and such was the novel relationship those fans enjoyed with their keeper, the *Liverpool Echo* sent their intrepid reporter, Bee to stand among them and report back with his findings.

These were the results:

> *Here was loyalty, here was belief; here was a trusting nature; they had commentaries on all phases of play, players, press and from their unequalled view they reckoned they saw things that the people in other parts of the ground could not hope to see. Yes, the Kop is the home of the loyalists.*
>
> *Two women were there, one in chocolate brown and another daring to wear a blue hat, a tricky thing of beret design, but the colour scheme did not seem to be quite inviting, as she was in the Anfield ground. Two swarthy sons of Ireland came beside me. They had come to see the MA of goalkeepers, Elisha Scott. One wore a black velvet beret and a film face that suggested a Valentino. He was plainly of Basque extraction and was silent as the grave.*
>
> *Where I had expected slashing attacks on players, I found praise and kindness. The kind way they talked of players astonished me… They were an object lesson to me… Their sportsmanship was a great feature; their language was fit and proper, and they treated the players encouragingly and in a*

sporting manner. Anfield's all right if they can keep this man at their back. They have tantalised him, he says, by some of their movements, but he's loyal to the core and he goes on talking his matches, debating his matches. The spectator is matchless.

Scott got it. Scott would stand in front of those fans and understand them, not only as football fans, but as people from backgrounds just like his own. Scott would run from the tunnel and be just as eager to be with them as they were to share their Saturday afternoon with him. He was keen to get their opinion on form, not just his but that of his team-mates. 'That made people feel intensely close to him,' remarked the football historian and club biographer John Williams. 'That made people feel he was really one of them.'

His team-mates – just as they became accustomed to all sorts of remarks from the never tongue-tied crowd – could expect plenty of chat from their goalkeeper. Much of Scott's ire was focused on Jimmy 'Parson' Jackson, a Cambridge University graduate who had studied Greek and philosophy and who – in 1933 – would become a Presbyterian minister.

Jackson was a dependable defender but should he allow a striker the sort of room that would allow for a shot at Scott's goal, he would hear about it with a few choice words. Should that striker happen to be Dixie Dean, those words were usually the very sort that would make the most modern of altar boys blush.

Jackson was good – he played 224 games for Liverpool – but Scott was inclined to think that the man from Clyde was too nice, that he went too easy on the likes of Dean and would tell him to 'rough him up'. A Dean hat-trick at Anfield in 1931 saw a particularly awkward afternoon for Jackson from both striker and keeper alike.

'William,' Jackson once said to Dean. 'I never want to play in front of that man again.' The Kop, privy to it all of course sided with their keeper and like everything he did in front of them, they couldn't get enough.

The fans loved to hear Scott scream. 'Rate' meaning right, was a common shout and his screams echoed their own, to the point when some must have wondered where they stopped and he began. Once a fan approached Scott outside the stadium and went into a tirade of football chat that Scott enthusiastically contributed to. 'Do I know you?' he asked after a while. 'You ought to,' said the fan. 'I threw the ball back to you from the Kop last Saturday.'

Scott – as well as being totally at ease with the people who supported him – had a way about him. He was tough alright. He had a steely eye and sharp cheekbones that made him look like a young Jack Palance and like the actor playing the villain Jack Wilson in the movie *Shane* and standing in the mud asking his next victim, 'Where do you think you're going?' Scott must have been able to frighten the most bulky of strikers with just a knowing glare.

He would run out to play, often with a tilted cap, the woollen jersey, gloves (rare for his day among mostly bare-handed keepers) and his knee-pads. He cut a striking figure. He had already conducted his strict pre-match routine which would see him arrive two hours before kick-off, warm up and then bounce the ball off the wall for an hour. Funnily enough, Bruce Grobbelaar would also hit a ball at the dressing-room walls but in his case he was trying to turn the light switch off.

Scott had more than that habit in common with Grobbelaar. Like the Zimbabwean, Scott wasn't tall. 5ft 9in wasn't physically imposing perhaps, but he made up for that with incredible bravery, unsurpassed agility and a command of his box that Grobbelaar would have marvelled at.

Scott was ahead of his time. He loved to punch the ball to safety and had no qualms about coming far from his line, fists raised and ready for action – a sight that must have brought cries of joy in a stadium so often used for prize fights at the time.

In 1955, writing about football he said, 'Punching is an art that goalkeepers these days have not completely learnt. You can hit it further with your cap than some of them can punch today. To punch a ball properly you must get poise, get set and do to it, no half measures. Make up your mind when the ball is coming over what you're going to do with it and don't change it. Many goalkeepers out there are frightened to leave the goal. They forget it will always be there when they get back.'

And then there were the saves he made. The agility that Scott used to keep Liverpool's goal safe warmed the heart for so many eager fans. Imagine in 60 years and an old man describing to his grandkids about what he saw at the Millennium Stadium in Cardiff on 13 May 2006? With just four cramped filled minutes left, they'd say, Steven Gerrard managed to get a flame to the fuse on his right foot and that dynamite of a shot destroyed West Ham's FA Cup hopes.

Stories from older fans making their way in the Boys' Pen in the early 1930s have an unworldly feel. They talk of a misty Anfield and thunderous shots from the likes of that dastardly Dixie Dean. They talk of the heartache about to be felt as that big leather wrecking ball careers towards the top corner. And then from nowhere, there's the gloved hand. It breaks through the mist and touches the ball over an impressed crossbar. Silence, followed by a delirious and unbelieving roar. Lying on the muddy turf is their goalkeeper, their hero. Elisha Scott.

No wonder one reporter later described Scott with such awe: 'He was a great football personality with the eye of an eagle, the swift movement of a panther when flinging himself at shots and the clutch of a vice when gripping the ball. In every sense he was a goalkeeper extraordinary.'

Scott described his form and saves with of course far less hyperbole; the down-to-earth Ulsterman was as understated as one of his goalkeeping jerseys. 'At one time I thought myself more or less invincible to headers, as the speed of the ball could never be really great. This notion was, of course, pretty well upset by such men as Dixie Dean.

'One particular effort, to keep out a header from [Charlie] Buchan, at Anfield, I can still clearly remember. Charlie was close in, and nodded it down, as he knew how. By a certain amount of good luck, anticipation, and a full-blooded dive, I got to it and pushed it away. Charlie lifted me up and patted me on the back.

'Another save that comes readily to mind, was one from Wilfred Chadwick, then with Everton, in a derby game at Goodison Park. Alex Troup was doing his stuff, that time for the Toffees. Alex's game was to bring the ball down the touchline, and then "square it" along the floor, in such a way that Chadwick with his mighty drives, could not miss.

'The idea worked wonderfully well. I was at the scoreboard end. Troup wheeled his way beautifully down the touchline, and when everybody was expecting a high centre he simply pulled it back to his pal. Coming at full tilt Chadwick let go a real ten tonner to the far side of the goal. I don't know how on earth I kept the ball out, but I did. The speed and power of that shot I recall to this day. On such occasions, I think it must have been grim determination not to be beaten that saved me. On derby day, the spectators require little to set them cheering. But this save, well I can hear them yet.'

Scott was spot on. The Kop had been expanded to house 30,000 fans in 1928 but it was those games against their blue brethren that were the highlights of a season and into the 1930s, with the success of the early 1920s as distant a memory as dancing the Charleston, it was their keeper's rivalry with Everton's Dixie Dean that so captured the imagination.

Times – like everywhere – were tough on Merseyside in the early 1930s. Unemployment was a constant feature of life, as was underemployment on the docks. Wages were better there than in most cotton towns, but the work was sporadic – averaging at three days a week. By the end of the decade it is said that plenty of men couldn't afford the shilling entrance fee but would turn up anyway, just to be part of the matchday crowd around the ground.

Matchday was a highlight of a hard week, and derby day the highlight of a sometimes-tough season. By now, Scott vs Dean was a derby within a derby.

Their rivalry went unmatched on Merseyside until the early 1980s when the positional tables were turned and Ian Rush took on Neville Southall. Rush might have scored plenty (in 1989 he broke Dixie Dean's record with his 20th derby goal) but like Scott, Southall moved mountains to stop it being more.

Everyone loves a sporting rivalry and usually the attraction lies in how different the two protagonists are. Ice cold Bjorn Borg against mercury busting John McEnroe. Sebastian Coe, smooth and established up against Steve Ovett, rough and instinctive.

With Scott and Dean though, you had two very similar and hard men, desperate to win and brave enough to put their head in where it hurts to make sure that that happened. When they came up against each other, something had to give.

As mentioned the two became great friends and goaded each other mercilessly. Prior to one game, Dean sent some aspirin to Scott's home – he'd need them once he'd finished with him, laughed the striker. Scott in turn would always meet Dean in the tunnel before a game with, 'You'll get none today, you black-haired bastard.'

Perhaps the most mood-lifting derby for Reds fans came in the FA Cup in 1932. The press wrote of locals wearing blue bowler hats and red sashes and that in their thousands they jostled to get in to view the game. 'They were a happy crowd. What was a bump or a push on a day like this?'

On the field there was plenty of pushing and plenty of bumping and that *black-haired bastard* Dean scored after just 15 seconds. Liverpool though found a new level and equalised before half-time before scoring a second with 15 minutes remaining. Then came Scott's moment.

Dean rose to head one of those bullets at goal but… well here's how the *Liverpool Post* saw things:

'Scott may have been at fault with the opening goal, but from that point onwards he gave one of his most superb displays, and his catch of an on-coming header from Dean in the last moments of play was the catch of the season. He seems to get a position that is right before the forward has decided which way he will take his shot. It is intuition.'

Scott, for all that intuitive brilliance had come close to leaving the club. In 1929, Liverpool offered Preston North End £9,000 plus their 35-year-old keeper for the services of Alex James. James's wage demands put paid to that. In 1930, Everton – yes Everton – had a £5,000 bid accepted but an ankle injury (one that it is said Scott made very vocal) meant the unthinkable never happened.

But then, it nearly happened again. In 1934, Scott was almost 40 and whilst past his dynamic best, he was still adored amongst the fans. When the local press reported that the club were ready to let their man go, fans were in uproar, writing letters. This one, signed merely 'Disgusted', summed up the feeling among the people:

'To think, the one and only Elisha Scott should have to submit to the indignity of a transfer is unthinkable, especi-ally as it is being proved week in and week out where the weakness is. He is the world's best. The "owld man" could do for me if he came out and played in crutches.'

It got worse. Once again it was reported that Everton were the club to which he would go and for a measly £250. A full-on campaign in the *Echo* to prevent the move to Goodison – champions at the time – was the least the fans could muster and so visits to the keeper's house followed, pleading for their man to turn down the call to arms from their bitter rivals.

A cartoon in the *Echo* summed up that relationship. It had the Kop, a heaving mass of fans behind the goal and it had Scott, his bags packed. It read, 'Can you imagine the Spion Kop without Elisha Scott? And can you imagine Elisha Scott without the Spion Kop?'

Going against type the directors listened to the punters and the deal was off. Scott made the decision to leave, but it wouldn't be for another English team; that clearly wouldn't do. He would return to Belfast where he would become player-manager at Belfast Celtic.

There he would be an incredible success. At Celtic he is up there as a manager where Jock Stein and Bill Shankly are in Glasgow and Liverpool respectively. His ten Irish League titles and six Irish Cups, among plenty of others, saw to that. 'Even today,' says Martin Flynn, a member of the Belfast Celtic Society, 'his name resonates with local footballing people.'

In 1949, sectarian violence occurred at a Celtic game against Protestant club, Linfield. One of Scott's young players had his leg broken and that night, he thought it would have to be amputated. For Scott that was enough. The club was disbanded.

That leg was saved, but like an amputee with an invisible scratch, Scott continued to come to the ground day after day, caretaking a club without a team. In 1959, he died.

That was the year Bill Shankly arrived at Liverpool as a manager. It is oft said that Shankly made a poor club great. That is only half true. The club had once been great and much of that was down to Elisha Scott.

On the last day of the 1934 season, Scott had been injured but he wanted to say his farewells. A microphone was set up and whilst no great orator, he addressed those who – for 22 years – he had stood before, making save after save. He said:

'We have always been the best of friends and shall always remain so. I have now finished with English association football. Last but not least, my friends on the Kop. I cannot thank you sufficiently. You have inspired me. God bless you all.'

With that he was gone. But never forgotten.

Albert Stubbins

1946–1953
Appearances: 178
Goals: 83

YOU have to feel for Albert Stubbins. He never quite got noticed. One of the most gifted centre-forwards of the post-war years but through no fault of his own, the amiable Geordie was always in the margins, unable to get fully under the spotlight.

At Liverpool – in the years straddling the 1940s and 50s – he was competing with Billy Liddell in an Anfield popularity race that was always only ever going to yield one winner and at international level, Stubbins only ever won one cap – and that was unofficial. Like so many defenders at the time he found Tommy Lawton to be an unmovable object.

Then there was that pesky war. Stubbins was at the peak of his powers during its latter stages but the country was too busy to notice. Even today, pictures of Stubbins should have him stand out, but his impressive head of bright red hair is lost to grainy black and white imagery. Yes, historical circumstance was never too kind to Albert Stubbins.

And what about his most iconic moment? Never mind what he achieved with a ball at his feet (or on his head), Stubbins will long be remembered for his appearance on the cover of The Beatles' *Sgt. Pepper's Lonely Hearts Club Band* album (the only footballer to be there). Fame and notoriety at last? Well yes, but even there he is sandwiched between a domineering Marlene Dietrich and an Indian guru called Lahiri.

Stubbins though didn't mind. He wasn't one to grumble. World wars and German actresses hogging his limelight weren't ever going to get him down. Instead he played with a smile and he scored goals. Plenty of them that won the title and helped take the fans to Wembley for the first time. Sure, many eyes were drawn to Liddell's array of skills, but in Stubbins, fans had an alternative hero and he was red-haired, talented and delighted to be there.

Liverpool had gone without a trophy since their First Division championship win in 1923 but the club kicked off the first full season after the war with a title win that owed much to the goals and footballing intuition of Stubbins. Three years later, Liverpool were in their first FA Cup Final in 36 years and despite defeat to Arsenal, the punters had their first taste of that heady trip to north London that would one day become as familiar as the walk home from the pub.

Stubbins was key to it all. The success of the title winning team in 1946/47 might not have kick-started an era of domination but it did bring welcome relief after the hostilities and the adventures that followed – attendances were more than healthy – had Stubbins firmly at their heart. He struck a chord with so many Liverpudlians, and four of them weren't even major football fans.

The Beatles released their album, *Sgt Pepper's Lonely Hearts Club Band* in June 1967 and earlier that year were putting the finishing touches to a cover that would become arguably the most famous ever seen. On it, they planned to feature an array of iconic heroes and historical figures, including those from sport.

The boxer Sonny Liston and the swimmer (come actor) Jonny Weissmuller were in, but there seemed to be an absence. Hunter Davies – a writer (he would go on and write the wonderful *Glory, Glory Nights* – a book on his beloved Tottenham Hotspur) who had become the band's official biographer and was very much in the inner sanctum – looked at the drafted artwork of the cover and had a thought.

'I suggested that, given where they came from, their heroes should include a Liverpool footballer,' recalls Davies. 'As a football fanatic, it was a disappointment to me that they had no interest in the game. In the end, John had stuck in Albert Stubbins, but only because he thought his name was funny.'

Post-war Merseyside needed a laugh. Being the country's lifeline to the 'free world' and a major port, the Battle of the Atlantic was coordinated from a Combined Operations headquarters at Derby

House in the city. The Mersey waterfront was vital in the war effort, undertaking shipbuilding and naval repairs. Hitler knew, and in no uncertain terms did his best to destroy it.

Outside of London, Liverpool was the most heavily bombed area of the country and the Blitz of May 1941 was a sustained attack that even the Luftwaffe generals boasted was, 'one of the heaviest ever made on Britain'. Amidst the rubble, Liverpudlians got on with their lives the best they could. Winston Churchill visited his port-city and said, 'I see the damage done by the enemy, but I also see the spirit of an unconquered people.'

Albert Stubbins, a draughtsman by trade had been exempt from the armed services and played plenty of football, excelling up front for his home-town club, Newcastle. In the Northern League in 1945/46 he scored 36 times, 25 more than Jackie Milburn who after his departure would become a Geordie legend.

Such was Stubbins's form (and despite the player's fondness for his home town where he hoped to set up a small business) his legendary status lay elsewhere and although a proud Geordie his move became inevitable. What wasn't sure was where he'd go and the way he decided to make his future red has taken on an almost mythical status.

Liverpool were in the market for a new centre-forward and had made a (perhaps cheeky) bid for Everton skipper Joe Mercer, but instead the striker went to Arsenal. Chelsea's Tommy Lawton was also enquired about but the Stamford Bridge hierarchy believed the 'fans would burn down the stand if he went'.

Stubbins fit the bill. Club historian John Williams describes him as, 'Powerful and fiercely quick but also "dainty", unpredictable and exciting, hardly attributes that had characterised recent Liverpool centre-forwards. Stubbins could bring a ball under control immediately from a great height, and he could bind together a forward line and bring others into the game.'

This wasn't a player then who would come on the cheap or without rival attention. Everton – having lost Mercer – were very keen and both clubs offered £13,000 bids in September 1946. It was now up to the player and it was whilst sitting in the Northumberland Street News Theatre in Newcastle that a sign flashed up on screen requesting that he report back to St James' Park immediately. There he would find (rather surprisingly as far as each club was concerned) officials from both Merseyside clubs, hoping to take home his signature.

Some say that Stubbins made the decision by simply tossing a coin. Not strictly true. The Newcastle secretary asked him whom he'd like to talk to first. He tossed a coin and it was Liverpool. The player later recalled: 'Bill McConnell, the Liverpool chairman and George Kay and myself discussed matters and I was impressed with them both, and with the possibilities of Liverpool, so [I] said I would go to Anfield. I also knew several of the Liverpool players at the time like Willie Fagan and Jack Balmer. That probably gave Liverpool the slight edge and in the end I never spoke to Everton because I had been so impressed with Liverpool's offer.'

Liverpool had caught the Geordie eye with their ambitious plans but they also offered to help with Stubbins's own career ambitions. 'While I was at Newcastle I wrote for the local *Evening Chronicle* and I was looking to a career as a journalist when I finished,' said Stubbins.

'Liverpool said they would arrange for me to write a column for the *Liverpool Echo* and after a meeting with the sports editor Bob Prole I duly began doing articles for the Saturday night edition.'

Liverpool were putting a squad together they hoped would seriously compete. George Kay had taken the squad to the United States before signing Stubbins and embarked on a inspired tour where not only did they win every game but the players gorged themselves on treats for so long rationed back home and a diet of eggs, steaks and orange juice built up a group of men who started to believe they could wrestle the league championship from their neighbours Everton who had won it in 1939 before the outbreak of war.

The people were desperate to get back to football. Food rationing was one thing but the lack of their favourite pastime was as big a miss as any cut of meat. 'The country yearned for top class football,' said popular centre-back, Laurie Hughes, 'and nowhere was it more eagerly anticipated than in the city of Liverpool.

'For six long years Everton fans had all the bragging rights in the town. Merseyside was such an upbeat place back then, despite the horrors of war. Gradually things were turning back to normal, and that meant regular football. The game meant so much and to have it back brought a spring to the city's step. It got everyone going. After all, what else was there?'

Liverpool played four games before the signing of Stubbins and the results proved that this was a team with plenty of ability but also a worryingly soft underbelly. 1–0 at Sheffield United was followed by a

1–0 defeat at home to Middlesbrough. A 7–4 victory over Chelsea at Anfield was followed by a 5–0 reverse at Manchester United. There were signs of greatness, but a vulnerability when key players were missing. Billy Liddell for instance was still undertaking duties with the RAF and missed three of those opening games.

Liddell had been acquired before the war – on the advice of the departing Matt Busby who was leaving the club to manage Manchester United. Liddell's – due to RAF commitments – was a talent not yet fully unleashed but his potential was there and the left wing would soon sparkle under his array of skills and the club's manager and board will have noted that with his presence in the team, they seriously needed a centre-forward capable of working with him.

Jack Balmer was a fine forward at the club but his game was not Stubbins's. 'Jack wasn't the type of player who would battle alone up front and take the harsh treatment that could be dished out by the country's defenders,' recalled Laurie Hughes. 'He didn't like the rough and tumble aspect of the game. Jack thrived on running onto balls and his speed often saw him race clear of those nasty centre-halves and that's how he got so many of his goals.'

What Liverpool wanted and needed was a striker to complement both Balmer and Liddell. Stubbins was the man. His manager at Newcastle, Stan Seymour was in no doubt that he was losing a complete forward. Tommy Lawton was England's main man at the time and the forward by which all others were measured but Seymour felt that Liverpool had signed a player every bit as good. 'The only advantage Lawton may have over Albert,' he said, 'is with his heading but Stubbins is cleverer on the ball.'

Just days after the drubbing at Manchester United and such a player had cost them £13,000, a fee only bettered by Arsenal's recent £14,000 spent on Bryn Jones and would last as a Liverpool record until 1960. Plenty of players had gone for big money but not lived up to the tag. Stubbins though had a calm disposition, a friendliness and easy-going countenance that belied the sport's professionalism and pressures.

'The fact that I'd scored goals for Newcastle gave me the confidence to think I could do it for Liverpool,' said Stubbins. 'In contrast to some players who later moved for bigger fees, I never felt any sense of strain over the price Liverpool had paid. It was never a worry to me. In fact, it was an incentive for me.'

The transfer might have been a record but there was no fanfare, in fact Stubbins arrived in the city completely unnoticed. Such was George Kay's fear that the deal could still go wrong, he was at Lime Street station at 10pm with his captain, Willie Fagan and a few journalists. No Stubbins. Kay panicked and ordered station porters to search the train. No Stubbins. Had he changed his mind or worse still gone to Everton?

Fortunately not. Such was the low-key nature of Stubbins he had simply walked from the train to the Hanover Hotel in the city's centre where the club had booked him a room and was – by the time his manager found him – settling down for a night's sleep.

Stubbins must have rested well because just days later he made a more than impressive debut at Bolton's Burnden Park. The new forward had only met up with his team-mates for the first time on the morning of the match but there was never any doubt that he'd go straight into the team. With Liddell now fully de-mobbed, the attacking five had an ominous feel about it and the Liverpool fans wanted to see it in the flesh.

Mass travelling crowds were reserved mainly for cup ties but on this occasion the fans made the short journey to Bolton in their thousands. Gary Shaw and Mark Platt, in their excellent book on the 1946/47 season, *At the End of the Storm* remarked that, 'Stubbins-mania quickly swept through the red half of the city. By midday on the morning after his arrival thousands of Liverpudlians were setting off to cheer him on in his debut at Bolton.

'The close proximity of Burnden Park meant Liverpool's away following that day was always going to be a healthy one, but the signing of Stubbins boosted the numbers considerably and meant the scale of the travelling support was more akin to that which would attend a cup tie.'

There was a particular spring in the fans' step; not in keeping with the mauling their team had taken just a week earlier at Manchester United. Stubbins had lifted the mood and so there they were, snaking their way to Bolton in high spirits. 'After all,' wrote a report on the day, 'it is not every day one has the chance of seeing £13,000 of footballer in one packet, and loyalist Liverpudlians just could not wait for his first appearance at Anfield.'

The game itself was played in wet conditions and Bolton – a decent side with a young Nat Lofthouse in their ranks – were in no mood to welcome the hordes of guests with an easy win. Liverpool's defence though proved much tighter than in Manchester the week before and

Stubbins himself was showing signs of a hunger and skill the side had previously lacked.

With five minutes left in the opening half, Billy Liddell, hitherto a peripheral figure in the match, sent a tempting cross in from the left. Stubbins wasn't on hand for a dream goal but the old South African right-winger, Berry Nieuwenhuys was and a powerful downward header saw Liverpool go in at half-time in the lead.

A downpour in the second half and an eager home side made things hard, getting a deserved equaliser in the 78th minute which looked like settling a plucky draw but then came Stubbins's moment, a moment that set the tone and made his popularity among the fans complete.

Eight minutes remained when the new forward picked up the ball in the centre-circle and moved ominously into space; space left by backtracking defenders who perhaps suddenly saw his price-tag hanging from his socks and in fear retreated. Stubbins moved through the mud like an anaconda, before unleashing a strike from outside the area that flew in via the woodwork.

A third goal – from Jack Balmer – settled matters but the name on the fans' lips was Albert Stubbins and they arrived back in Liverpool gushing about his goal. 'The Burning Stub' they called him because of his flame-coloured hair and it was clear they had a burgeoning addiction to a new hero.

Stubbins was impressed with his new team. Especially the centre-halves who managed Lofthouse so admirably on the day. 'Seeing how the Liverpool defence coped so well with their attack gave me so much confidence because I knew the players around me were all capable,' he later remarked.

For one of those defenders, Laurie Hughes, the admiration was mutual. 'We had signed a player who would complete a fantastic forward line and help us challenge for and ultimately win the title,' Hughes said. 'Albert, like Liddell, was a match winner, and unlike Jack Balmer, he loved the rough stuff. He actually thrived on the treatment given to him by defenders. I used to note how much he loved rubbing up against the enemy. If a defender was going to try and intimidate Albert he was going to have his work cut out. Our Albert was always up for the challenge and would simply use his shoulders to see off his opponent, all the while keeping complete control of the ball. That takes some doing.'

The Anfield crowd had to wait to totally join the Stubbins love-in. Two more goals on the road at Grimsby further proved his worth but it wasn't until the end of October – over a month after he signed – that Stubbins got his first goal at his new home.

Once again the weather was awful (a sign of things to come that season) but nearly 45,000 packed into Anfield to see their now high-flying team take on Brentford. Thanks to the signing of Stubbins and the now impressive team around him, expectations were high, so high that Anfield became a frustrated place in a goalless first half.

Bee, the *Liverpool Echo* reporter noted in his match report that the natives were prone to get restless. 'Spectators at Anfield are the frenzied type who expect everything in red to be a speed merchant and all opponents to be veritable caterpillars. It is not for the game's good that footballers sacrifice craft at the altar of speed. We are inclined to be greedy now the club is being hailed as 'League Champions'. It is a long, long trail but they can get there by measured football not by frenzied stuff.'

Wise words but in a much better second half it was an early Stubbins winner that once again had the fans frothing with hope as the side moved up to third in the table. Bee was impressed and wrote of Stubbins, 'The big man is a great endeavourer with what others would consider unconsidered trifles and plainly wants football and not headball. His delayed success had got on the Kop nerves. All is over now. Tension ended.'

Not quite. Further good results were quashed by a 5–1 mauling at the hands of title favourites Wolverhampton Wanderers in front of a huge – and shell-shocked – 53,000 crowd. A 1–0 defeat at Goodison Park at the end of January further cooled title hopes, but they were nothing when compared to the cold air blowing into the UK for what was turning out to be the most extreme of winters. 'Warmer in the Antarctic' declared one paper and games everywhere were affected.

Liverpool were getting games played though and a visit to Leeds United at the beginning of February was pivotal in getting their title chase back on track. Stubbins put the side one up but they succumbed to an equaliser on the hour, only for the 'Burning Stub' to pop up with a late winner and send the team home with belief running though their chilled veins. They were fifth in the table, but momentum had shifted and at the heart of it was Albert Stubbins.

Liverpool were unbeaten in their next six league games as winter thawed and Stubbins scored a goal at Anfield to beat title rivals Manchester United. There was four games left to play and Liverpool were in fourth place, but there was great hope. A Stubbins hat-trick the following week at recent FA Cup winners Charlton cemented the optimism and when they won 2–1 at Highbury in the penultimate match, Liverpool were top of the league, albeit having played a game more than second-placed Wolves. And their last game, well that was at Wolves's Molineux.

Results meant that the team were level on points and Stoke City were also in the running. Liverpool had to win. Wolves – the side containing Billy Wright and the great Stan Cullis – were formidable foes. For the latter this was to be his last game of a brilliant career and an emotive 50,000 fans were on hand to give him what they hoped would be the perfect send-off.

'The fans weren't the only ones,' recalled Laurie Hughes who had enjoyed a fine season at centre-half. 'Wolves's players said later they were desperate to win for Stan and so we faced an even more hyped-up team and set of supporters.'

It was a boiling hot day but George Kay had kept cool, calmly telling his players to play the match, not the occasion. They were the form team and on what could have been an energy-sapping afternoon, Kay's men played with a knowing confidence and just after the 20th minute Jack Balmer put them ahead.

Stubbins had looked at his opponent at centre-half and whilst he had nothing but respect for what Stan Cullis had achieved, he saw a weakness. 'I had a word with Bob [Priday] and I told him if he received the ball in a deep midfield position to knock it straight down the middle for me to chase. The first opportunity he got he did exactly that and it took the Wolves defence completely by surprise.' Cullis was caught flat-footed and on went a rampant Stubbins to put the Reds two up. It is said that Cullis should have pulled Stubbins back to stop him but was far too much of a Corinthian to do so.

Wolves pulled one goal back in the second half but it wasn't enough and the Reds finished their season with a famous win. The title though wasn't yet secured. Players, staff and fans would have to sit and wait until 14 June (the cricket season was well under way) as Stoke City had to play at Sheffield United, knowing a win and the title was heading to the Potteries.

Liverpool were playing Everton at Anfield in the Lancashire Senior Cup Final in front of 40,000 fans who had their eyes on an always hotly contested derby game but both ears waiting for news from Yorkshire.

Five minutes left in the game at Anfield and the director George Richards came on the stadium tannoy. 'Sheffield Wednesday 2 Stoke City 1'. Cue pandemonium.

The *Liverpool Echo* wrote:

'The roar which greeted this announcement made the Hampden Park one sound almost like a childish whisper. The crowd threw their hands up in the air, many lost their hats and did not bother to look for them after they tossed them high up in a burst of joyful celebration.'

Nine months earlier, Stubbins had been sitting in a Newcastle cinema before being called to make the biggest decision of his footballing life. Now here he was, a champion starring in his own heroic matinee. Twenty-four goals he had scored to help the cause and here he was, the flame-haired hero among a sea of adoring Scousers. His smile would have stayed on his face if Stoke had nicked it but now it beamed bigger and brighter than ever before.

It had been a remarkable start to life in Liverpool and the player himself later acknowledged that those who cheered his every move had very much helped him. 'The support of the fans helped me settle. I always felt I had their support and I'll be eternally grateful to them for that. Later, even if I had a bad game, the crowd would never crucify me like they would some players. As a player it is so important that the fans take to you. Fortunately I had no such problems at Liverpool and everything went so well.'

Liverpool, the champions, had also got close to a first Wembley cup final. Knocked out in the semi-final by Burnley, the cup run was memorable for a Stubbins performance and goal that lived long in the memory.

Birmingham City were the visitors to Anfield on a snowy March Saturday in the FA Cup sixth round. Such was the interest and the hope that Wembley might be reached that the club declared this the first ever all-ticket match in the city of Liverpool and a huge crowd gathered when they were released on general sale. A request from a moored ship in the port for 500 Kemlyn Road tickets was given short shrift but 52,000 luckier locals got in to witness a brilliant performance by team and striker alike.

Stubbins opened the scoring with a fine strike just past the half-hour and got more than players back then bargained for in way of congratulations. 'Phil Taylor came up and kissed me on the cheek,' laughed Stubbins. 'In those days this was a wild extravagance, because usually if you scored a goal you would turn away and maybe get just a handshake off one or two team-mates. But with this being such an important cup tie I think Phil got a little bit carried away.'

Birmingham, themselves roared on by a healthy away support, managed to equalise in the 56th minute but Brummie joy lasted only a minute when Jack Balmer nodded a Billy Liddell free kick past the England goalkeeper, Gil Merrick.

It was, however the goal that sealed victory that those present so gushed about. Again it was supplied from the sweet spot of Liddell's left boot with the Scot's driven free kick hitting the space at the back post that was attacked by Stubbins, but such was its velocity, it looked too much to ask.

For nearly ten years, kids had marvelled at the comics of Superman and now those in the Boys' Pen must have thought the man from Krypton was among them and wearing their red and white uniform. In a flash an unmarked Stubbins flung himself through the air, and parallel with the ground he headed past a bewildered Merrick. Is it a bird? Is it a plane? No it's Liverpool's number nine.

'It was an amazing goal by Albert,' commented Liddell. 'Nobody who saw it could ever forget it. It went in like a rocket, giving Gil Merrick absolutely no chance, and Albert slid on his stomach for several yards on the frozen surface before coming to a stop.'

Stubbins was ever mindful of Liddell's brilliance. 'Free kicks were a tremendous part of Bill's armoury,' he later said. 'In a game against Preston at Deepdale we got a free kick just outside the box, slightly towards the left flank. Billy came up to take it and was going to hit it with his right foot when the wind rolled the ball towards his left one.

'Most players would have stopped to re-place the ball as Billy was entitled to do. But he just let it run, hit it with his left and it went in like a rocket. He was great with either foot. It didn't worry Bill at all.'

Stubbins was also once asked by former colleagues at Newcastle prior to a game in the north-east, how best to handle Liddell. Stubbins was not going to give away any trade secrets and so offered only this, 'If Billy picks up the ball and you're not close to him when he does, then you're dead.' Stubbins later declared it was, 'More a warning than advice.'

The glories of 1946/47 couldn't be matched and what followed that championship success was steady decline but the team did give the fans that first trip to Wembley they so craved. The special train from

Lime Street to London left at 5.50am full of eager fans enjoying beer for breakfast and a three-year-old, Eric Stubbins, clutching a favourite red teddy bear, perhaps confused about his rowdy fellow travellers but excited about seeing his daddy later that day.

The youngster like all those who made their way to Wembley were dampened by the rain but the match tickets were much desired and in nearby bars were being swapped for all sorts of 'luxuries' such as silk stockings and whisky. Those Liverpool fans who resisted such temptations could certainly have done with some Scotch as Liverpool lost 2–0 to an impressive Arsenal side captained by Joe Mercer who being from the city, trained with the Merseysiders every week whilst playing in London on weekends.

Liverpool would have to wait for that elusive and much craved FA Cup but the team were greeted back in Liverpool by thousands of proud fans who lined the streets, ten deep in places and cheered their team home, making – according to the *Liverpool Echo* – 'one's ears ring with their cheers, rattles, bells and what nots'.

The *Echo* continued to praise its constituents when it stated that, 'I doubt whether any club in the country can possibly possess such a fine bunch of supporters as Liverpool. No wonder Hitler's hordes couldn't break the spirit of Merseyside, in spite of all their efforts.'

Stubbins continued to score frequently (his record is almost a goal every other game) but, now in his early thirties, the form of his early days was less consistently presented and like the team itself, he found things harder and harder. Not that his popularity ever waned. He left with many friends and his smiling face left a mark on a club who – despite having plenty of famous number nines – always appreciated his enthusiastic efforts.

Such was that appreciation that in the late 1990s, a group of fans set up an appreciation society they called 'The Albert Stubbins Crazy Crew', and the chant *'A-L-B! E-R-T! Albert Stubbins is the man for me'* could often be heard by the sons of grandsons of fans who had cheered his every move in the 1940s and '50s. 'My son, Eric says they'd never have started a fan club had they ever seen me play,' joked Stubbins six years before his death in 2002.

Stubbins had carried out his ambitions of becoming a sports journalist and admirably covered football for many years. Brian Glanville, that doyen of football scribes was impressed with the man and the writer. 'He was a good writer and the most delightful of gentlemen,' says Glanville. 'He was a highly skilled centre-forward, good both with his feet and in the air. The England team could do with him today.'

For Liverpool fans of a certain vintage, it will always be Stubbins's actions in the penalty box – not the press box – that bring a smile. This was the man who brought them joy, goals and that league title and many of them will have echoed the message sent to the player from Paul McCartney along with a copy of the newly released *Sgt Pepper* that simply said, 'Well done Albert for all those glorious years of football. Long may you bob and weave.'

Jimmy Melia

1955–1964
Appearances: 286
Goals: 79

T HE late 1950s and the young people of Britain are changing. Unlike the early part of the decade where teenagers were glum miniatures of their parents, struggling with post-war conditions and the memories of the war against Hitler, the youth now have a new spring in their step.

They identify with things their elders don't understand. The boom-boom-boom of never ending air raids no longer means anything to them – just stories told by weary-eyed adults. In the late 1950s the young people of Liverpool weren't looking to the past, they were looking out from their sea walls and looking to America, to the future. And with that change, came new heroes.

In February 1957, Bill Haley brought his Comets to the Liverpool Odeon and rocked around the clock with such verve that it brought delirium from the crazed teenagers getting high on his new sound.

A month later a young singer called Elvis Presley was making such a stir and selling so many records that he bought a new home in Memphis called Graceland. This was a sound that resonated to Liverpool where – being a port – the records were more readily available and local youngsters loved what came their way.

The police who rushed into the Odeon the night Haley was performing to be told that seats had been torn from the floor expected to quash a riot, instead they found kids, barefoot and dancing in the aisles. Five months later, in a church in Woolton, a boy with a band met another boy with a guitar. John and Paul were acquainted and ready to go to work.

In the world of cinema, Marlon Brando's 1953 *The Wild One* had ushered in new desires. Young people could watch Kirk Douglas, Tony Curtis and James Dean – with their rebellious streaks and wavy quiffs – and see far more of themselves than they ever did with Bogart or Cagney.

And what of sport? The early years of the 1950s saw boys'-own idols like the Compton brothers adorn the bedroom walls and scrapbooks of young boys everywhere. Leslie and Dennis played cricket too and with their matinee idol good looks and Brylcreem contracts, these were the nation's sporting sweethearts.

Things though were changing. Johnny Haynes of Fulham was now England's main man but he had an edge; the swagger of Tony Curtis, the cleft chin of Kirk Douglas. Stanley Matthews was a national treasure and playing into his middle-age, but as the 1950s became the 1960s the youngsters who made their way to the match saw and admired their players as if stars of the silver screen.

At Liverpool, Billy Liddell had remained the hero; in fact he had been more than that. The Scottish forward was *the* reason for many to support Liverpool, or Liddell-Pool has they liked to call their team. The side had slumped to relegation and so whilst John Lennon and Paul McCartney were strumming their first notes together in that local church, the football team were making only dud sounds in their quest to get back to the top of the hit parade.

Bill Shankly would soon come of course and in the 1960s new players would arrive. Players able to make heroic contributions whilst looking every bit the heroes of film and pop. Roger Hunt with his glut of goals and huge blonde quiff. There was a hero to get their teenage teeth into, a player who could usher in a new era far away from the baggy shorts and laced-up balls of Billy Liddell's era.

Playing alongside Hunt in 1960 was a strange-looking little inside-forward with – in spite of his young age – a balding head. Jimmy Melia was far from matinee idol and far from anyone's poster-boy, a fact that might go a long way to explain why, despite his efforts and goals between 1955 and 1964, plenty of the Anfield crowd found it hard to connect, found it hard to idolise.

But that diversion can make a cult. Rebellion can be a two-way street and plenty saw Melia as an anti-hero, cool in the fact that he; well, that he wasn't very cool. Melia might not have been able to convince a majority desperate to pin their hopes on style as well as substance, but to pockets of the crowd he was the team's great bald hope, a player that linked the gloom of the 1950s with the revolutionary 1960s. He was also a damn fine footballer.

Jimmy Melia was a Scouser and brought up in the Scotland Road district in the north of the city, not far from Anfield. A cultural and ethnic hothouse, Scotland Road was said to be the beating heart of the city. Yes it was poor but it encapsulated the varied but all at once close-knit community that was Liverpool.

On board the RMS *Titanic* – with its links to the city – was a lower deck corridor that ran the length of the ship and was referred to by the crew as 'Scotland Road'. Far from palatial and housing most of the crew, this though was the stretch from which everything seemed to stem.

Melia – having cut his young footballing teeth in the inter-street football leagues set up on nearby roads around the 'Scottie Road' – joined the Liverpool groundstaff in 1953, aged 15. Melia had supported Everton as a boy but he was close mates with Bobby Campbell who would also make the first team, and so went with his pal to Anfield.

Whilst cleaning and painting the stadium, Melia had starred alongside the likes of Bobby Charlton in the England Schoolboy team and on his 17th birthday, in November 1954, he signed professional forms.

The day that the young man put pen to paper fell between a 3–3 draw for the first team at Lincoln City and a 2–1 win at Anfield against Hull. Two weeks after he signed the team lost 3–2 at Luton Town. Yes, Liverpool were very much in the cloudy and dense waters of the Second Division.

Relegated in the spring of 1954 they were – bereft of match-winners, ambitious board members and confident fans – a club doing their best to merely stay afloat in these difficult waters. Defeat at Kenilworth Road saw the side drop to 15th in the division. Not a good place to be for a set of fans who four years earlier were at Wembley and seven years earlier were the champions of England.

Not good either for a team with a player like Billy Liddell at his peak. Such was his skill and their adulation; fans were almost apologetic of their team. Week in and week out Liddell would lighten up an otherwise grey afternoon's work. Left from the championship winning team of '47 were Laurie Hughes and Ray Lambert but both were in the dusk of their careers. What was needed was new talent but in charge were a board whose idea of 'new' was thinking about replacing a broken light-bulb at their decrepit Melwood training ground.

One supporter, old enough to remember the last relegation in 1904, wrote to the *Daily Post* in no doubt where the blame lay. 'When they last went into Division Two it was because they lacked money. Today they must be fairly well off. I think the way the club has been run in the past couple of years has been scandalous. To start this season without a single decent signing to replace the old faithfuls was shocking and an insult to their most loyal of supporters.'

And things were about to get worse. In mid-December 1954 Liverpool went to St Andrew's in Birmingham on a frosty afternoon and returned to a far cooler city having been beaten 9–1, still a record defeat at the club. The staff blamed the wrong studs in the boots whilst the board told a press pack and a set of fans demanding answers and action that the scoreline should, 'not be taken too much at face value'.

One fan, calling themselves simply, 'Fed Up', wrote to the *Football Echo* a week later stating that, 'Liverpool's debacle at Birmingham calls for a full inquiry. They are going from bad to worse, and I fear for the future. Don't ask us to keep on cheering, we haven't the heart. They have no reserves of any promise.'

Whilst the fan's sentiment was right, the last line wasn't. In charge of the club's reserves was Bob Paisley. The former left-half, who had joined the club as a player just before the outbreak of war, had taken over the role after the club's relegation and as the affable Durham-born man began to master his trade, the young Melia started to be noticed as a young player able to make the grade.

A year after the Birmingham bombardment – December 1955 – Liverpool took on Nottingham Forest at Anfield. The team were lying seventh in the Second Division and so a debut for a local boy was about as exciting as it got for some; the small 29,000 crowd reflected the apathy around the place.

Melia was still doing his National Service in Catterick barracks when asked to take the plunge with the first team and he recalled how in awe he was of running out to play a match *with* Billy Liddell, his boyhood hero. 'He was just unbelievable. At the time there was a massive playing staff. There were about fifty professionals. It was far too many and it was just crazy. But Billy was something else. A fantastic player.

'There is nobody in the modern game who could equal him. He was a living legend to the fans and did everything for the team. He took the penalties, free kicks, corners – and scored most of the goals!'

Melia though wasn't on the pitch that day to merely collect autographs. Six minutes in he cleverly sent centre-forward John Evans clear to score an early goal and then, in the first two minutes of the second period, Melia himself popped up to score a second goal in front of an impressed Kop. The *Echo* remarked that, 'The coolness and confidence shown by Melia in taking his opportunity belied his years.'

Melia could only play four more games that season as he still had work to do for Queen and country. Other, less uniformed members of the nation's young were also busy and by 1956 there were signs of drunken gangs travelling to Liverpool games. 'Filthy mouthed, beer swillers,' commented one aggrieved fan in the local paper.

Yes, football and youth culture were beginning to blur into something more tribal but for the de-mobbed Melia his concentration lay only with cementing a place in a still struggling Liverpool team.

The club's manager was now former player Phil Taylor and under him, Melia managed 27 starts, scoring six goals and showed enough and contributed enough to get the team to third in the table. Not enough for promotion but the young Melia was a standout and alongside Liddell a player to pin hopes upon.

The club lacked a spark. They played it safe, avoided risks and whilst crowds remained relatively healthy, stagnation filled the Anfield air. Fans knew. They would go for their post-match pint and sip in frustration, knowing that unless the board released funds, the likes of Melia would have nothing to work with and who knows, ask to leave themselves. The chairman, a T.V. Williams told shareholders the club was, 'His sole concern and his whole life,' but the fans didn't buy it.

The chairman's 'whole life' simply wasn't working. The 1958/59 season was the same old story. The team lost too many games in the league with tepid performances, the most standout being a 5–0 turnover at the hands of Huddersfield, managed by one Bill Shankly.

It was a cup tie though in the far from footballing mecca of Worcester that was the death knell in the club's apathetic approach. A 2–1 shock defeat and enough was enough. Moves had to be made at board level, things had to change or Liverpool Football Club were going to drop and drop until defeat at the likes of Worcester would no longer be considered disastrous.

The campaign though was a breakthrough one for Melia and underlined his importance and maturity in the side. He finished with 21 goals, the club's top scorer and to fans looking at things with more than their Liddell-tinted glasses on, he was the standout footballer. Alan A'Court had been to the World Cup a year earlier with England but for real talent that might just prosper in the top division, Melia seemed it.

Not all fans thought so. They would argue their doubts about the man not being the real deal and when compared to Liddell he wasn't deemed up to the heroic job. It was unfair. Such was Liddell's ray of talent, not many – especially young players – could come out from his shadow.

Melia wasn't a bustling, all-conquering winger who would beat two men and fling in an inviting cross or bury a 30-yard screamer. Melia was a cerebral footballer, a man willing and able to link with his centre-forward whilst also dropping deeper to start attacks. In modern spiel, he played, 'between the lines', looking to make things happen with stealth rather than Liddell-like dynamism.

Melia was very aware of what he was up against. Even in the autumn of 1959, when as the previous season's top scorer, he stepped up to take a penalty in what was Liddell's comeback game from a lengthy absence, the locals let him know what they thought of his taking the spot kick.

'Even though Billy was playing, the boss had told me to take it as I'd already scored from a penalty in a game when Billy was injured,' recalled Melia. 'So, I put the ball down and suddenly the whole of Anfield started booing me!

'I could hear Liverpool fans saying, "The cheeky little bastard taking the penalty when Billy's out there." I could hardly believe it. I blasted the ball into the net, thinking that would at least win the crowd over. But they carried on booing me. It just showed the amazing esteem Billy was held in.'

The board had other things on their minds. Whilst hardly being decisive they did make their change in November of 1959 and with results as erratic as ever, Phil Taylor left the club after a 4–2 loss at Lincoln.

The board didn't have a replacement to immediately come in but they had an idea of whom they wanted to ask. Bob Paisley, the reserve team manager and club trainer was – like other backroom staff – concerned about his future role under a new boss. Much has been written about Bill Shankly's arrival but perhaps Paisley with his brilliant understatement summed it up when he said, 'When Phil finished I put a letter to the board asking to clarify my position. They said I would be staying at the club. Then Shanks came.'

Then Shanks came. There it was. Shankly came to the club whose fans he had admired from afar for a long time and whilst shocked at just how rundown the place was, he saw huge potential. Despite losing his first game 4–0 at the hands of Cardiff, Shankly had a plan. Melia was moved to the right wing, not a position he relished but Shankly felt the reserves lacked experience.

Things didn't start well for Melia. Following a 3–1 cup defeat to Manchester United at Anfield, he was dropped completely. Billy Liddell replaced him and with new striker Roger Hunt, playing and scoring up front with former Everton hero, Dave Hickson. Melia cut a forlorn figure from the sidelines.

Shankly though watched Melia in training, he took stock and saw that he had a player capable of playing the deep-lying forward role as well as anyone on the books. Melia was restored in March of 1960, part of an exciting front five that as well as Hunt and Hickson, included Liddell and Alan A'Court. Liverpool won the game and whilst Liddell's wonderful days were numbered, Shankly's methods were starting to take effect.

The *Liverpool Echo*, remarkably stating early in his tenure that he was, 'Not a man with the gift of the gab,' but rather more accurately they saw that here was a new manager with a worldly footballing knowledge that was too great for the English Second Division. 'Shankly is a disciple of the game as played by the Continentals,' they wrote. 'He will make his players learn to kill the ball and move it all in the same action, even when it is hit at them hard and maybe awkwardly; he will make them practise complete mastery of the ball.'

And that's what he did. The 1960/61 season was another close call with the side again finishing just one place off that promotion spot but the following season with the board finally dusting off their chequebook and Shankly's changes at the training ground bearing fruit, the team took the division by an impressive eight points.

The key was the team's fitness. Yes they were learning to play a high-tempo brand of football not seen, but the work on the fitness they put in at Melwood was vital to their success. The season started with a 2–0 win at Bristol Rovers and Melia remarked, 'That was the first time I'd played in the first match of the season and felt I could play again afterwards.'

Melia did play afterwards. In fact he played in all of the next 41 games (just one of four ever-presents) and was now very much an integral part of Shankly's plans. He scored 13 goals from midfield but total hero status would elude him. Liddell had gone but now the fans had his successor Ian Callaghan, Hunt and new striker Ian St John to worship.

Not that Melia's skills went totally unappreciated. Plenty of fans saw the work he put in and loved him for it. Peter Marshall today is a BBC journalist who has covered global events for programmes such as *Newsnight*, but back in the early 1960s he was a small boy, taken to Anfield by his big brother and when not fixated with the activities in the Boys' Pen, his attention was taken by the bald Jimmy Melia.

'Of course Roger Hunt was the main man back then,' recalls Marshall. 'He was the one people noticed. A blonde bombshell. He looked like Heinz Burt, the guitarist from The Tornadoes. Hunt was that obvious hero but the guy that always impressed me was Jimmy Melia. He was a wily inside-forward, the creator of goals and I was immediately struck by him. He made everything happen. Often a simple pass would do but it was always the right pass. He was the antithesis of the quiffed goalscorers of the game.

'I wrote to him once in 1962. I was nine and I told him I was a big fan and that I was sure he would soon play for England. I asked if he could sign a picture. He sent me back a piece of Liverpool FC headed paper with every player's signature on it and a black and white picture of him signed, "To Peter". Today they both hang, framed in my toilet and I'm sure if my house caught on fire, they would be the first two things I'd save.'

The atmosphere around Liverpool's squad was now one of get up and go. The turgid apathy that enveloped the 1950s had gone. The dressing room was now full of characters who weren't there to go through the motions. Success was the end game but with big personalities came big clashes and for Melia, relations with one new player were strained from the off.

It was thought by some of the newcomers that the old local guard, players such as Melia and Ronnie Moran were sceptical of an influx of Scottish signings. Ian St John called them 'The Liverpool mafia,' and at one training session at Southport beach, tensions spilled over.

'Long before it happened I knew I was on a collision course with Jimmy Melia, the midfielder and former lord of the dressing-room, and his team-mates Ronnie Moran and Johnny Morrissey,' recalled St John.

'They were the local lads who had come up through the city's schoolboy football system, and they didn't like their Scottish manager showing a preference for the products of his home country. His move for me and Ronnie Yeats suggested strongly to them that the old order was changing rapidly and on a trip to Czechoslovakia I felt the first negative vibrations. I caught full-back Moran referring to "Scottish bastards".

'The violent climax to that resentment came when Shankly, driven almost to distraction by the effects of the heavy winter of 1962/63 on his training programme, announced that we would have a day out by the sea. What he had in mind was the perfect surface of the beach when the tide went out. The sand was wonderfully level and Shankly was so happy he might have been Lawrence of Arabia catching his first sight of Damascus.

'His mood changed quickly, though, when Melia took a snide kick at me and I went straight for him, with the lads trying to cling on to both of us and break us apart. The manager always liked to think he was in charge of a fiercely united family, and that this fondness for each other would be shot through our performances on the field. Now he was seeing his midfield general and his striker trying to land the big knockout punch. Shankly bellowed, "Fucking hell stop," and eventually we were separated. On the bus back, I bombarded Melia with threats, one of the milder ones being, "When we reach the ground, I'm going to get you." There was a little gym down the corridor from the dressing room, and I said to Melia, "I'll see you there – right now," but he refused to come. That signalled the end of the Liverpool mafia. In a way I could understand how the bad feelings developed. The pity was Melia was a good player, a terrific passer of the ball, who might have had a run with England had it not been for the competition of Johnny Haynes and Bobby Charlton.'

Melia did get his first England cap in a game against Scotland at Wembley (annoyingly for Melia, St John played for the Scots in a 2–1 win against the auld enemy). He was a player at the peak of his powers, the Kop would even chant 'Melia, Melia' every now and then and he was still able to make things happen. Everton were beaten at Anfield early in the 1963/64 campaign 2–1 with Callaghan getting both goals. 'I remember Jimmy Melia laid off a two-yard pass and I battered one in past Gordon West from 25 yards,' recalled Callaghan. 'Jimmy then did exactly the same for my second and after the game, whilst I'm looking to take all the plaudits in the dressing-room, he comes over to me and says, "I don't half lay them on for you kid." He wanted all the credit!'

Then, whilst enjoying this good form in the middle of December 1963 – with Liverpool pushing for what would be their first title under Shankly – Melia got injured. It was the beginning of the end. Being injured at Shankly's Liverpool wasn't a good idea. The Scot famously ignored those not fit and then there were the newfangled machines used by physiotherapist Bob Paisley that were enough to scare the hardest of footballers.

Melia confessed to a twinge in his knee and so unwittingly became a guinea pig for a new machine brought in, designed to heal. In front of the squad, Melia's knee was strapped to the piece of kit, whilst Paisley started to fiddle with knobs and dials. Nothing was happening and Shankly was getting a bit irate at the lack of healing.

'Jesus Bob,' the boss said. 'Haven't you read the instructions?'

'The instructions are in German, boss,' said Paisley, the rest of the squad fighting off giggles.

'You were in the war weren't you, Bob?' said Shankly. 'Didn't you learn German?'

Paisley fired up all the dials to maximum before realising he hadn't plugged it in at the mains. When he did, Melia's leg shot uncontrollably towards the ceiling and he screamed for it to be turned off. The miracle machine wasn't going to work and the writing was on the wall.

'I had a couple of goldfish,' recalls Peter Marshall. 'One was called Roger Hunt. The other was called Jimmy Melia. Roger Hunt ate Jimmy Melia.' More accurately it was his old nemesis St John who devoured Melia's Liverpool career.

With new striker Alf Arrowsmith arriving and scoring goals in Melia's absence, St John had been withdrawn to a deep-lying position behind the strikers by Shankly and did so well, there could be no way back for Melia. His last appearance was a 3–1 defeat at Goodison Park before he moved on to Wolverhampton Wanderers in the March of '64. Liverpool went on to claim the title and Melia fittingly was awarded a medal for his contribution.

'I was absolutely devastated,' says Marshall. 'It was such a shock and I couldn't believe it. When you're 11 years old, it is hard when a hero leaves. I was at school when I heard the news and I remember being cross with the club, so cross that I became an Everton fan for the day. Everton! This was a team I used to call "Stinky Pongos" as a kid but that's how cross I was that Jimmy had been sold. I was only 11 and I soon came to my senses but yes, it hurt to say goodbye.'

Melia had felt the writing was on the wall and whilst he found it hard to leave the club he had grown up with, he got on with his career and always came back with that bald head held high. Having moved on to Southampton, he helped the south coast club back into the First Division in 1966 and was instrumental in his side's 2–0 win over Liverpool at The Dell in August 1968.

He then came to Anfield as player-manager of Aldershot in 1971 for an FA Cup tie that Liverpool only just won, 1–0. Melia was given a hearty welcome, as he was in 1983 when he sent his Brighton team out for an FA Cup fifth round tie.

The competition had always eluded Bob Paisley and so in what was the great man's final season, the cup run took on extra significance. Melia's Brighton though put an end to any cup dreams thanks to a goal by another old Jimmy, Jimmy Case. The midfielder's strike won the game 2–1 and on the final whistle as the players ran to their fans in the corner of the Kemlyn and Anfield Road stands, there was Melia, the top of his head bobbing along the Anfield turf like old times.

Like a schoolboy, he didn't know what to do with himself and at one point he seemed to be instructing his players to follow him to the Kop end to take the applause. His players thought better of it and whilst the Kop can be a compassionate entity, Melia only got so far before coming to his senses.

And that was that. Melia can be seen at Anfield from time to time today. He lives and coaches in Dallas, Texas and at the end of the 2013/14 season he came with coaches to see Liverpool beat Manchester City, 3–2. Prior to the match he was able to take his coaching colleagues onto the pitch, and to one patch in particular. 'I told the coaches, "This is the spot where I scored my first goal." From a Billy Liddell cross, I crashed it in with my left foot.'

It wasn't the famous old stadium's biggest moment and he wasn't the club's most lauded footballer, but Jimmy Melia did his bit and to a few, he did it absolutely brilliantly.

Ian St John

1961–1971
Appearances: 425
Goals: 118

*T*HEY say breakfast is the most important meal of the day. *They* say that get your *brekkie* right, you are set for the whole day. *They* might be right. For it was over breakfast that one of the most important signings in Liverpool's long and illustrious history first materialised.

It was the spring of 1961. Bill Shankly's house in West Derby, near Liverpool's Melwood training ground. The season is about to end but already the manager is thinking about how he takes the club on. His team will finish third in the Second Division, not enough for promotion and the manager knows he needs to make the right decisions to lift the club to the levels that he and they belong.

Shankly comes downstairs to eat. It was a Sunday. A difficult day for Shankly as officially it was a day off. Shankly didn't do days off. Liverpool had drawn at Sunderland the day before and the manager's head is crunching over his forward line and the need for reinforcements.

He sits down, pours his tea, takes a bite from his toast and turns his *Sunday Post* newspaper to the sports pages. There it is. The headline might as well have been in neon. A smile comes to his handsome face. This was the news that would change things. This was a good Sunday. 'St John Wants To Go', it says. It's time to get to work.

Motherwell, St John's club, were phoned immediately to check the story wasn't press mischief-making. It wasn't. Next T.V. Williams the chairman and his vice-chair Syd Reaks were wrestled from their own

Sunday slumber and told to get themselves and the club's bank account into action. The board member Eric Sawyer was instrumental in making cash available and he was quickly reassured by Shankly that St John was, 'not just a good centre-forward...he's the only centre-forward in the game.'

This remark might have been tainted with slight Shankly overhype. The manager had been seeking another striker to complement Roger Hunt ever since he arrived. Dave Hickson was far from the player adored at Goodison Park and so Shankly's mind had long been on getting another.

At Huddersfield he had managed a certain Denis Law, a fantastic forward who would surely complement Hunt very nicely. Law for one was prepared to make the move. 'There was nothing else in my mind other than following Shanks,' he later said. 'But Liverpool, like Huddersfield were in the Second Division when he went and they didn't have the money that Huddersfield required, so that was the end of it. It was a disappointment. Shanks was like a father figure when I first moved from Scotland, but it wasn't to be and I ended up joining Manchester City.'

By 1961, with Sawyer on board, cash flow was no longer a trickle but still there were targets and frustrations. Brian Clough was the most sought-after of strikers. Scoring plenty of goals at Middlesbrough, Shankly had his eye on the player and buoyed by his board's new approach made a £40,000 bid plus an extra £10,000 should Liverpool be promoted. Middlesbrough rejected the offer. Shankly was keen and able to spend money but he wouldn't be played. Clough went to Sunderland for £55,000 and for Shankly it was back to the drawing board, or should that be breakfast table?

Now Shankly was in the vice-chairman's Rolls-Royce and heading to Motherwell in North Lanarkshire, not a million miles from where Shankly was brought up. St John had been on the Shankly radar from his days managing Huddersfield and he wasn't missing out this time.

Shankly made the Fir Park club an offer of £37,500. Liverpool's transfer record still stood at the £13,000 they paid for Albert Stubbins back in 1946 and the most Shankly had ever spent was £4,000, but things were changing.

Negotiations were off and running, confused slightly by Charlie Mitten, the manager at Newcastle United arriving with offers of signing-on fees and property. St John's ears pricked, but the Motherwell hierarchy were smitten with the Liverpool man and wouldn't be starting a bidding war.

Shankly met St John and his wife at their flat. They were – like everyone – impressed. The manager talked but he was eager, excited, and keen to get his man and his family down to Merseyside and signed. Mitten had gone away for now but he and others might be back. 'Let's go now,' he said to the St Johns.

'You do know we have a young baby don't you Mr Shankly?' said Betsy St John.

'Take the baby to your mother's, we have important business.'

Soon St John had signed, was moving into an apartment in the Maghull area of Liverpool and he had enough money as way of a signing-on fee to buy a new Vauxhall. Shankly had seen that headline on the Sunday. St John was now a Liverpool player. It was only Tuesday.

Days later St John was popular; a hat-trick in the Liverpool Senior Cup Final against Everton is always a good start (even if the side do lose 4–3). Months later he was cherished, his goals after all had helped the club back to the top-flight and years later he was idolised for his part in making Shankly's team among the best in Europe.

Clubs make signings that can change the trajectory of the club. Great players come and go but only a few have the sort of impact St John had. His arrival changed things and turned the team from Second Division also-rans into the most feared around. Later John Barnes's transfer created a new, exciting team and made a good team great. Kenny Dalglish's arrival made a team already the best in Europe somehow better and for longer. Luis Suarez lifted the gloom from the Hicks/Gillett era and ushered in a new dawn. St John is up there with these greats.

St John's cult lay in his demeanour and will to win. Like his manager he was single-minded and would stop at nothing to score goals and win football matches. Roger Hunt was the more prolific goalscorer but he was wholesome, a nice guy. St John was far from a nasty man but he had an edge, a glint in his Scottish eye that appealed to so many fans. Like them, he came to win.

The, 'Clap-clap-clap-clap-clap-clap-clap-clap-clap-clap St John!' that went up was thought to be the first regular song for a player since Elisha Scott's, 'Lisha! Lisha!' It was to be a chant exclusive to special players, later taken on by Kenny Dalglish and Robbie Fowler. St John in many ways was a combination of the two. Like Dalglish he was a skilful Scottish number seven who would bully defenders before they could bully him, and like Fowler, he had a natural eye for goal to go with a mischievous streak as wide as the Mersey.

Ian St John was born and raised in a Motherwell tenement, one of six children and the young St John would spend hours in front of his home's wireless, brimming with excitement as Scottish internationals such as Jimmy Mason and Willie Waddell were brought into his living-room via what he called, 'The magic box'.

It wasn't just football had that the young man under its spell. St John loved cricket. Motherwell was far from a hotbed of the game enjoyed on English village greens, but St John loved the heroics of West Indian bowlers Alf Valentine and Sonny Ramadhin. St John spent hours of his summer holidays trying to perfect the art of spin bowling. It probably appealed to his cunning nature, a trait he later brought to Anfield.

St John made his debut for his local club in 1957 under manager Bobby Ancell and hit the ground running with a glut of goals that included a famous hat-trick in just two and a half minutes against Hibernian in 1959, the quickest in Scottish football history.

That same year, St John made his international debut for Scotland against West Germany and so when he came to Liverpool two years later, whilst he may not have been a household name in his new city, he quickly proved to be the clever centre-forward the fans had been dreaming of.

Like the club's previous record signing, Albert Stubbins, St John immediately made the forward line better, pleasing fans and accountants alike. Liverpool won ten their first 11 games, practically securing promotion by Halloween. Not that it was easy. Seven years of hard graft in the second tier of English football had proved that, but this team now had a way about it that bamboozled opponents. They were quick and they were skilful and they were very, very strong.

Teams were engulfed, often doing their best to quell Shankly's men but even if they enjoyed a resolute day, Liverpool had a knack of getting late winners; such was the fitness of the team. Reuben Bennett who had worked with St John at Motherwell was now the fitness man in Shankly's burgeoning boot-room and with Shankly overseeing matters, results were emphatic.

'When I arrived at Melwood for training it was a wonderful surprise,' says St John. 'We played two-a-side on small pitches, it was all work with the ball. Nothing but work with the ball. I loved it. It underlined the neglect in my earlier years at Motherwell. If you asked for a ball back then they frowned at you and said, "If you don't use one today, you'll be hungry for it on Saturday." What nonsense! How can I use the ball when I haven't trained with it? It's like asking a boxer to fight without having sparred.'

Much is made of the simplicity of Melwood training sessions and whilst small-sided games and ball work were priority, Shankly went to huge efforts to change the philosophy of the place. Yes it was simple but the players had to work. Individual training and dietary requirements were enforced. Players would cool down after training and take the bus together to eat at Anfield. A simple but modern, forward-thinking approach.

Shankly stood back on the sidelines and watched, sensing his work and his thoughts were getting through to the players and the club as a whole. 'In no time at all,' winger Alan A'Court remarked, 'both Anfield and Melwood were buzzing with an electric atmosphere. It was rather as if you were on board a powerful new racing car and he had just switched on the engine.'

St John revelled in his new home. Hunt scored 41 goals that season, a record league return that still stands but St John's 21, coupled with the perfect dovetailing with his partner, caught the eye. Hunt, blonde quiff and softly spoken Lancastrian ways; St John crew cut and a face that even when silent looked like it was swearing. Soon the best defenders in Europe would struggle to contain them; those poor guys in the Second Division had no chance.

Promotion was secured and St John relished playing the big boys. The strikers at the time – Jimmy Greaves, Bobby Smith, Denis Law – were huge stars, but St John played with the confidence and arrogance necessary to mix it with the best of them. 5ft 7in, but with a leap that seemed to spring from a desire to beat the biggest of defenders, St John was lethal in the air, scoring plenty of headed goals. He had a tenacity that defenders hate and a cunning to stretch any back line.

He'd drift wide and he'd drop deep, all the while making space for others. Like the spin bowlers he grew up idolising, St John's style of play was his team's very own *doosra*.

He was hard too. Very hard. In Motherwell as a boy he had been enticed into a local gym and immediately loved the place, full of characters and all the better for its lack of glamour. 'The first thing that hit you was the smell of stale sweat,' St John said.

'A rickety ring, a few punch bags and the odd skipping rope made up the equipment, but the atmosphere was full of life. No one likes getting that first serious belt in the face, especially without the headgear, but I came to terms with that quickly enough and boxing gave me a lot of confidence. I gained a strong belief in my ability to handle myself, both on the football field and in the street. This was particularly useful when my brother Billy got into scrapes and I was obliged to sort things out.'

Shankly will have seen that edge and loved it. The manager was a huge fan of the pugilistic arts – he loved the likes of Gene Tunney and on a tour to New York in 1964 made a beeline for Jack Dempsey's Bar on West 33rd Street hoping to meet a hero – and had no problem with his striker 'sorting things out' if necessary. Centre-halves in the 1960s were far from shrinking violets and for a forward to get by, he had to be of the resolute variety.

Sometimes that could spill over. In February 1966, on their way to another title, Liverpool went to Fulham and lost 2–0. In the 88th minute, consumed by frustration, St John took a hack at Mark Pearson who came back at the Scot, grabbing his hair and there it was. St John was back in the Motherwell boxing gym, the smell of sweat filled his nostrils and he turned with a right/left combination that saw the Fulham man flat out admiring the London sky.

Shankly would have been impressed by the flurry of punches but didn't want to lose his player to suspension and so became the first manager to use video evidence in an FA hearing. He failed. He went to even greater steps a year later when once again St John had been show to the dressing room for throwing his fists around.

This time it was at Coventry, on Boxing Day 1967. The Sky Blues' Brian Lewis had seen fit to grab St John in a spot Scots like to cover with a sporran. St John was shocked, and of course Lewis's chin took the full brunt of that surprise. After his early shower, Shankly asked what had just happened?

'He grabbed me by the goolies, boss,' said St John.

'Come in and see me tomorrow,' the manager barked.

St John told the story again and Shankly called in Bob Paisley and told St John to get undressed and up on the treatment table. Paisley got to with some boot polish, iodine and an old cloth, rubbing it all over St John's 'groin and genitals'. The player lay there wondering where this was going, 'I hope you're getting as much pleasure as I am out of this, Bob,' laughed St John.

When Paisley was done, St John looked like he had been hit by a truck and so when Shankly called in some selected press to see the bruising caused at Highfield Road the previous day, he got the required response and the back pages were full of stories of mass provocation. The FA were less taken in and the player's suspension stood.

St John had his run-in with Jimmy Melia but he could also pick on players not his size and despite being the best of friends, he and Ron Yeats once had a run-in at Melwood. Yeats had taken a kick at him and so St John retaliated with interest. Yeats went for him again and as St John later put it, 'All bets were off. We were dragged apart and when the players gathered to have the traditional cup of tea, it started up again.' Welterweight against heavyweight maybe but what did St John care? 'I wasn't frightened of anybody,' he later said.

The two men didn't fall out for long though and on another occasion were fighting side by side. In Milan after defeat in the semi-final of the European Cup in 1965, Yeats and St John had joined a couple of fans. The bill arrived and it became clear to the tourists that they were being conned. Words were followed by actions and before you could say *buon appetito*, punches were being thrown. 'At one point I seemed to be fighting everyone,' said St John. 'Ronnie and I fought a rearguard action up the stairs and out on to the street. This gave me a certain height advantage, something that for Ronnie was not a dire need. We were, as they say in street fighting circles, giving them plenty.'

En masse, Liverpool fans were singing, 'She Loves You' by the Beatles or 'Anyone Who Had a Heart' by Cilla Black, but factions of supporters were more inclined to do their talking with their fists, and trouble at football was a growing phenomenon. 'Special' trains back from London were often smashed up and whilst far from a major problem, certain fans will have been drawn to a player who would throw a punch or two in the name of Liverpool Football Club.

Most though just loved the goals, the trophies and the glory he helped bring to their corner of the footballing world. St John's role in the team that took the First Division in 1964 was key. He played much of it up front with Roger Hunt of course but such was his tactical nous, St John would also drop deeper into midfield, allowing the prolific Alf Arrowsmith to chip in with vital goals.

St John played in the midfield with fellow Scot Willie Stevenson just as well as he did up front with Hunt. He was a footballer's footballer, a man who could take instructions from his manager and make a team tick. An evangelist outside the stadium once wore a sandwich board, asking sinful passers-by, 'What Would You Do If The Lord Came?' One fan, clearly appreciative of his hero's tactical nous wrote underneath, 'Move St John to inside-right'.

It was at Wembley in 1965 though that St John cemented his place in red hearts with his extra-time winner that brought the FA Cup to Anfield for its first ever visit. Liverpool were by now a talking point, a top team competing with the best in Europe, their fans the subject of BBC documentaries and their manager becoming more than just some coach.

On the week of the final, Shankly did BBC radio's *Desert Island Discs*. In homage to his roots, he chose Jim Reeves and Kenneth McKellar but the latter sang My Love is Like a Red, Red Rose. Shankly was a Scot but he was also a Liverpool man now. Through and through. He also picked Danny Kaye and Louis Armstrong's rendition of When the Saints Go Marching In, and that day under the Twin Towers at Wembley it was his Saint that helped his team do just that. They marched in, they won the cup and they marched home.

Street parties had raged all weekend as Liverpool's first coronation had lit a fuse under an adoring public and St John was the man, the man who had won the cup. At 1–1 and with the game a seeming stalemate, Ian Callaghan found a burst of energy that defied the heavy pitch and weather and ran at the Leeds full-back, Willie Bell.

'I knew I could beat him for speed,' said Callaghan. 'Having put the ball past him though, I doubted I could catch it as I had hit it maybe too hard. I hared after it and just managed to get my foot around the ball before it went over the byline and whipped it across. Because of my struggle to reach it I couldn't get much height on the cross, but my only concern was getting it into the box. That was all that was on my mind. The ball was only a few feet off the turf and actually behind Ian, but he twisted in mid-air and somehow turned the ball in with a glancing flick. He was a wonderful header of the ball. On this occasion it was his supple ability to alter his body shape whilst airborne that allowed him to score that crucial goal.'

Shankly had told his players prior to kick-off, 'This is a great day in our lives.' He could have been talking for the fans too. One supporter, with a handkerchief on his head to keep the rain off, invaded the pitch to be with his heroes, as Kenneth Wolstenholme, the commentator took the words from his mouth, telling the world, 'Ee-ay-addio, We've Won the Cup'. Supporters would come home that night or the next day, well oiled on success and booze.

St John himself actually felt slight anti-climax after that final but the club had another big game just days later when the unofficial world champions, Inter Milan came to town for the European Cup semi-final first leg. It was a classic Anfield night, the first of a famous breed when Liverpool players have been driven on in Europe by rampant fans made even more fervent by a night sky.

Inter's famous manager Helenio Herrera would call the fans animals after the game, such was the noise they produced that night, their passion ignited further by the sight of the FA Cup paraded prior to kick-off. His bitterness brought on by not only the atmosphere generated by the locals but also the way Shankly's team set about his great side.

St John fondly recalls that night in May. 'Inside Anfield, the fans were going crazy and even the Italian players, used to the boiling atmosphere of the mighty San Siro, were clearly affected by the scale of the reaction on the terraces. It was so intense, so intimate. In the San Siro you were in a great cathedral of the game. In Anfield, even more so than today, you were in a cockpit. In the tunnel at Anfield that night, the eyes of the Italians showed surprise, concern, the flickering of doubts – whatever it was it was not such a distant cousin to sheer fright.'

Liverpool went after the Italians from the off. Wave after wave of attack was greeted with wave after wave of bigger and bigger noise. Roger Hunt scored early and whilst Alessandro Mazzola took advantage of a defensive lapse, Liverpool had too much belief and too much guile to be held back further.

A brilliantly worked free kick saw Callaghan restore a lead and then in the 75th minute St John himself added a third from close range. A controversially disallowed goal prevented a fourth but the Kop, singing 'Go Back To Italy', went home in fine spirits.

Liverpool though did have to go back to Italy for a second leg that would prove heartbreakingly tricky. An Italian journalist had told Shankly that his team, 'Would not be allowed to win,' and so it transpired. Liverpool, thanks to some dubious refereeing decisions, lost 3–0 and were out. Lessons though had been learnt.

Liverpool and St John licked their wounds and moved on. Manchester United had won the league in 1965 and a rivalry was growing. The Charity Shield was drawn 2–2 at Old Trafford but Shankly wanted to recapture the title, a prize that he would later call the club's 'bread and butter'.

Liverpool lost their first game at Anfield in August 1965, but their home team was imperious and the title was taken – Don Revie's Leeds once again the closest victims to Liverpool's success – by an impressive six points.

Alf Arrowsmith had been injured in the Charity Shield and so St John once more partnered Hunt up front. Hunt would get his customary 30 league goals whilst St John with a less impressive ten strikes was more about his ability to create, both chances and space.

'Those were the days when there was more man-to-man marking,' wrote Shankly. 'St John would take a walk and the opposing boy would go with him and we would say, "It's alright, bring him in here and we'll give some tea!"'

In September, Liverpool won at West Ham 5–1 with their team full of soon to be World Cup winners. At the end of the month Everton came to Anfield for what was the most satisfying of derby day demolitions.

One up after 34 minutes through Tommy Smith, Roger Hunt started the second rout in its fourth minute and after a fine lob from Willie Stevenson and another from Hunt, the Kop with the smell of blue blood in its nostrils demanded a fifth. 'We want five', they cried. In the last minute the obliging St John battered a header past Gordon West and the Kop had their scoreline. They still sing about it today. '*And we played the Toffees for a laugh and we left them feeling blue…1-2, 1-2-3, 1-2-3-4-5 nil.*'

On 27 November, after a 2–1 win over Burnley, Shankly's men topped the table and there they stayed. It was a glorious team. St John and his comrades were royalty. In their all red kit with the huge Liver bird on their breasts, they were knights. 'We were not so much a football club as an empire, and I lived at the heart of it,' St John said.

'I walked down the street in Liverpool the master of everything I saw, as did all my team-mates. Maybe we lived in modest houses that we didn't own, and we would never earn similar fortunes to the pop stars – who seemed to be springing up in every corner of the city – but as footballers, we were in the right place at the right time, following the lead of the right manager. He made our footballing lives.'

St John, his team-mates and the staff gave the fans their life. If the players strutted around town, fans did too and on matchdays they would taunt anyone and everyone. The style in which their team would beat all-comers was contagious and the fans loved every smug minute. Billy Wright's Arsenal were beaten 4–2 at Anfield in December – '*London Bridge is fallin' down, fallin' down, fallin' down, poor old Arsenal*'. Matt

Busby's men were beaten 2–1 at Anfield on New Year's Day 1966 – *'Man United, Man United, you're not fit to wipe my arse! You're not fit to wipe my arse!'*

Chelsea were beaten at Anfield 2–1 in late April and the title was once again Liverpool's, with the use of only 14 players, a record. 'Champions, Champions,' screamed the Kop. 'Shankly, Shankly,' screamed the Kop and of course, *clap-clap, clap-clap-clap, clap-clap-clap-clap, clap-clap – St John* screamed the Kop.

It was the most wonderful afternoon. Those players who had formed Shankly's first great team reached their zenith. Peter Etherington, an Anfield regular recalls the day in his excellent book, *One Boy and his Kop*, 'The celebrations went long and loud and it was a good job we savoured them as it would be another seven years before we would experience the like again.'

The following season the side were comprehensively beaten in the European Cup by Ajax of Amsterdam and a young player called Johan Cruyff. 'Maybe the best player we ever faced,' said St John.

The young Dutchman had taken the team apart both home and away but Shankly was finding it harder to do just that. Players had passed their peak and whilst the team were still very competitive trophies weren't being won. St John and his team-mates – now with their fuller sideburns – were struggling to keep up with a new breed of opponent; younger and fitter. Shankly loved the team and found it hard to make changes. So hard that when he did drop St John for a game at Newcastle in the autumn of 1969, he went about it in the wrong way.

It was Newcastle hero and now a football writer Jackie Milburn who told St John he'd been dropped, not Shankly. St John was furious. He knew teams had to be broken up. His team-mates Geoff Strong, Willie Stevenson, Ron Yeats and even Roger Hunt were being moved on but he had adapted, he was fit and dropping deeper, he was still playing well. In early 1971 St John left, but there was a bitter taste to what should have been a glorious exit. 'I cannot shake the belief that, at the end, Shankly let me down,' he wrote in his autobiography. 'I was terribly disappointed he didn't handle it better. Neither Shankly nor I could change the realities of football, or the ageing process, but he could have shown me more courtesy.'

Shankly had found it tough to do but now his focus was on the future and more glory. St John – his name etched on the decade – is still one of the greats, one of the pioneers. Years later working on local radio he was very vocal and critical of Gerard Houllier's methods at Liverpool. On fan forums plenty of supporters were angry with this ex-player's constant gripes. Others though saw the bigger picture. If anyone was entitled to voice an angry opinion it was the likes of St John.

The man himself no doubt would have liked to talk face to face. Internet chat room fights are never as good as the real thing. Centre-halves, team-mates, Italian waiters; St John stood up to them all. In the summer of 2014 it was announced that he was battling cancer. You fancy it is a battle he will win.

Shankly loved St John, loved what he brought to this team. 'My first great buy,' the manager later said. 'Clever, canny, bags of skill, made things happen. Liked a scrap too. Jesus, did he like a scrap. I sometimes wanted to tie his fists behind his back. Great player though. Gave everything on the pitch. What a player.'

Ron Yeats

1961–1971
Appearances: 454
Goals: 16

T HERE is a photograph within the glorious album of Liverpool's history that will please Bill Shankly, for it sums up everything he ever wanted from the club he took on and made great.

Taken just minutes before his first FA Cup Final with the team, at Wembley in 1965, his skipper Ron Yeats is shaking hands with his counterpart, Bobby Collins of Leeds United. That's it. That's the image.

No action, no goals, just his captain shaking hands with another. Look at it though and you will notice that Yeats dominates the photo. In his all red kit (a change made by Shankly just months earlier) he dwarfs the Leeds man and Bobby Collins – Evertonians will tell you as well as Leeds fans – was, despite his small stature, a difficult footballer to dominate.

That's all that Shankly ever foresaw, all he ever wanted; for Liverpool to dominate. 'My idea was to build Liverpool into a bastion of invincibility,' Shankly later said. 'Had Napoleon had that idea he would have conquered the bloody world. I wanted Liverpool to be untouchable. My idea was to build Liverpool up and up until eventually everyone would have to submit and give in.'

Here that vision was a reality and in Ron Yeats he had the perfect specimen. Shankly wanted to make his club a huge angry volcano and the players he sent out to represent him were to be the spewing red ash that devoured all in its path. His team then had to be fast, committed, strong and where it mattered, huge.

Shankly met Yeats in an Edinburgh hotel in 1961 and walked around him as if marvelling at a great old oak. 'Jesus,' said Shankly. 'You must be seven feet tall son?' Yeats, not knowing quite how to take this enigmatic man shyly put him right. 'No, I am only six feet two.'

'Well, that's near enough seven feet for me.'

And there it was. Shankly could make the players who played for him feel 7ft, he could make the fans think their heroes were 7ft and he very much made opponents think they were about to play against players who were 7ft tall. Yeats was the personification of that, and the manager and the fans loved him for it.

Shankly's first team – that exciting bunch who won two league titles and the club's first ever FA Cup amid a soundtrack of Merseybeat classics – was brimming with heroic figures for the fans to pin their allegiances to. Roger Hunt, blonde and bombastic. Peter Thompson, handsome and creative. Ian St John, fantastic and stubborn. All were attacking players but at the back, Shankly knew he needed a solid base and they didn't come more solid that Ron Yeats.

He wasn't a match winner but he helped win matches, and he did it with a smile. A gentle giant who away from the glitz and glamour of goals, meant so much to fans falling deeper and deeper in love with the club that Shankly was building.

Liverpool had long missed the domineering type at the centre of their defence. Laurie Hughes had been impressive in the successful post-war team but when Shankly arrived in 1959, Dick White was, like the team itself, struggling to fully impress.

A big centre-half was top of Shankly's shopping list. The young Jack Charlton at Leeds was a target but the board wouldn't sanction the money to make the transfer happen. Frank McLintock at Leicester was another target. The young Scot was at Leicester City and after their FA Cup Final appearance against Spurs in 1961, Shankly gatecrashed the club's banquet to convince the player to join him. Again, no joy.

It wasn't easy. Shankly had a way about him sure, but he was trying to talk the country's most promising players into coming to a Second Division outfit and smooth-talking charisma alone wouldn't cut it. Money was an issue. Liverpool's coffers were hard to breach and the board needed convincing to part with cash as much as any player needed persuading to come.

That had to change and thanks largely to Everton Football Club, it did. John Moores, of the Littlewoods Pools Moores', was the chairman at Goodison Park and was about to embark on his own successful spending spree there, but he also had a stake in Liverpool and understood that having two thriving teams in the First Division would benefit each club, and the city as a whole.

Moores put Eric Sawyer on the Liverpool board, the account manager at Littlewoods and a man who knew that to accumulate, you had to speculate. Shankly and Sawyer immediately hit it off. The businessman was enthralled by the football's man insights. Shankly laid out his vision and Sawyer promised to do all he could to finance it.

'The people [of Liverpool] were craving for success and I knew what was needed to get it,' Shankly wrote in his autobiography. 'But I had problems trying to convince the directors that you couldn't get a good player for £3,000.

'I would tell them, "Look we need a goalkeeper." They would look doubtful and say, "Oh, the one we have is good enough."

'That is how they went on every time I wanted to move in those early days. Some of the directors thought the club was all right.

'When Mr Sawyer joined the board, he knew were not good enough. We had lots of discussions together. "Bill," he said. "If you get the players, I'll get the money." Ron Yeats and Ian St John were still the players on my mind, but when we discussed possible transfer moves at board meetings the tune was still, "We can't afford them."

'That's when Mr Sawyer stepped in and said, "We cannot afford *not* to buy them."'

Yeats was perfect for Shankly. The manager, for all his sharp suits and managerial genius was a frustrated player. He longed to be in red, playing the game he so loved. He would have loved to have played in front of the Kop for Liverpool (a few guest appearances during the war were not enough to satisfy that dream), he would have loved to have won games with muddied knees and a sweated brow. Instead he built a team who won games for him, by playing with the tenacity and speed he would have if he could have.

'A man who's a manager whose players are honest with him and he's honest with them, he can transmit his thoughts to them and I'm certain I've headed some balls that have gone into the net and I've kept them out and I've scored a few goals as well,' Shankly once said. 'So I've willed somebody to do something, and they've done it.'

Yeats was perfect in this capacity. A player cut from the same cloth. Not just the tartan variety but with the same will to win, the same grimace when losing but also the same likability that belied his massive frame.

Born in Aberdeen, and growing up when the town was more famous for beef than oil, Yeats worked in an abattoir from the age of 15. Slaughterhouse shifts took up half the young man's time, football took up the rest and in 1957 – whilst still working with cattle – he signed for Dundee United. He would work night shifts, get some sleep and turn out for the Tannadice club, before his National Service took him away. His ability with a football though saw him captaining the British Army side and there, he caught the eye of many an admirer.

In his autobiography, Shankly recalls how as manager of Huddersfield, he first noticed this big, young man in action. '[His coach] Eddie Boot and I drove up through the moors one night, up on to Kendal and on to Falkirk to see Ron Yeats and Ian St John, who were playing against each other in a Scotland versus Scottish Second Division select match. Ronnie was in the Second Division with Dundee United. I saw him before the game and I saw him on the field. The quickness – and the size of him!'

Huddersfield couldn't afford either player but now, four years later with Anfield's purse strings finally loosened moves could be made. It was the summer of 1961. July. A month later the East Germans would start construction on a giant wall in Berlin that they hoped would keep out enemy factions.

Shankly drove with his vice-chairman, Sidney Reaks to an Edinburgh hotel with the same motives in mind. He had been on at the Dundee club for a while and in time had convinced them to at least let him talk to a player Shankly hoped would be the main brick in a wall that would keep out enemy factions.

Yeats had been told by his employers that a big English club wanted to sign him and arrived at the hotel expecting to meet people from Manchester United or Tottenham. Yeats knew nothing of the confident manager that greeted him or even where Liverpool was on the map. 'Liverpool are in the First Division,' said Shankly. Yeats might not have known geographically where this team were, but he knew a bit about football. 'I thought they were in the Second Division,' he replied.

'With you in the team we will soon be in the First Division.'

The Shankly charm started to work and soon Yeats was coming under his spell. 'I always remember this,' recalled Yeats. '[Shankly] was a lovely dresser: lovely suit and tie, and white, white teeth. That really impressed me. I thought there and then, I like this man.' Yeats bought into Shankly's vision and – with a £22,000 transfer fee agreed – was soon driving to Merseyside with his new employers. 'I couldn't believe it when we were coming down the M6, with vice-chairman Sidney Reaks, who had a Rolls-Royce at the time, and me and Bill in the back. I was only 23 and didn't know what to say. Bill just turned round and said: "Ron, I want you to captain the side. You will be my eyes, my ears and my voice on that pitch." I thought to myself, "Bloody hell." It's a big thing at 23, and I'd never even seen Liverpool.'

Shankly and his sartorial prowess had stood out to the young Yeats and the admiration was mutual. 'Big Ron was a fantastic looking man, with black hair,' Shankly later remarked. 'The first time I saw him he was wearing a light-grey suit and I said, "It should be Hollywood you're going to." He looked as if he could outclass all the film stars. When he came to Liverpool, I got the press boys and said, "Go on, walk around him. He's a colossus."'

Members of the press corps did just that, such were Shankly's hypnotic powers of persuasion and as for 'Colossus' it was a tag that stuck and whilst physically only 6ft 2in, fans and opponents alike saw him as a 7ft giant.

Just weeks later, Yeats was running out at Bristol City's Ashton Gate and helping his new side to a 2–0 win. The press who had recently been asked/told to walk around this new colossal footballer were impressed with how he played. Horace Yates in the *Football Echo* was one such scribe.

'There was much about Yeats that I liked. The advantage which his height gives him made him a great asset in the air, for even if he did not always direct his headers to advantage at least he served to break up aggressive Bristol intentions. He is still settling in and if he can satisfy in his first game the odds are that he will be very much more impressive as time goes on. He does not move with quite the agility we have grown accustomed to seeing from [Dick] White, but he has a sound sense of positional play.'

A week later, Sunderland came to Anfield with Brian Clough up front, a young in-form striker who Shankly had tried to sign. According to Shankly, Yeats 'Bottled him up' and how the manager must have purred from the dugout at his new acquisition.

With formations housing single centre-halves, Dick White was moved out to right-back and on Boxing Day 1961, with White injured

Shankly handed the young Yeats his captaincy. The game, away to Rotherham, was a rare defeat, but Liverpool were four points clear of Leyton Orient in second spot and flying toward promotion.

The team now had the beginnings of a spine. Yeats, Gordon Milne in midfield and St John alongside Roger Hunt. Throw in Gerry Byrne at full-back and later, Ian Callaghan on the right-wing, and Shankly's first great team had its embryonic shape and the Second Division was won with ease.

The details were seen to after a 2–0 win at home to Southampton and with an impressive five games to spare. April showers engulfed Anfield, but no matter; a party eight years in the making was under way. Michael Charters of the *Football Echo* was moved from the press box to write, 'The skies wept, the atmosphere was grey and dismal, but it was still a glorious unforgettable day at Anfield.'

On the final whistle a fan ran onto the pitch and stuck a red and white hat on Yeats's head and a kiss on his cheek. Shankly and the chairman, T.V. Williams tried to address the crazed crowd but unlike the team, the PA system had been neglected and with the Kop screaming for the players ('We want the Reds' they sung), the players came back out but such was the melee, the lap of honour was far from neat. Many of the players retreated back to the dressing room but their captain had been thrown into the Boys' Pen by his many admirers and they weren't going to let him go. 'Jesus Christ son,' said Shankly when a slightly dishevelled Yeats made it back to safety. 'I thought we'd lost you forever!'

Michael Charters finished his article in the *Echo* prophetically. 'So it's First Division ahead and Liverpool have the spirit and confidence to make their mark there.'

Confidence and spirit. There was no doubt where that came from. The manager left his mark on each and every one of his players and within the dressing room was a crackling atmosphere that was fully charged by the boss.

Now in the First Division and holding their own, a new young keeper had been given his chance. Tommy Lawrence, a fellow Scot would become a firm favourite, but Yeats recalls how he was soon on the receiving end of Shankly's wit. 'Tommy Lawrence was frightened to death of Shanks,' recalled Yeats. 'I'll always remember we were playing Arsenal for the first time in eight years because Liverpool had been in the Second Division. We were winning 1–0 with ten minutes to go and I thought, "what a good win this will be at Arsenal." I can't remember the

Arsenal striker's name that hit the ball from 25 yards. I am not joking, but he stubbed his toe first and then hit the ball. It trickled by me and I went "it's yours, Tommy". Tommy was on the line and opened his legs and the bloody ball went right through him. I couldn't believe it.

'I am thinking to myself all this time, "When we get into that dressing room I am going to get into the bath before Shanks comes in." Little did I know that the ten players I was playing with thought the same thing. Everybody was trying to hurry into the dressing room but we weren't quick enough. The door opened and in came Shanks. His face was blue and I am thinking, "Here it goes." He went, "Where is he?" I didn't realise but big Tommy Lawrence was behind me. I was three inches bigger than him and didn't know where he was. His finger went up and he said, "I am here, boss."

'"Where?"

'"Here, boss. Before you say anything, boss, I want to apologise to you and the lads. I should have never opened my legs to that ball." Shankly said, "It's not your fault. It's your fucking mother who should have never opened her legs."'

It was typical of the man and the camaraderie he was hell-bent on orchestrating. Togetherness and pride were now traits running through the city itself, with Merseybeat the pride of Liverpool. Between April 1963 and May 1964, a Merseyside act had topped the hit parade and on the Kop those songs were now revived. The fans swayed giving the Kop a sense of an independent, living organism and the team it came to watch just got better and better.

There was a belief that – after a slightly stuttering start – coursed through the side, a sense that they were simply better than their peers. In late September 1963, the reigning champions Everton were beaten, in late October the 1962 champions Ipswich were beaten at Portman Road and then later, in March, Tottenham the 1961 champions were beaten in north London.

It was a win though at Old Trafford in November that will have had Shankly knowing that this was a side capable of building those invincible bastions. His old mate and former Liverpool skipper, Matt Busby was building a new side at United and from the tragedy of the Munich air disaster, juicy shoots of renewed brilliance were appearing.

It was a strangely subdued day at Old Trafford. 54,000 people constituted a lowish attendance but John F. Kennedy had been shot dead the day before and probably affected the crowd. Liverpool got on with things, and Ron Yeats particularly set about making his presence felt.

Moments before half-time the big man jumped with United's keeper, Harry Gregg for a corner. Gregg felt all 14 and a half stones of Aberdeen meat and was stretchered off with a broken collarbone. Striker David Herd went in goal and Yeats completed his day's work in the 75th minute with a first goal for the club and the points were going home with a now resurgent Liverpool side.

Shankly was ecstatic and never one to shy away from hyperbole, the manager stated that Yeats, 'Is the greatest centre-half in the world today.' Was he? Who cares, this was now a side who believed everything its manager said.

Liverpool went on a six-game winning run that took in the Easter programme and meant a win at home to Arsenal would bring the championship back to Anfield just two years after promotion and 17 years since its last visit.

Liverpool, now the buzzing centre of the universe, intrigued the nation, even the newsy types at the BBC's *Panorama* were interested in the relationship between the football club, the fans and the city's thriving pop culture. A plum-voiced BBC man stood before the Kop intellectualised the Kop's behaviour as it sang the latest songs of Cilla Black, the Beatles and of course Gerry and the Pacemakers.

He did though strike a chord when he noted, standing in front of the swaying mass of fans that, 'It used to be thought that Welsh international rugby crowds were the most musical and passionate in the world. But I've never seen anything like this Liverpool crowd. On the field here, the gay and inventive ferocity they show is quite stunning. The Duke of Wellington before the battle of Waterloo said of his own troops, "I don't know what they do to the enemy, but by god they frighten me" and I'm sure some of the players in this match here this afternoon must be feeling the same way.'

Among the crowd that day and visiting Anfield was Peter Etherington, an eager ten-year-old who had earned the two bob needed and was now off to the match with his mates for the very first time. Etherington went on to write a great book on those days called *One Boy and his Kop* and evokes every young fan's memories when he writes:

'We queued for two hours, but I didn't mind. The sight of people going in and out of the Albert pub, the smell of onions, the sound of people in the ground singing Beatles songs, the size of the big police horses, all left me completely enthralled.

'Finally I got to the front of the queue. A shilling handed over, a push and a click of the turnstile. I had entered the Promised Land. It was a world I had heard about but not seen.

'My first sighting of fifty thousand people all gathered together: twenty-eight thousand of them on a swaying, singing, bouncing Spion Kop, is something I will remember forever. "You'll Never Walk Alone"sang the masses in a moving, colourful display of togetherness.'

Arsenal were put to the sword by Liverpool who took the title in style with an emphatic 5–0 win. It was everything Shankly envisaged. It was quick and it was clinical. Football as a scalpel cutting through soft tissue and all done in front of a crowd that like the team they so adored never stopped moving. It was team and crowd as one. The *Daily Mirror* noted that, 'Liverpool fans don't just watch a game. They take part. They live it.'

Neither team nor supporter though had the pleasure of seeing the championship trophy though. The Football League hadn't brought it with them but that wasn't going to stop the skipper.

Prior to the game when Yeats led the team out onto the field, a young fan had given the him a home-made trophy created from papier-mâché and so, on the team's glorious lap of honour he sought out the fan and took the trophy once again and it ended up in the dressing-room and eventually the club museum. 'Ee-ay-addio we've won the league' screamed the crowd as the party went on into the April night.

Yeats and his mate Ian St John wanted to be more than just players, they felt an affection for the fans and so took themselves off to a pub on the nearby Scotland Road called The Maid of Erin. There they sank a river of Guinness with an adoring public. These weren't superstars giving fans a treat with their presence. This was players and supporters congratulating each other and revelling in the glory *both* had helped create. 'For a few hours,' said St John, 'Ronnie and I were breathing the joy of the fans.'

There was of course plenty of time to revel in heady achievement and pride but this was just the start. Shankly had too many plans to allow this football club to sit back and wallow. The following year was going to be even more memorable.

The start to the league campaign was far from smooth. A 4–0 defeat at home to Everton wasn't nice and by the end of November Liverpool were in 15th position. They were however in the European Cup for the first time and going into the first round (they had beaten Icelandic champions KR Reykjavik in the preliminary stage) Shankly had an idea.

One day at Melwood, he threw a pair of red shorts at Yeats to go with the red tops. 'Get into those and let's see how you look.' It was like the afternoon in the Edinburgh hotel when the two had first met. Shankly was impressed. 'Christ, Ronnie,' he said. 'You look awesome, terrifying. You look 7ft tall.'

Shankly added all red socks to his new uniform but had more than colour on his mind. Liverpool's opponents in the European Cup were Belgian side Anderlecht. Shankly had seen Belgium hold England to a draw at Wembley and as the Anderlecht side housed most of the national team, he knew he was in for a tough game.

Tommy Smith had made his debut earlier that season but was a raw teenager and Shankly was unsure whether to play him in such a big game. The manager took Yeats (his 'eyes and ears') to one side and asked his skipper if it was too soon for the local boy. Yeats was impressed with Smith and told his boss he'd be fine.

Smith though was in Shankly's mind to play alongside Yeats in a rare back four as security to what he felt might be a weakness in Yeats's game. 'Shanks said we were going to shore up the defence and I would be Ron Yeats' right leg as a second centre-half,' recalls Smith.

'Ronnie never could kick with his right. Great player the big man, but no right foot. I had played up front and at inside forward so could use the ball and I played well that night. Everyone thought that it was Alf Ramsey in 1966 who started playing with two centre-backs. That's a load of shite. It was Shanks and Liverpool in 1964.'

Liverpool won 3–0 and progressed in Europe nicely. The quarter-finals were won against German champions Cologne but only after two goalless draws, a 2–2 draw on neutral ground in Holland and the toss of a coin – yes a toss of a coin.

Yeats did plenty of fantastic things with foot, head and body in the name of Liverpool but this game of pure chance was among one of his most iconic and glorious moments. 'I got in first to the referee and said, "I'll have tails." Lucky for me the referee said, "OK, Liverpool tails, Cologne heads."

'Up it went and Christ didn't it stick in a divot. I said to the referee, "Ref, you're going to have to re-toss the coin," and he said, "You're right Mr Yeats." I thought the German captain was going to hit him. He was going berserk because it was falling over on the heads. He picked it up; up it went again and came down tails.

'We were coming off and who's standing there but Bill Shankly. I was first off the pitch and he went, "Well done, big man. I am proud of you. What did you pick?"

"I picked tails boss," I said. I was waiting for the adulation but he just said, "I would have picked tails myself," and off he went.'

Liverpool were beaten in the semi-final of the European Cup by Inter Milan. A tie famous for one of Anfield's most famous nights – a first leg in which the side played superbly against a superpower of the European game to win 3–1, and a second leg that Shankly felt – so poorly was it refereed – was the victim of foul play.

Europe had been a wonderful adventure but for Liverpool's fans, the big story of the 1960s was their win at Wembley for the first time in the club's 74-year history.

Yeats would take the trophy from the Queen in May but back in early January, a skipper faux pas almost cost Her Majesty the pleasure of his company. Liverpool had been drawn at West Bromwich Albion in the third round and with the score at 0–0, Yeats bent down and picked up the ball. He picked up the ball! Penalty. The big man argued that he had heard the referee's whistle. Instead it was a whistle from the crowd.

Albion missed the penalty and Liverpool went on to win 2–1. Had they lost thanks to Yeats's mishap, Shankly's reaction might have included a C-word but it wouldn't have been 'Colossus'. Instead Liverpool went on and on. Stockport County, Bolton Wanderers, Leicester City and Chelsea; all were beaten and so for the first time since 1950, Liverpudlians were heading south for England's showpiece occasion.

Like the day in 1962 when Liverpool won promotion back to the top flight, the weather wasn't befitting the occasion but no matter, Liverpool and their fans were at Wembley and Shankly walked his team out alongside Leeds' Don Revie with his shoulders back and his head high. A white pocket-handkerchief matching his pristine shirt, and behind him equally as pristine his captain, resplendent in all red and big enough to intimidate the twin towers.

The team were relaxed. Entertainers Frankie Vaughan and Jimmy Tarbuck had been cracking jokes and singing songs in the dressing room but then Shankly had said, enough, it's time for business. He got his team in a huddle and looked each of them in the eye. 'You're going to win today because you're the best team,' he said with a grimace.

'Leeds are honoured to be on the same field as you and you're not going to disappoint the greatest supporters in the world. If necessary – and it won't be – you should be prepared to die for them.' You got the feeling that Yeats and his team-mates would have done just that.

The game was a tight affair, a stalemate at times. Yeats dominated but so did Jack Charlton for Leeds. Don Revie's young team were on the up and the likes of Billy Bremner and Johnny Giles were brilliant talent. Hard too. But so were those in red.

Liverpool's left-back Gerry Byrne was injured early but played on despite a broken collarbone. He went on and on into extra time, never shirking the demands of a big match on a big pitch.

Roger Hunt – from a Byrne cross – gave Liverpool the lead but a Bremner equaliser was a blow until Ian St John nodded in a famous winner. It was a tense finish and in the last moments, the ball bounced invitingly in the Liverpool box but before a Leeds man could break hearts, Yeats's famously telescopic left leg cleared the danger and minutes later it was the big man who was walking up the steps to take the cup from the Queen.

Such was the captain's confidence, he had rehearsed what he would say to his monarch but such was the excitement – and with the travelling Liverpool fans singing, 'Ee-ay-Addio, the Queen is wearing red' he forgot his lines. 'It looked hard,' said the Royal punter. 'It was' said Yeats and with that the trophy was aloft.

It was the moment that defined Yeats, the Liverpool skipper. He went to his manager and gave him the trophy saying it was all down to him. Shankly though knew better. 'I'm proud of you, Ron,' he said. The fans were too but Yeats typically thought of them in equally as exulted terms. 'I just wanted to throw [the trophy] into the crowd,' he said, underlining that thriving relationship between player and fan.

Yeats would go on to lift another title the following season and play in the Cup Winners' Cup Final (an unfortunate Yeats own goal lost the game at Hampden Park) but it was that afternoon at Wembley, alongside his never ending respect for the fans' role in the side's success that made him so popular.

'As captain, I received a tremendous amount of mail after the final, congratulating me on our victory,' Yeats later said. 'Some letters were from older supporters who actually wrote that they could now die in peace after Liverpool had won the FA Cup.'

Yeats, this colossus of a man had come to their club and made a difference. No he didn't beat wary full-backs, and no he didn't go in for the glamorous art of goalscoring. He did though lead the team from Shankly's dressing room and made sure that the manager's words stayed firmly ringing in his team-mates' ears.

He was also a fantastic defender – among the best the club ever saw – but like every great team changes were soon made. Shankly found it very hard to let go of the players, such was the esteem he held them in and perhaps his mistake was not evolving sooner but in 1971, Yeats left for Tranmere Rovers. He would return to the club as a successful chief scout and is still very much loved at Anfield.

Mention Yeats to fans of a certain vintage and they will usually say his name using their best Shankly voice. 'Big Ron Yeats! Aye he was a colossus.' The manger knew his captain's worth, calling him the cornerstone to success and, 'The beginning of the big march.' A march that goes on today.

Emlyn Hughes

1967–1979
Appearances: 665
Goals: 49

TEN years is a long time. A lot can happen. It's late winter, 1967. Liverpool are the champions of England. Ten years earlier they were scratching around the Second Division and had just been knocked out of the FA Cup at Southend.

Things have changed. A manager with a vision has seen to that and now he is making a beeline for a new player, a young footballer he is sure will move the team on to further glory. Bill Shankly is about to sign Emlyn Hughes and in another ten years, that same player will be lifting the European Cup toward a Roman night sky.

When Shankly saw the player he liked, it was always an instant attraction. Like a lothario at a debutant ball, his eyes would light up and he would pursue his target with one aim, making him his.

Shankly had seen Hughes make his debut for Blackpool at Blackburn Rovers at the end of the 1965/66 season. The manager travelled to Ewood Park with no particular mission. It was the last game of the season, his Liverpool team had won the title and the World Cup in England was weeks away.

Some managers might sit back and admire their achievements. Shankly drove through Lancashire. 'Who's playing tonight?' he asked Blackpool's manager Ron Stuart.

'There's a boy from Barrow playing his first game,' said Stuart. Shankly sat back and watched. Shankly sat back and was soon drooling. Hughes was on a mission to impress, not necessarily the footballing royalty in the director's box but everyone there. Playing at left-back – far from a glamorous position – he set about doing everything.

Tackling, heading, marauding, fouling, crossing, shooting, passing, there was Hughes. The home crowd got on his back; he just worked harder, taking energy from their hate. Shankly was hooked. It was as if footballing harps were playing to mark his new love, their sweet sound ringing out over the West Pennine Moors.

The only other individual to catch Shankly's eye is Matt Busby. The Manchester United manager has come along too, so Shankly acts fast. There and then he offers Blackpool £25,000 for Hughes's services. 'This is somebody special,' he said. The offer was turned down, the seaside club were due to sell England international Alan Ball so weren't desperate for cash. Shankly would have to wait before he consummated his love.

And then the phone calls began. Every Sunday morning the phone would ring at the teenager's house. Every Sunday at 8.30am. Hughes the teenager had an even higher pitched voice than Hughes the adult and when the young man answered the phone, Shankly would often greet Mrs Hughes and ask if he could speak with her son.

'I'd just be about to make short work of a plate of eggs, bacon and black pudding when the phone would ring,' recalled Hughes years later. 'It would be Shanks. "Hey Emlyn, son, don't eat that stuff you've got on your plate there," he'd say. "I'll be signing you shortly. I want you lean and hungry son. Lean and hungry!" Thirty years later, I still associate the smell of bacon with the telephone ringing at 8.30am sharp on a Sunday morning.'

Hughes made more than his manager smitten. Liverpool fans in the late 1960s whilst adoring the old crop of players who had brought them so much glory, were looking for someone new to idolise. The likes of Tony Hateley came in for big money and was a brief poster boy but from the off, Hughes had his public enthralled, many didn't know what to make of this energetic bundle of enthusiasm but it was clear he was going to be the shot in the arm that an ailing side so needed.

Hughes had made his debut against Stoke at Anfield in a 2–1 win but the team then stalled. Everton knocked them out of the FA Cup and defeats at Burnley and Tottenham saw the side lose major ground to Manchester United in the title race. Next to Anfield was Newcastle and having made a steady if inconspicuous start to his life in red, Hughes was about to make himself very noticed. He was after all, only following orders. Shankly took him to one side before the game and said, 'Go out there son and give them something to remember, they need a new hero.'

That didn't look likely in the first half hour as Newcastle's winger Albert Bennett was giving the teenager a torrid time. Again and again he skipped past his lunge to get crosses in and so Hughes took things into hand. Having once again been beaten and with Shankly's words ringing in his ears, Hughes lunged. *'…Give them something to remember…'* Hughes grabbed Bennett by the neck and rugby tackled him to the ground. The ground fell silent and then roared with laughter.

Shankly and Bob Paisley were laughing, even the referee was laughing, so much so he could only muster a slight telling off for the impetuous new boy. The Kop had a hero. The game was won, but the roars of approval were saved for Hughes. It is thought that Evertonians present at the game went home mocking a player they called 'Crazy Horse', and the tag stuck. Liverpool fans took it as a badge of honour. Hughes had arrived and was going to fit right in.

Actually, 'fit in' isn't all-together accurate. Sure, Liverpool fans took to his mad enthusiasm immediately. This was the late 1960s. Hughes was *Far Out Man*. His team-mates, slight more conservative than those who flocked to the ground, never quite knew what to make of this very different man. Tommy Smith especially, a hard man who put the 'Ow' into 'Scouse', was particularly unimpressed with Hughes, the man.

More of that later. Hughes was born in Barrow-in-Furness, a seaport in Cumbria. His father, Fred was a rugby league player who represented Great Britain. Hughes junior showed great skill in the game of his father, but also excelled at cross-country running (any fan who watched Hughes rampage through the muddy football fields of England and Europe will tell you he never lost that ability) and of course football.

His father was very ambitious and convinced Blackpool to take a look. The manager, Ron Stuart, was a native of Barrow and that local loyalty ensured a trial at the seaside club. Hughes was still small in stature but showed enough for Blackpool to offer him games for their 'B' team. Hughes moved to digs in the town, got down to work and was soon a regular in the youth team's midfield.

Hughes progressed through the ranks. He turned pro in 1964 and soon that first team debut was his to grab with indisputable zest. Not that his dad hadn't continued to play his part. Fred had written plenty of letters using pseudonyms, asking such questions as, 'When is the young lad Emlyn Hughes going to be given a first team chance?' At home games with the reserves, Fred would stand near the director's box shouting, 'Hells bells, this lad at full-back looks useful. He's getting better every game!' You can see where Hughes got that manic enthusiasm.

Having got his chance and played himself firmly onto Shankly's radar, Hughes played against Chelsea in the autumn of 1966. Peter Osgood was the new darling of Stamford Bridge, but Hughes cared little for reputations. Both players were at each other, Osgood not taking to this northern upstart who was nipping at his well-polished Kings Road heels. 'Emlyn nipped Peter in a tackle,' recalled Shankly later.

'In the next tackle Peter tried to "do" Emlyn, but Emlyn was either lucky or cute and broke Peter's leg, unfortunately. I still think that Peter was as much responsible for it as Emlyn. I was more convinced than ever that I wanted him and eventually I got him for £65,000. Emlyn was one of the major signings of all time.'

Hughes was immediately smitten with Shankly. He recalls his first car ride with the manager:

'We had to get to Lytham St Anne's to complete the signing so I could play straight away in Liverpool's next match and Shanks drove us both down there. It's only about ten minutes from Bloomfield Road, but he was the worst driver in the world. He had this old brown Corsair and just as we left the ground he half went through a set of lights and a woman shunted into the back of us and smashed all the lights in. Next thing, a police car flags us down and the young officer comes up to the car and Shanks winds down the window. "What is it officer?" he asked.

'"I'm sorry sir you can't continue the journey in that car as you've got no lights," said the policeman.

'"Do you know who's in this car?" said Shanks, and I thought he was doing the old, do you know who I am? routine."

'"No", said the officer, "I don't recognise you."

'"No not me you fool," he said, "I've got the future captain of England alongside me."'

Hughes's first few seasons at Anfield underlined not only his appetite for life but also a versatility that saw him wear the number ten, three and six shirts. It was the latter that he would wear with most distinction and in it, he replaced the always stylish and popular Willie Stevenson in midfield.

Liverpool challenged for honours but were just falling short. Hughes was the energy in a side perhaps lacking it. An England cap came his way in November 1969 and just weeks later, Liverpool lost an FA Cup tie at Watford that convinced Shankly that the old guard's time was up.

Hughes's form and hunger probably made Shankly's mind up too. The manager needed to be sure he had players with the required talent before he offloaded the great men who had made his team so wonderful in his early seasons. In Hughes he had a golden boy, a player who shared his confidence, who shared his desire to run through walls. Shankly only ever had daughters. Some felt that in Hughes he had a son and others didn't like that relationship at all. Hughes was far from popular.

'The first thing that struck you about the young Emlyn was he was totally self-absorbed,' recalled St John in his autobiography. 'In the bar, Emlyn was always eager to get his hands on the first drink and picked up the first one, whatever the order had been. The older players quickly became restless, mumbling remarks along the lines of, "Who's this kid coming along taking drinks that he hasn't even ordered?"'

Of course it wasn't drinks that those players were really worried about. It was a place in the team. As the 1970s unfolded, old players such as Ron Yeats, St John and Tommy Lawrence were replaced by Larry Lloyd, Kevin Keegan and Ray Clemence, as Shankly's second great side took shape and at its heart was Emlyn Hughes.

In April 1971, Southampton were the visitors to Anfield but were beaten by Hughes at his marauding best. Intercepting a pass on the edge of his own box, Hughes fed Ian Callaghan midway in the Liverpool half. With Callaghan checking and playing a simple pass to Tommy Smith at right-half, Hughes is off.

In that moment he is a cross-country runner again at school. The Kop end is his finishing line and with his head back and blinkers on, he skims over the Anfield turf. Smith finds John Toshack's head on the edge of the Southampton box and a beautifully cushioned nod down finds the space being attacked – make that invaded – by Hughes. A first-time shot and the ball is in need of medical attention as it swivels in the back of the net.

It's the reaction to what has happened, as much as his part in it that made Hughes so likable to the fans. As the ball strikes the goal, the Kop surges in mass appreciation and Hughes does exactly the same. His arms are up, his mouth is agape, and he wants to celebrate as if his life depends on it. The Kop got that. They loved it.

A shared enthusiasm for the game is never a given between fan and hero but with Emlyn it was there in abundance. 'I have played at Spurs on a Saturday afternoon, caught the train to Liverpool and then driven north to Barrow late on Saturday night in order to turn out for a Sunday League team,' Hughes once wrote.

'I did that run when I was a current England international. If the authorities would have found out I would have been in terrible trouble, but I had so much extra energy that after those Sunday morning matches I was looking for a game of tennis in the afternoon.'

Two years after that Southampton screamer, those arms were flailing around above his head once again, like drunken snakes. This time the title was on the line and the opponents were Everton. 55,000 were at Goodison to witness a tense and tight affair in the March mud. Liverpool's strikers Kevin Keegan and Phil Boersma couldn't break down a stubborn Everton rearguard and with ten minutes left it looked like Liverpool might drop points in what was becoming a four-horse title race.

Inspiration though would come from midfield. Callaghan as ever probed and spotted another purposeful run from midfield from Hughes who broke the offside trap, took the ball past David Lawson in Everton's goal and knocked it between the posts. Cue red pandemonium.

Eight minutes later, Hughes again took himself into the box, this time volleying in a low shot to make the derby, the points and ultimately the title safe. Arms aloft he runs to his public. His sideburns are the only giveaway that this is a man and not a child doing what he loves best.

Liverpool won the UEFA Cup as well as the league title that season. Tommy Smith was the skipper by now, but that changed in the summer of 1973 and with Hughes being the replacement, an already strained relationship completely broke down.

It is thought that Hughes himself had gone to Shankly, suggesting the captain be changed, as some of the new younger players in the side struggled to cope with Smith's, shall we say, slightly more frank approach to passing on orders. That it was Hughes who got the job, plenty felt he was once again being opportunistic.

Smith was hurt. Hughes was an England player, a future England captain and now he was Liverpool skipper. Fans were never fully aware of the ill feeling between the two but it was there, simmering away without ever affecting the team's ethic or success.

Even to those fans that did have an inkling, Hughes's determination to plough ahead on their behalf, no matter who disliked him might have further added to his allure. This was a player who seemed hell-bent on winning tackles, games and trophies. Winning friends was way down his priority list.

He cared little for names and reputations. He hadn't the day Shankly watched him fracture more than just Peter Osgood's ego. Later the Chelsea man laughed at how little Tommy Smith thought of the man they called Crazy Horse.

'I remember this game at Anfield once. Chopper's [Ron Harris] done Emlyn Hughes after 15 minutes and he's gone down squealing. Tommy Smith sprints in from 20 yards away, but he sprints straight past Emlyn, his team-mate, gets to Chopper, hauls him up and says, "I could get to like you, Harris."'

Peter Cormack, himself a new player in Shankly's rebuilding programme in the early 1970s commented on Hughes and Smith in his autobiography, *From The Cowshed To The Kop*, and it was clear that Smith was the more popular one among the players. 'The regular chant away from home was, "Emlyn Hughes, you're a wanker, you're a wanker", and whilst Crazy Horse enjoyed the attention I think most of the Liverpool players smiled when they heard this and hummed along with the chant.

'For what it was worth, I told Smithy that he was still the club captain as far as I was concerned, even though it was Emlyn who tossed the coin on match days.'

The thing is, Hughes really didn't care. On he went. On he went running all over the pitch in the name of Liverpool FC and most noticeably, on he went beaming out that smile. Eventually players would appreciate his efforts. Even Tommy Smith. 'Crazy Horse would run all day,' he said years later. 'We didn't get on off the field, but who cares?'

That was the thing. Who cared? The staff? The other players? The fans? So what if there were disagreements? These were men who were treated like men and because of that, whatever happened elsewhere, on the pitch a torrent of success flowed more incessantly than the English game had ever known.

By the 1973/74 season, Shankly's 'new' team looked complete. They had won the title; they had taken a first European trophy thanks to a win over two legs against Borussia Moenchengladbach, a team they would get to know well over the next half a decade.

Ray Clemence in goal was among the best in Europe, Alec Lindsay at left-back was dynamic up and down the wing. In front of him Steve Heighway was a cacophony of tricks, dribbles and goals. Kevin Keegan was not a young buck but among the best strikers in the European game. Ian Callaghan was still brimming with energy and John Toshack was the perfect foil for Keegan's movement up front.

This was a team once again in Shankly's image. Industrious, cute, hard as nails and quick-witted. It was also modern. During the season, Hughes – once again showing his incredible abilities as a footballing all-rounder – moved from midfield to the centre of defence. Tommy Smith had stormed off early in the season when told he'd been dropped, inadvertently giving his position to his nemesis, Hughes. Smith of course was far too good a player – and just as versatile as Hughes – to be out in the cold for long but for now it must have stung.

Hughes was to partner young local boy, Phil Thompson. An elegant player who, like Hughes had converted from midfield and whose skill far outweighed his bulk. Thompson, all skin and bone was deceptively strong, could time a tackle and most importantly had a keen eye for the right pass.

Hughes and Thompson were a very modern defensive partnership. Gone was the notion that one or both of your centre-halves had to be the bruising type. Heading the ball clear was one thing but now coaches were looking to start attacks from the back.

'It was a clever decision by the boss and his staff,' wrote Thompson in his autobiography. 'They were ahead of their time. All of a sudden we were looking to play from the back. If it took fifty passes to score we didn't care. The coming together of Emlyn and myself in that partnership was the start of the Total Football that would be made famous by the Dutch that same year.'

Liverpool went to Wembley in buoyant mood. They had overcome their bogey side Leicester City in the semi-finals and were rightly favourites to claim a second FA Cup. Their opponents were Newcastle, a team that had won each of its previous five visits to the famous old ground. Their striker Malcolm 'Supermac' Macdonald was confidently telling anyone with a notepad what he'd do to Liverpool's central defence but Hughes had a strong glint in his eye as he walked behind his mentor and manager onto the Wembley turf.

The noise that greeted them might have been heard back in Anfield. John Moynihan in his match report for the *Sunday Telegraph* wrote, 'Was there ever such a bedlam of noise as this in sporting history? On our left there were the chanting banks of solid red representing Merseyside; on our right the black and white minstrels from Tyneside.

One thing was certain. This would be the noisiest Cup Final of all time.'

The first half didn't match the vibrancy of its surroundings but Liverpool came out like a heavyweight boxer off from his stool and thinking enough is enough. Alec Lindsey had a superb goal wrongly disallowed for offside but in the 57th minute, the brilliant Keegan smashed one in from the edge of the box and with over half an hour left, the game looked won.

Newcastle weren't in it. They couldn't muster any space up front and despite Macdonald's bravado, the elegant certainty of both Hughes and Thompson was the foundations on which the side built one of its greatest ever performances.

Steve Heighway made sure of the win in the 75th minute and with just two minutes left on the big Wembley clock, Kevin Keegan scored from a yard out but it was the final touch of one of the great moves. Every player touched the ball, patterns were weaved on the green turf and Newcastle players were dizzy as Smith (back in the team and playing at right-back) crossed for Keegan's finish. BBC commentator David Coleman summed it up perfectly when he said, 'Newcastle were undressed'.

Liverpool had finished the game with a sublime arrogance. Hughes when quizzed by the press afterwards matched that swagger. 'We outclassed them didn't we?' he told John Moynihan of the *Sunday Telegraph*. 'We thought we could because when we played them in the league, they didn't get a kick.'

Hughes went up to get the trophy and there was that smile. Some players had mischievously prodded Tommy Smith to the front of the queue to get the club but as ever, such frivolity didn't matter and there at the top of the stairs with the trophy in his hands, the first trophy he had ever lifted, the big one, the FA Cup, there was that canyon-like smile.

But then came shock. Just two months after the joy of Wembley Bill Shankly announced his retirement. Television crews scouring the city for opinion were given short shrift by passers-by, suspecting a prank. Then the penny dropped. News began to filter through. Stunned silence. Disbelief. It was true. But why?

Shankly gave personal reasons, stating he wanted to spend more time with his family, but you could argue that such was the manner in which his team swatted away Newcastle to win the FA Cup, that he wondered where else he could take them. The arrogance of that third goal; Phil Thompson was right, it was *Total Football* before that tag was swathed in Dutch orange. Everything he had envisaged for the club had, in that 45 minutes, come to fruition.

Perhaps this was as good as it could ever get for the great man and the fact that Emlyn Hughes – the player he had seen, wanted and then nurtured into the team's leader – was lifting the trophy must have added to his sense of perfect endings.

Hughes cried when the squad were brought together and told the news. Smith of course didn't appreciate that, not his style but Hughes was an emotional man. The smiles came easily but then so did tears and in Shankly he had lost a father-like figure as his boss. Sadness though could only last so long. There was more work to be done.

Football's public loves a dynasty but the fun part is watching one fall. All eyes were on Anfield and the new – reluctant – boss, Bob Paisley. The affable Durham-born man had been an integral part of Shankly's success but he was no clone. As far as partnerships go, compared to Shankly, he wasn't just a silent partner, he was catatonic.

No matter, he had been talked into taking the main job and being a football man brimming with knowledge, he would let his teams do the talking and he set about the task with quiet verve.

When it came to Hughes, the man, Paisley was one of the doubters. 'Emlyn always struck me as a player who could have been an even better one if he had been a slightly different personality,' he once wrote. Quite strong stuff but no matter, having taken over there was never any doubt that Hughes would remain the team's captain.

It wasn't as if he had a lack of options either. Smith, Clemence, Keegan, Terry McDermott, Phil Neal, all big personalities capable of leadership. Ian Callaghan, a quieter man but with so much experience. Any of them might have been made skipper but Paisley knew enough about the squad to know that was something that needed no change.

In any case, Paisley had more on his plate. Shankly still came to Melwood frequently. His players called him boss, they called Bob simply Bob. Results weren't perfect and the press, even the local guys, printed their concerns. Paisley – sterner than he looked – adapted, Shankly was politely (if a little awkwardly) asked to stop the visits and slowly, Paisley's team took shape.

Many people dismiss Paisley's achievements. They say he simply inherited Shankly's great team. Inherited? Try telling those who replaced Sir Alex Ferguson that inheriting greatness makes life easy.

No, Paisley took the pressure that comes with following a legend; he slowly made changes, slowly moulded the team into his and then went on a winning spree that even Shankly couldn't have envisaged.

His first season was trophy-less but it was to be the last trinket-free campaign for ten years. In 1975/76 Hughes lifted the UEFA Cup and the league title. The title was won with a 3–1 win at Wolves and Hughes came back into the dressing-room with that broadest of grins, his fists clenched and with Ronnie Moran, now a vital part of the boot-room draped around him as way of appreciation. This team was getting better and better and now, the big one was on their minds.

Hughes was at the centre of it all but found success with the horses a bit harder than he did in the red of Liverpool. He had got to know the racehorse and legendary local hero Red Rum's trainer, Ginger McCain. McCain had yet to hit the big time in his field but Hughes with his team-mate and horse lover Terry McDermott tried to get the rest of the squad to come in and buy shares in one McCain's horses. No matter, Hughes led the way and bought a big stake.

When McCain took them to the field to see his horses, the trainer whistled and all of the horses galloped over, expect one who didn't move other than a swat of his tail. 'Which one is ours?' asked Hughes. McCain pointed to the one now lying down at the far end of the field. The squad on hearing the news joked that Hughes had the back end, McDermott had the front. The horse ran one race and had to be destroyed.

Hughes in his red and white jockey outfit though was now a thoroughbred. The league title was once again won and so with five days left of an epic season, Liverpool had an FA Cup Final and a European Cup Final to seal the most momentous of campaigns.

Hughes walked out at Wembley against Manchester United as the newly crowned Football Writers' Player of the Year. The team walking behind him though was perhaps the wrong one. Paisley had opted to 'rest' Ian Callaghan and went with David Johnson up front with Kevin Keegan. The team played well enough but lost 2–1. They trudged off the pitch, licked their wounds and then simply got pissed on the train home before flying to Rome with memories of the Twin Towers merely a blurry memory. The European Cup Final against German champions Borussia Moenchengladbach in the Eternal City now had their full focus.

Paisley famously told his players he hadn't been in Italy's capital since he liberated it during the war. He had beaten the Germans, now they could go out and do exactly the same. Paisley reinstalled Callaghan and had Keegan roaming alone up front. It worked a treat. Liverpool played brilliantly. Tommy Smith partnered Hughes at centre-back and despite the fact they would often talk to each other via others ('Tell that fat bastard to pass the ball', Hughes was known to ask a team-mate) they marshalled the Germans expertly. Smith himself scored effectively the winning second goal in a 3–1 win and so it was Hughes who stepped up the short staircase at the Olympic Stadium to lift the beautiful trophy the club was taking out on the first of many dates.

It was *the* iconic moment. The moment that is etched on the minds of fans of all ages. Camera flashes, smiles, deafening roars, and Hughes lifting that trophy to his travelling masses, and for all the talk of the captain's self-obsession and lack of empathy with older team-mates, his thoughts as he lifted that trophy are of nothing but respect for those who wore Liverpool's red before him. 'As I walked up those steps, I was thinking about the past teams,' he said later. 'Players like Ronnie Yeats and Ian St John – it was their efforts that allowed us to win it. As a team we'd done it, but the victory was about the whole club and its efforts over a number of years.' Hughes and Smith were even seen embracing that night!

Twelve months later and Hughes and Liverpool were back for a second date with the famous trophy, this time in London but by now Hughes knew that his days were numbered at the club. Like he had come in to replace an old guard, the likes of Alan Hansen and Kenny Dalglish were now coming in to do the very same thing.

'I was captain for that 1978 European Cup victory, but Bob knew I was nearing the end of my time,' Hughes later said. 'I'd been there for 12 years and it's never nice to be replaced, but it was the correct thing for the team and that was Bob's priority.'

In 1979, Hughes left for Wolverhampton Wanderers. In 2004, Hughes died after treatment for a brain tumour. He was only 57 years old. He had done so much. Scored thunderous strikes that with either foot bruised the rigging. He lifted trophy after trophy in what was the club's halcyon era. He headed, he passed, he tackled, he fouled, he celebrated wildly and he smiled. He smiled because he loved what he was doing and whom he was doing it for.

He upset plenty of people, most of them the closest to him. Even when he retired, a tabloid column would upset the staff, players and fans at the club but his cult never diminished. In his autobiography he talked of Tommy Smith in glowing terms, acknowledging his team-mate's inspirational qualities; a player he had antagonised for over a decade. That was Hughes all over. A paradox. A crazy mix of boyish giddiness and desperate competitiveness that would see him leave sweat and blood all over the pitches of Europe. Crazy Horse indeed.

The man who brought him to Anfield, Bill Shankly once said, 'I want to build a team that's invincible, so that they have to send a team from bloody Mars to beat us.' What a game that would have been but with Hughes charging around the pitch, his arms flailing around, his mouth wide open, looking more Martian than human, it's obvious that the spacemen would have moved heaven and earth to sign him.

Peter Cormack

1972–1976
Appearances: 178
Goals: 26

PETER Cormack only joined Liverpool Football Club because of an STD (and that doesn't stand for Serious Transfer Demand). In the summer of 1972, Bill Shankly was on the lookout for attacking reinforcements. His new young buck Kevin Keegan had enjoyed a bombastic first season and was thriving alongside his strike partner, John Toshack, but Shankly wanted more. More creativity and more goals. He wanted a player who could support his two strikers; a midfielder of considerable talents was on the shopping list.

His choice? Frank Worthington. Worthington had been scoring goals for Shankly's old team Huddersfield and had a spark about him that the manager liked. He also had a reputation that grew in the coming years for being a bit of a lothario and enjoyed nights out as much as he enjoyed his football.

Now the official line was that, having agreed a deal with Huddersfield for Worthington's services, the move was temporarily postponed by Shankly as the player failed a medical; apparently with high blood pressure. That was the line. It has been alleged since that actually Worthington had a sexually transmitted disease.

Shankly was keen on getting his man though and so sent Worthington on holiday, told him to rid himself of his ailment and come back at the end of the summer to sign on. Now Shankly was a genius and all that but sending Frank Worthington away to sunny Spain to rid himself of an STD is like asking a fireman to pour petrol on a fire.

Worthington went to Magaluf , came home and was far from cured. The deal was off.

Tommy Smith recalls approaching Shankly to enquire about the transfer. 'Hey boss, what was wrong with Worthington?' he asked.

'Don't talk to me about that fella,' Shankly screamed. 'I'll tell you one thing, no one is playing for my Liverpool who's got the fucking pox.'

Shankly looked elsewhere and had heard from his brother Bob, a distinguished football man north of the border, about Peter Cormack, formerly of Hibernian and now at Nottingham Forest.

Cormack had come to England in 1969 with a fine reputation and at Forest he had caught the eye with his graceful attacking play. Typically Scottish, he had a mixture of granite tenacity and silky imagination. He jinked and he probed but kick him and he kicked back, harder.

By the close of the 1971/72 season the back pages in England were full of where he might go next. Manchester City were trying to get back to the top of the pile and were keen. Arsenal had relinquished their title and wanted to strengthen their squad, and they were interested. Tottenham were building a new, young team and saw Cormack as the ideal fit.

The player himself was very aware that a move was imminent and so when he was called to his manager Matt Gillies's office at Forest, he guessed an offer had been accepted. He presumed it was Bill Nicholson at Spurs.

'No it's not Bill,' said Gillies. 'It's Shanks.' Cormack presumed it was Bob Shankly scouting on someone's behalf.

'It's no' fucking Bob Shankly. You daft bastard,' bemoaned his manager. 'It's Bill Shankly. He wants you at Liverpool now for a medical.' That afternoon, the medical successful (no STDs here!), Cormack was a Liverpool player. Quick and ruthlessly efficient, even Forest were surprised with how fast Liverpool made their move.

Today, Cormack is back in his native Edinburgh and he chuckles at how that very afternoon spun him around like a top. 'It was crazy,' he says. 'Liverpool hadn't been mentioned at all when it came to my future and suddenly there I was on my way to a city I knew little about. I had a massive decision to make, but such was Shankly's desire to sign me, it became clear that "no" was not an option. My wife and I settled in very quickly.'

Cormack was born in the Leith area of Scotland's capital in 1946. Leith with its docks was a hub of shipbuilding, but constant bombardment during the war caused havoc with employment and the area suffered, becoming a tough place to live and grow up. Being good at football was a massive help when it came to avoiding a good beating. The area was full of Hibernian fanatics and a youngster with talent avoided the rough treatment. Who wanted to hurt a future player?

The author Irvine Welsh grew up in nearby Muirhouse and recalls the locals at the time. 'People were either good fighters, proper hard cases or they could play football. You would be labelled by those two skills.'

Cormack was – whilst not being shy of throwing a punch – the latter and soon Hibernian came knocking. He made his first team debut in 1962 aged only 16 and he scored. He went on to be a star for his local team, idolised by youngsters, not far off his age. 'In the 1960s, in the playground you wanted to be Cormack,' recalls Welsh of his schooldays.

Cormack had a certain style. Great looking, he looked like one of the pop stars from England and played with all the imagination befitting that superstar image. His greatest moment in green and white came in a high profile friendly against the now world famous Real Madrid at Easter Road.

By now Jock Stein was the boss at Hibs and used his already considerable weight in the game to get the Spaniards over for a game and Cormack, just weeks after his 18th birthday, whilst excited wasn't overawed by sharing a pitch with Puskas and Gento. In fact so relaxed was he that he put his team ahead after 13 minutes and won the man of the match award after a famous 2–0 victory.

In fact, Cormack made a habit of gracing football pitches with the world's best and in 1966, two years after his Real Madrid exploits he made his Scotland debut against Brazil at Hampden Park in a warm-up for the Brazilians prior to the World Cup in England. Cormack again played well against Pele, Jairzinho and Gerson.

Yes, arriving at Melwood for the first time, whilst daunting to so many players, held no fears for a player used to such exalted company. 'I wasn't nervous at all,' says Cormack with a spark. 'I was slightly lucky that there were plenty of new, young players finding their feet at the club. Clem [Ray Clemence], Brian Hall, Steve Heighway. All pretty rubbish players right enough.'

Cormack had cost a club record equalling £110,000 but no matter, such was his confidence, he breezed into that summer's training without a doubt in his mind and he certainly passed Tommy Smith's initiation tests. On arrival, Smith approached the new boy and having played against him on several occasions, enquired about Cormack's distinctive running style that saw him lift his knees high to his chest. 'See the way you run, Peter,' said Smith. 'You look like a fucking poof.'

Cormack grinned. 'Smithy, you're safe on two counts,' said the new signing. 'Firstly I'm not a poof, and secondly if I was, you'd be the last person I'd fancy.' Smith and his team-mates laughed but an hour later, the hard man was picking Cormack up from the Melwood turf after a hefty challenge just to underline who was top dog. 'Welcome to Liverpool Peter,' said Smith. 'You'll do for me, lad.'

Cormack loved his surroundings immediately. His team-mates, the training methods, the fact that his manager insisted that no player drive a blue car; all of it spoke of a club he could feel at home at. 'I didn't have any reservations about being there,' recalls Cormack. 'Such was the confidence I had in my ability that I really thought I was as good as anyone around. I was right.'

His team-mates immediately took to him. Kevin Keegan and Cormack hit it off from the start. Practically lookalikes, they formed a great relationship on and off the pitch, cemented early on in a pre-season friendly in Germany, in which Keegan was sent off for a gem of a right hook. It was Cormack who offered to take the blame, saying he was more likely to get off a suspension and anyway, he'd be proud to have thrown the punch.

It was that sort of effervescent cheek that soon had fans onside too. Peter Cormack is not in many fans' all-time XIs. His name is not mentioned when punters sit around a pint and discuss Billy Liddell and Kenny Dalglish. For three seasons though, Cormack was an integral part of Liverpool's success.

In the playgrounds of Liverpool, Kevin Keegan was the poster boy of course, but for the cool kids, who looked for more than just the glory of goals, he was the player to call your favourite. Like smoking or buying a motorbike, having Cormack as your hero made you stand out from the crowd.

Liverpool had started the season in indifferent fashion. They'd started with wins over both Manchester clubs but had lost to Leicester and Derby. The press were predicting a barren future. Shankly, prior to a home game against Wolves took all the cuttings into the dressing room, crumpled them into a ball and volleyed them into the bin. 'What a load of crap, lads. Now go out and show those fans they've got a team to be proud of.'

Liverpool won 4–2 and Cormack, on his home debut was brilliant on the right side of midfield, scoring his first goal with a header from a Heighway cross that put the team 2–1 up to set up a victory that kick-started the campaign and sent Liverpool on their way up the table and firmly into the title race.

That night, Cormack sat in his new home near Southport and watched *Match of the Day* and was struck by the Kop's surging swell as his header struck the net. He had caused that wave of delight and sitting on his sofa that night, he realised just what and whom he was playing for.

A month later, things got even better. Everton were this time the visitors to Anfield for a nervy kind of derby, the kind that has fans growing more and more terrified that should the enemy score, there will be no way back. In the 77th minute Cormack struck again. Once more it was Heighway down the left who got free and put in one of his inviting crosses.

Cormack on the other side of the field was always alive to play on the opposite flank and was encouraged to take a gamble. There he was, at the Anfield Road end, leaping to head the ball past David Lawson in the Everton net. The stadium erupted. Cormack was swamped by team-mates and as Larry Lloyd, the big centre-half helped him to his feet, he said, 'You'll be a fucking hero here for life mate.'

Cormack had arrived in style and whilst John Toshack was *the* aerial threat in the side, it seemed the striker had a rival in the far more diminutive Scot. 'I put a lot of work into my heading,' says Cormack. 'I was around 5ft 9in but I had an exceptional leap and to score that day against Everton was incredible. I floated off the pitch at the end. "I've won them over," I thought to myself, and from there I was flying.'

So were Liverpool. Cormack's form was fantastic. Shankly called him, 'The final piece in the jigsaw' and when he was sent off for a retaliatory punch at West Brom, whilst disappointed, Shankly was at his supportive best. 'You have exceeded even my expectations in your first couple of months here and those Liverpool fans worship you,' said the manager to his player. 'They work hard all week and what keeps them going is their Saturday afternoon watching Liverpool Football Club. Always remember that what you do on that park will determine if their next week at work will be a good week or a bad week.'

Those fans were enjoying mostly good weeks and as spring approached and with the added interest of a successful UEFA Cup campaign, things were getting better and better. The penultimate game of the league season saw Leeds United come to Liverpool and Shankly's men knew a win would all but guarantee the title. It was played on a Bank Holiday Monday afternoon and the old stadium had one of those special atmospheres that guarantee special games.

The first half had finished goalless but two minutes in to the second period, Cormack latched onto a loose ball and struck it in at the Kop end. Keegan wrapped up the result five minutes from time and with Arsenal failing to win, the title was won. The team took their plaudits. Cormack looked up at the Kop and was thrilled to have won, not only his first trophy in England but to have done so for a set of fans who 'Always brought out the best in the team.' One fan ran on and dropped to his knees in front of Shankly, for he had become so much more than merely the manager.

Scarves were thrown on to the pitch to be picked up by the players and Shankly noticed a policeman kicking one off the turf. 'Don't do that,' Shankly growled. 'That's precious.' Cormack certainly got what part the fans played in the team's success. 'You sensed the intensity from them,' he says. 'As soon as you came out you felt what they felt and you loathed to lose. That's why we hardly ever did.'

It was that form at Anfield that saw Liverpool through to their second European final. They won all four of their matches in the UEFA Cup at home and having seen off Eintracht Frankfurt, AEK Athens, Dinamo Dresden and then Tottenham, Liverpool were through to a two-legged final against Borussia Moenchengladbach of Germany.

The rain was absolutely pouring down on the night of the first leg in Liverpool and whilst waiting in the tunnel to go out at Anfield, one Liverpool player said, 'Here we are for the final of *It's a Knockout.*' The game was abandoned after half an hour but when it was replayed the following night the only thing pouring over the visitors was attack after Liverpool attack and a 3–0 win ushered in a night of celebration with even Ray Clemence getting in on the act, saving a late Borussia penalty.

The Germans though were a fine team on the up. Bertie Vogts, Jupp Heynckes and Rainer Bonhof would all win the World Cup for West Germany the following summer and so despite their three-goal advantage no one was taking anything for granted.

It was the club's 66th match that season and there were leggy performances in Germany. The hosts went 2–0 up but then, thanks largely to a dominant display by the captain, Tommy Smith, they held on and for the first time in their history, a European trophy was making its way to Liverpool.

The team paraded both their trophies to an exuberant Liverpool public. Cormack chose to hold the league trophy rather than the far heavier UEFA Cup but as he got off the bus with two manageable medals in his pocket he couldn't believe just how well his first season had gone. His manager felt the same way.

'Peter Cormack has more than fulfilled what I hoped he would do,' he said in an interview with the *Liverpool Echo*. 'I thought he'd score ten to fifteen goals for us and he's done that. He'd have scored more if he hadn't suffered a few injuries. He has been brilliant in his shielding of the midfield and the back four as a semi-defender and I have never seen him beaten in the air.'

The manager was right. Cormack had looked the complete midfielder. Emlyn Hughes was alongside him and took a lot of the strain, but Cormack was silk, keeping the team's rhythm ticking with his movement and passing. He loved every minute of it. 'Training was geared to simple football and that is why we did so well in Europe,' he says. 'People ask me why the team didn't come under more pressure. Defenders such as Smithy and Chris Lawler weren't blessed with much pace after all so why didn't teams get in behind us? What they were though was fantastic passers of the ball. Teams couldn't get it off us. Our full-backs would have made great midfield players in most teams and every one of us was so comfortable.'

It wasn't only cool blokes in parka jackets that had taken to Cormack either. Their sisters were also partial to a poster of the new player up on their walls. Cormack with his flock of black hair, cheeky grin and Edinburgh tones was a hit with Merseyside girls. It had been the same in Scotland and 'The Peter Cormack Female Fan Club' had been set up before his move south.

An agent, employed somewhat sceptically by Cormack at Liverpool promising to make his client rich away from football, had reopened the fan club and at one point had over 500 members, all getting T-shirts, membership letters and signed photos.

Not that Cormack could count on huge wealth. Alan Ball at Everton had been paid large sums to wear white boots at the time and Kevin Keegan was also offered £2,000 to do the same. Big money back then. Cormack was offered £100. Clearly the boot manufacturers hadn't heard of The Peter Cormack Female Fan Club.

Not that that put Cormack off from his entrepreneurial exploits. A new venture saw him design and model a fashion range called, 'Cormack Creations'. Cream flares, knee-length leather trench coats, denim shirts and Cuban-heeled boots and all modelled by a clever midfielder with a new Burt Reynolds moustache. Cormack had helped Liverpool to glory in Europe but his fashion label wouldn't ever trouble Paris and Milan.

Unperturbed though, Cormack also dipped his toe into the music business. Cormack's agent had heard that his client was prone to picking up a microphone in clubs and could more than hold a tune. His version of 'Route 66' by the Rolling Stones didn't make its mark on the charts in the summer of 1973 and his team-mates didn't let up when hearing his efforts.

In Shankly's last great team, it might have been Keegan and Toshack who were seen as the side's Mick and Keith and when performing 'Route '66', Cormack will have sung the lyric, *'Just take my way, that is the heighway, that is the best.'* Steve Heighway too was one of the headline grabbers, the glory providers; but Cormack, especially in 1973/74 was as vital as any of them. There on merit and a player able to dictate and influence as much as any of his peers.

In the league, Cormack was an ever present and played in all but one of the nine games that saw Liverpool win their second FA Cup. The big scare came in the third round at home to Doncaster when the Yorkshiremen had the temerity to go 2–1 up at half-time against a weakened Liverpool side fielding lesser known players, Trevor Storton and Dave Rylands.

In the end it was their very known player, Keegan, who saved red faces with a second goal against his home-town club. At half-time Shankly had told his team-mates he wanted no part of what was unravelling into a huge embarrassment. 'I can assure you, lads,' he said. 'This is one bit of English football history I don't want Liverpool Football Club associated with.'

Cormack scored in the replay and Liverpool went on, beating Carlisle, a young and brilliantly managed (Bobby Robson was already being touted as a future England boss) Ipswich Town, Bristol City and, in the semi-final, Leicester City.

The Foxes had long been a bogey side, especially in this most tantalising of stages of the competition. In 1963 and then 1969, Leicester had beaten Shankly's men and the fixture was eagerly awaited by fans and tabloid hacks alike. Frank Worthington had – after failing to convince Shankly of his clean living – joined Leicester from Huddersfield and he was splashed over the *Sunday People* suggesting he would prove Shankly very wrong and boasted about how he would be the difference come the big match.

The game at Old Trafford finished 0–0 thanks mainly to Leicester's keeper, Peter Shilton, who was brilliant on the day. Even England's Number One though couldn't contain a rampant Liverpool side in the replay at Villa Park and goals from Brian Hall, Keegan and Toshack secured a 3–1 win and another trip to Wembley.

The win against Newcastle at Wembley must rank as one of Liverpool's greatest ever performances, especially the second half when the Geordies were blown away by Liverpool's slick and hypnotic passing game. Every outfield player looked like they had been born to play the game on Wembley's gigantic pitch. Newcastle were torn apart and whilst Kevin Keegan and Steve Heighway got the goals in the 3–0 win, Cormack was brilliant in the centre of midfield, playing perhaps his finest game for the club.

Shankly had of course also played his part. Prior to the game during the extensive television build-up, the two managers had been interviewed by the BBC's Jimmy Hill. Like a televised Presidential debate, the body language of the managers was scrutinised and whilst Shankly – that most natural and dynamic of orators – revelled in the cameras and the attention, his counterpart at Newcastle, Joe Harvey, shifted awkwardly in his seat. Having been thanked by Hill, Shankly, still on air, took off his headphones and said to someone off camera, 'Jesus Christ, Joe's a bag of nerves.'

The manager knew exactly what he was doing. He knew his players were watching back at the hotel and this was his way of saying, we're better than this lot, they are fortunate to be here with us. 'For us, it was like being given a goal start before a ball had been kicked,' said Cormack.

Liverpool returned by train the following afternoon, each station they passed on their way into the city more packed than the last. Over one million locals turned out to greet the team home that day. A long way off from the hundreds that greeted Alex Raisbeck and his title-winning team home through the steam in 1901 and an indication of what the club had become.

Cormack's abiding memory is of a female fan in the Old Swan area of Liverpool throwing up her skirt to show off a red pair of knickers with the Liverpool crest in pride of place. 'Shanks for Prime Minister' proclaimed one banner, and the manager himself professed to the hordes of disciples that this was his proudest moment as Liverpool manager. It was also his last.

Cormack had gone with Scotland that summer to the World Cup in West Germany. To his great disappointment, he hadn't played a game and he returned to Merseyside to the news that he would be playing for a new manager in Bob Paisley.

It was a shock but Cormack was pleased with the appointment. 'I had been at Hibs when the great Jock Stein left so was used to managerial shake-ups,' he says. 'We were all pleased with Bob coming in. As a player you much prefer it being in-house and as well as having enormous respect for Bob, we didn't want an outsider coming in and shaking things up.'

Cormack remained a vital part of Paisley's first team. Results weren't quite good enough to stop Dave McKay's Derby winning a second league title but Cormack looked to be firmly in the new man's plans. The following season too, Cormack had started well. He had managed to go back to Hibernian's Easter Road in the UEFA Cup and despite losing that fixture 1–0, a 3–1 win at Anfield set Liverpool on their way to a second UEFA Cup victory in three years.

Sadly, Cormack would play no part. On 27 December 1975, Cormack scored the winner at Anfield that beat Manchester City to ensure Liverpool stayed at the top of the table. He also severely aggravated an old knee ligament problem and never played for the team again. In his absence, Ray Kennedy was moved back into midfield and excelled.

Cormack was too busy a footballer to warm benches and so in the November of 1976 he left for Bristol City. It might have lacked the back page hyperbole of Keegan's departure at the end of that season but to a contingent of supporters who relished his efforts, Cormack's departure was a sad day for the club.

He did play against his old club on a few occasions and in April 1978, managed to miss a penalty during a 1–1 draw at Ashton Gate. Cormack had scored in the game but no matter, the travelling Liverpool fans happily sang, 'Cormack's still a Kopite'.

'I loved my time at Liverpool,' Cormack says today. 'I was playing for the best club in the country, winning league titles, FA Cups, European trophies and playing with the great players of my era. It was magnificent. I have all my shirts from those famous games, all my medals. Now and then I get a visit from some swanky collector in London who wants to buy it all. He'll knock on my door and I'll say it's not for sale. I will invite them in though for a biscuit and a coffee and again, he'll make me an offer. "Listen pal," I say. "Did you not hear me? These are my greatest possessions from the greatest time of my life. They're no' for sale.'"

Ray Kennedy

1974–1982
Appearances: 393
Goals: 72

T HE 1970s. Supposedly the decade that taste forgot. All avoc-
ado green bathrooms, brown cars and orange polyester. A
ten-year span bereft of style. Try telling that though to those
football fans about football's mavericks; the players who brought style
over substance and played the game with a nonchalant swagger. The
1970s as a mecca for these men and their cheeky ways.

There they were, socks rolled down around their ankles, sideburns
enveloping their cheeks. Cheeky smiles and naughty glints. Tales are
aplenty. Stan Bowles at Queens Park Rangers sneaking a quick drag on
a fan's fag before whipping in a corner at Loftus Road. Charlie George
at Arsenal flicking the V-sign to a set of fans whilst telling a linesman
to stick his flag up his arse, the lovable rogue. The whole Leeds team
brazenly turning on the showmanship against a hapless Southampton
side.

This was football played as if the last orders bell had just been rung.
Individuals entertained and they fought for notoriety. The result be
damned. At Liverpool things were different. Sure, the players had their
individual and energetic brilliance but there was a team ethic that would
trample all over any brazen circus acts.

'We had great individuals, but we didn't rely on them,' recalled Ian
St John years after leaving the club. 'What we were trying to achieve,
we were trying to achieve together. We would not have stood for a
Rodney Marsh.

'I'm not knocking Rodney, he was blessed with fabulous talent, but at Liverpool the team came before the individual. We were selfless and we helped each other. If you were having a bad game then fine, keep working and others will try and bail you out. You just didn't get the selfish headline grabbing, glory hunter because Shankly simply wouldn't have allowed it.'

And then there was Ray Kennedy. Far from selfish or affected by a desire for self-glory, Kennedy was laid-back, the hard work he put in was hidden by the very wrong idea that perhaps he didn't really care. It was his style. Goals were calmly celebrated. Loose balls were jogged toward rather than sprinted to. He had his own blasé style, that some fans mistook for laziness. Whilst a Kevin Keegan, a Graeme Souness or a Phil Neal covered a pitch with impetuous desire, Kennedy had the air of a player whose mind was somewhere else.

It wasn't true of course. Kennedy cared and he strove and he did his utmost to bring the club untold success. Sure a goal wasn't met with the sort of crazy antics of Emlyn Hughes but the simple arm up and jog back to the touchline was just his style.

In a decade that celebrated the unpredictable and the off the wall, Kennedy's cult lay in his difference. Here was a very cerebral footballer. Unlocking defences was a mathematical problem that needed care and attention, his fine array of passes could have come with a compass and his left foot would have made Pythagoras re-think things.

In the late 2000s, young Liverpool fans sang about having the best midfield in the world. Xabi Alonso, Mohamed Sissoko, Steven Gerrard and Javier Mascherano were the objects of their desires, but the older fans, the ones who can trump anything ever said in any pub debate, would have given only knowing smiles for they knew of an even better quartet.

Sure, those assembled under Rafa Benitez were very good but Kennedy was part of a foursome that you'd struggle to match, not only through the club's history but in that of the British game.

In 1978, Kennedy was joined in Paisley's midfield by Graeme Souness and with Terry McDermott and Jimmy Case very much part of the furniture, Liverpool had a formidable group. If your midfield is a team's torso, Bob Paisley had killer abs!

This was a midfield without wingers. Width was provided by clever movement rather than blistering bursts of pace. This was a midfield that didn't have the likes of a young Ian Callaghan on the right or later the excellence of John Barnes on the left.

Kennedy (originally a striker but converted to midfield by the always astute Bob Paisley) had the sweetest of left feet but he wasn't one to beat a man with a jink or a trick. His talent lay in his passing and his ability to drift and exploit space. In the middle were Terry McDermott, all bustle and drive and Graeme Souness, a one-man wrecking-ball who wouldn't suffer anything other than brilliance.

On the right was local boy, Jimmy Case. Case would become a firm friend of Kennedy's, his partner in crime, but on the pitch he offered the energy and dynamism that Kennedy's more considered approach didn't need. Whilst on different sides of the pitch, the two became a potent duo and would use each other just as much as they used their strikers.

'Tactically Ray was in a different league,' Case recalled. 'He had a delicate touch, a sweet left foot and his movement was phenomenal. I used to cover much more ground and tackle more and he'd cover less ground but use his head more. We worked well together. His best point had to be his timing. I'd have the ball, I'd look up and he was gone. A perfectly timed run; ghosting in from the left, losing his marker. I'd put in the simplest of balls and bang! One nil.'

On the opening day of the 1979/80 season, Crystal Palace came to Anfield. The Londoners, coached by a young Terry Venables, were the much-lauded young 'Team of the decade', touted to be the next big things. Liverpool though hadn't quite finished with their dominance and underlined how far the young bucks had to go on the half hour, when Case drifted in from the right, fed Kennedy who had come in from the left and could only admire as with two deft touches he had put the ball in at the Kop end. It was a footballing pincer movement and it was wonderful.

Kennedy might not have got the rave reviews and he certainly didn't court them, but his contributions certainly went noticed within the game itself. Bob Paisley said that he was the player who he had the most enquiries about from other, green-eyed managers. Jimmy Greaves said that Kennedy was the best British player of the 1970s.

That midfield won a European Cup and two league titles in three seasons but it was the side that took the First Division championship in 1978/79 that stands out. The team swept all before them. Built on solid foundations (they only let in 16 goals) the team could restrict teams before swamping them with attack after attack.

Kennedy played in all 42 games that season. Kenny Dalglish up front was the brilliant pivot but it was that midfield that did the most collective damage. At Maine Road in August 1978, Liverpool took Manchester City apart and a Kennedy goal set the tone for a season. Dalglish comes deep dragging defenders with him. McDermott fills that space with a run from midfield, looks up, squares it to Kennedy who has come in from the left and who, first time, slams the ball past Joe Corrigan.

They were a hard bunch too. The most famous victory that season came against Tottenham in August. Spurs arrived with World Cup winner Osvaldo Ardiles, who was quickly greeted by tenacious tackles from midfield and the onlooking Tommy Smith, no stranger to 'Welcome to Anfield' challenges, was impressed.

'They can't expect to come here and play fancy flickers,' said Smith after the game. 'That tackle was to say to him this is a man's league – and he didn't like it. I think Spurs ought to buy a good stock of cotton wool for such poseurs. He can't expect not to be tackled just because Argentina won the World Cup.'

Who would question Souness, McDermott or Case but Kennedy – less obviously tough – was no shrinking violet. Like so many Liverpool legends, Kennedy came from the North East, a place with great kinsmanship to Merseyside and like so many footballing legends in general from that coalmining hub, his prospects as a child were the pits or football.

Kennedy's father Martin worked those pits, from midnight to 8am for years. Kennedy enjoyed a happy childhood and those who saw him play won't be surprised to hear that he got out of many scrapes. At birth he had his umbilical cord wrapped around his neck, but he managed to twist free. As a young teenager he was caught eating the carrots and turnips in a nearby cornfield by the farmer and a band of savage dogs. Kennedy, very much like his footballing incarnation avoided trouble with stealth, slowly crawling through the corn on his knees to safety.

He excelled at football, playing against boys bigger and older than himself. They'd try to use size and age against him, but he was more than willing to stand up to them. His father encouraged self-reliance, advising him from a young age if he were to ever get into a fight don't be afraid to pick something up if your fists alone won't do. Kennedy once chased an assailant home with a brick in his hand and threw it into the bigger boy's living-room window.

When his brother Trevor was being bullied, Kennedy waited quietly for the boy, threw him from his bike and chased him down the street. Trevor never heard a word from his bully again.

That bullishness on the football pitch went noticed in youth circles. A free-scoring forward, Kennedy had locals talking. He had a fine pair of continental football boots bought with his mother's bingo winnings and the family were dumbstruck when Stanley Matthews, only recently retired at 52 and now the manager of Port Vale, came to their home on a tip from a local scout that here lived a fine young prospect.

Kennedy made the trip to the Potteries but after a while scratching around the youth and reserve teams, the youngster was let go and returned to the North East a dejected young man. Matthews himself had written a letter to the Kennedys explaining his decision not to take their son on. 'I now feel that Raymond will have difficulty in making the grade in football to take it up as a career,' he said.

'He is sluggish in his movements and it is only fair to let you know I consider he will be wasting his time here when he could find alternative employment.' Those words must have hurt and Kennedy himself cried when told the news and returned home feeling a failure. He did though continue to play and score in local youth football and that eye for goal kept scouts coming. One of them with links to Arsenal. Kennedy was going to London.

Just 16 and living in the capital was hard and Arsenal were far from the superpower they had been. Bertie Mee, the manager was building a new team though and with the likes of Frank McLintock, John Radford and Charlie George, the teenager blossomed and before his 20th birthday in 1971, had won the Double, scoring the goal that claimed the championship at Tottenham and days later, helping beat Liverpool to claim the FA Cup.

Kennedy later admitted he struggled to cope with such early success. Where does a young man go from a Double? Kennedy trained less, ate too much, enjoyed a pint. He put on weight and soon Arsenal were buying new strikers and listening to offers. One of them came from Bill Shankly, who despite wrestling with his own demons bought the player and announced the new signing on the very day he also retired.

Kennedy's £180,000 transfer was buried as far as news went, but fans got a taste of the new player early in the 1974/75 season as Keegan had been banned for a Charity Shield scrap with Leeds' Billy Bremner. The new striker certainly hit the ground running, scoring in his first three outings.

He had enjoyed a hard-working pre-season, losing a stone and being as fit as he was winning that Double. An onlooking Bill Shankly said his last signing reminded him of former heavyweight champion Rocky Marciano.

Ever the soul searcher though, Kennedy had questioned his own worth, why Arsenal had let him go and despite Liverpool's better form, Kennedy did tease his team-mates that compared to Arsenal's champagne and smoked salmon approach, theirs was a, 'Pork-pie and pop outfit'.

Despite such impertinence, his new team-mates immediately took to Kennedy and in time he very much took to them and his new surroundings. Sure his manager could be a confusing communicator, hardly ever finishing sentences and calling things and people 'Doins' rather than a name that had escaped him, but he was clearly a genius football man, and able to talk Kennedy's language, literally.

Not that those early goals were as free flowing as he and the fans would have hoped. Keegan returned from his ban and with Kennedy struggling, John Toshack was back in to partner him. Five goals in Kennedy's 25 league games in that fruitless season for Paisley was a concern. Wolves came knocking to take him and Paisley seriously considered it.

The manager though was too curious to sell. There was something in Kennedy he liked, something he couldn't quite put his finger on. Liverpool started the 1975/76 season in decent fashion but Kennedy was still unsure in front of goal. Like legendary television detective, Colombo, Paisley put on his old raincoat and went back to the North East to do some digging. There he tracked down an old friend who happened to also be Kennedy's old schoolteacher and discovered his man had played a lot of his football in midfield. A light bulb went on over the manager's head.

A run out in the reserves went well and so at Middlesbrough in November 1975, Kennedy – thanks to a knee injury to the usual left-sided midfielder, Peter Cormack -- was going back to his roots. If this were *Roy of the Rovers*, what would follow would be a tale of Kennedy's brilliance, a glut of goals and assists. This isn't *Roy of the Rovers*.

Liverpool lost and the *Daily Post* was far from impressed with the midfield exploits of the Liverpool man. 'With poor Kennedy looking a most temporary left-half, the nimble Armstrong, Souness and Mills outnumbered the loyally-working Callaghan.'

Paisley wasn't swayed by newspaper ink though and he continued with his experiment. He had seen in training that Kennedy had lost that spark needed up front but there was a footballing brain there that used correctly could be more than useful.

Paisley had had a heart to heart with Kennedy but the insecure player thought that being asked to move was just a prerequisite for selling him. He didn't count on Paisley following a hunch. 'Moving Ray was the best switch I ever made,' said the manager years later. 'He had really lost his appetite for playing up front but he was surprised I'd found out that he'd played midfield as a schoolboy. He got his weight back down from 14 stone to 12 stone 10 and went on to play for England.'

He also went on to win the league championship. A thrilling finish to the season saw Liverpool needing to draw at Wolverhampton to claim the prize and whilst losing at half-time, they went all out attack in the second period and scored through Keegan, Toshack and then Kennedy himself.

Kennedy was now an attacking midfielder and whilst the Toshack/ Keegan duo was as ever the talk of the town, it was Case and Kennedy behind them that offered Paisley another goalscoring partnership from deep, pitching in with 12 goals between them. It wasn't just on the field that the two men crackled either, now firm friends, Kennedy and Case were known to paint the town the same colour as their footballing shirts.

Case and Kennedy were kindred spirits. Case the raucous, fun-loving Scouser, as spirited off the pitch as he was on it. Kennedy, more considered but no less up for it. 'Batman and Robin' their team-mates called them. Kennedy joked that hotel receptionists would see them coming into their foyers and duck behind the desk in lieu of the impending chaos about to strike their establishments.

Players would return from dinner and find beds overturned. Wondering how on earth this happened when only they had the keys, they had missed the slightly open window and the fact that Case and Kennedy were prone to crawl along window ledges and gain entry by any means necessary.

When cup final tickets allocated to the players were to be sold on to major ticket touts in London, it was Case and Kennedy on the case. Women were picked up on long trips abroad – one of the perks of many European adventures. Kennedy was a hit with the women. One Aer Lingus stewardess described him as, 'A big affable Geordie who was strong, muscular and sturdy. Any girl would have fallen for his swarthy Mediterranean good looks and his easy manner… He always spoke fondly of his mother.'

Being a close-knit group, sexual activities were often done in packs. Once, with a few girls enjoying a few players in a hotel room, Kennedy turned to his colleagues – both of them recently awarded with honours by Her Majesty at Buckingham Palace – and said, 'If only the Queen could see you now.'

All typical football fodder but Case and Kennedy could go too far. One 'incident' finished up with both men in court, charged with affray, a charge to which they pleaded guilty and were fined £150 each. It was 1980 and the team were treated to a few days' 'relaxation' in The Bryn Howell Hotel near Llangollen in Wales.

Case and Kennedy enjoyed their dinner slowly with two bottles of Chablis and the company of the hotel owner. The other players were off out quickly and so Kennedy told Terry McDermott to call him from whatever bar they found themselves in.

No call came and so having drunk in another pub and now once more enjoying some wine at the hotel bar, both were suitably inebriated when McDermott walked in. It was 2am and suddenly Kennedy took offence to his team-mate's lack of contact.

Maybe he was a kid again hell-bent on punishing the bully but words were exchanged and fully riled, the owner's son asked if Kennedy's name was Alan. Kennedy didn't take kindly in this state to being mistaken for Alan Kennedy and struck out; the owner was hit too and then so was McDermott. Case wasn't going to miss out and he threw a bar stool at the owner. Mayhem. The police were called and Case and Kennedy were hauled into a van screaming for help from the boot-room.

These skirmishes and misdemeanours were isolated and trouble on the pitch, or in training were practically zero. The only problem Paisley had with Kennedy was keeping him motivated. The player had a habit of losing focus. As he had at Arsenal when he won the Double and put on the pounds, Kennedy's mind could wander at the end of a glittering season. Paisley didn't mind, by addressing the issue he could flex his ample managerial muscle. Kennedy was cajoled and simply went again.

What a player he was. His contribution was huge but his goals underlined his vast range of skills. A goal at Aston Villa in April 1978 was as deft a lob as you could wish to see. The perfect sand wedge out of the Villa Park turf and over a bewildered Jimmy Rimmer. And then there was a goal at Derby County, a brilliant run from deep that bamboozled the Derby defenders, a subtle take of a raking McDermott pass, the drop of a shoulder to drop the goalkeeper to his knees and the cool finish into the open goal. Just brilliant. No thrills, no spills, just wonderfully effective and clever football.

Kennedy was a major part of the club's first European Cup triumph in 1977. By now a fully-fledged member of the Liverpool midfield, this was a quartet not yet blessed with Graeme Souness but very much benefiting from the experience and industry of Ian Callaghan who had moved infield from the right wing. That was the thing with footballing men like Bill Shankly and Bob Paisley. They assessed players, watched them, studied them. If a player was slowing down why simply move them on? If a player wasn't enjoying one position, why simply just sell them? As Shankly had looked at Callaghan and discussed his move to the centre of the park, Paisley had brilliantly moved Kennedy to the left side of midfield and so the team marched on Rome in high spirits.

That march started in Northern Ireland at Crusaders with a comfortable win and then came the long trip to Trabzonspor in Turkey. Kennedy had caught the eye of a belly dancer on a 'quiet' night prior to the game and such was the basic state of the team's lodgings, the side flew home glad of just a 1–0 defeat. The second leg was an easier affair and a 3–0 win saw the team through to what became an iconic quarter-final.

St Etienne, the French champions and the losing finalists in the previous year's European Cup Final. This was now serious. The air stewardess on the Aer Lingus flight noticed that not one drop of alcohol was touched and not one racy comment to her or her colleagues was uttered. Liverpool Football Club meant business.

The game itself was lost by a single goal and so it was back to Anfield for one of the great nights. Anfield was full hours before kick-off. Ghosts of those pioneers who had crammed in to cheer on the likes of Elisha Scott must have been there because the noise made that March night came from more than the 55,000 in the ground.

Keegan, rather fortuitously, levelled the match early in the game but the French struck back with a brilliant Dominque Bathenay strike six minutes into the second half. Liverpool would need two more to go through against a fine, fine team. The Kop believed, the whole ground believed and the volume went up and up.

Eight minutes later, Kennedy picked up the ball outside the box and drilled a low shot past Ivan Curkovic, the French side's Yugoslav keeper. Anfield was on full blast but the team needed a shot in the arm. John

Toshack despite assisting Kennedy's effort was pulled off and on came David Fairclough, a player accustomed to changing football matches.

There were no tactical inswingers from Paisley, no over the top instructions, instead he just told his sub to, 'Run around and try to get on the end of things.' Well with six minutes left, those things to get on the end of happened to be a perfectly weighted lofted pass from Kennedy. Watch it. It looks like a mindless lob upfield but Kennedy knew there was space to exploit and he knew the pass's target was quick.

Fairclough was onto it, controlled the bouncing ball, bided his time and slipped the ball into the net and his name into Liverpudlian folklore. What followed was a party that has passed down the generations. The travelling French fans, sporting green (the club colours) Beatles wigs joined the Scouse soiree, many of them so taken with their victors that they travelled to Rome to watch the final.

The semi-final against Zurich was, in comparison, a damp squib and a 6–1 aggregate win had fans dreaming of a Roman holiday. By then the league had been won and the FA Cup Final lost. That day against Manchester United was a blow (Kennedy had hit the bar late on) but the team travelled back north whilst hordes of their supporters made their way to Dover from London for an epic journey that the Roman legions themselves would have been proud of.

The game against Germany's finest, Borussia Moenchengladbach, was a study in tactical nous and team spirit. The nous was laid down by Paisley, who picked a hugely-forward thinking XI that had Keegan up front alone with Steve Heighway drifting in front of a midfield four of Kennedy, McDermott, Callaghan and Case.

It worked a charm. Up front, Keegan ran the German World Cup winning centre-half Bertie Vogts ragged, pulling him this way and that and allowing those industrious folk behind him to exploit the holes his runs were ripping in the German defence.

The first goal was a case in point. Callaghan had robbed the Germans in his half, and immediately Heighway was drifting, receiving the ball on the right wing. Keegan kept Vogts busy on the far side of the pitch and as Heighway progressed, McDermott sprinted beyond him into the gap left by Vogts and buried the spotty ball in the slack Olympic Stadium's netting.

It was never going to be easy and Liverpool were penned back by a second half goal, but a thunderous header from Smith and a Phil Neal penalty won a famous victory. Arguably the most famous of many.

The celebrations were long and deservedly blurry. Kennedy had had a quietly effective game. Joey Jones at left-back might have been a target for the Germans but Kennedy remained disciplined and used all his experience to stifle that avenue of attack. For his efforts he now was a European champion.

Most sweet would have been in the dressing room after the game when in walked Stanley Matthews to congratulate the team. There were no hard feelings of course but how Matthews's words on that letter home from Port Vale must have been etched on Kennedy's brain. *'He is sluggish'*… *'Raymond will have difficulty in making the grade'*… *'find alternative employment'*. Kennedy couldn't help himself. 'Seen one of these before, Stan?' he said, showing the great man his winners' medal.

Kennedy was due his gloat. He was part of Europe's best team, a fact underlined the following season in London when they became the first British team to retain the trophy with a tightly fought 1–0 win over Belgian side, Bruges.

The unfancied Belgians had beaten Panathinaikos, Atletico Madrid and Juventus (the team Bill Shankly believed to be the strongest in Europe) on the way to Wembley but they were overly cautious against Liverpool and whilst they packed the defence, it took some magic from Souness and Dalglish to crack it.

Crammed streets greeted the team as their open top bus trudged through the city as the players sipped champagne and enjoyed their public. A lady in a negligee showed her appreciation whilst one fan lay down in front of the vehicle, making himself the only man to stop Paisley's men in a very long time.

All was well. Paisley hailed Kennedy as his 'Euro King' such was the player's abilities to follow tactical instructions, slow a game down and dictate a tempo to suit his team. 'He had a keen football brain,' Paisley later said. 'When he got in the box he was as dangerous as anybody. His talent was never fully recognised in this country.'

The last comment is interesting. Paisley is right but also underlines why Kennedy's cult among travelling Liverpool fans might have been so high. As the 1970s became the 1980s, supporters were following the team all over Europe and coming back with hitherto unknown continental fashion brands, often with the security tag still on them.

Like their new tracksuit tops or polo shirts with the strange green crocodile on them, Kennedy was unrecognised and uncelebrated at home but to these fans, that's what made him so cool. Ray Kennedy to the travelling fans was their own Sergio Tacchini tracky.

More was to come. Kennedy was getting on but his considered approach meant losing pace was never a huge issue and the 1980/81 campaign saw him cement his legend with a decisively cool finish in Munich to knock Bayern out of the semi-final, despite a glut of injuries that saw the likes of Howard Gayle, Colin Irwin and Richard Money add their unlikely names to Liverpool's pantheon of European glory. Kennedy was out drinking heartily with the Scousers that night in Munich's beer halls, toasting his role as skipper on the most memorable of nights.

Kennedy also got an assist in the final, albeit a throw-in to his namesake, Alan who hammered home a late goal to beat Real Madrid in the Paris final. Alan had enjoyed playing behind Ray (Paisley famously said that, 'They shot the wrong Kennedy' after a poor debut) but Ray joked that he found the partnership harder work.

'He took five years off my career,' said Ray of Alan. 'Whenever I wanted a short ball, he'd hit it long. If it should have been long, I'd get a short pass. Alan had no nerves and not much brain, which was why he was lethal at penalties.'

Paris was Ray Kennedy's high. He felt totally at ease with himself, the footballer, perhaps knowing that his time at the club was coming to an end. In 1982 he left for Swansea but in 1986, only five years after winning his third European Cup winners' medal, he got news from his doctors that he had Parkinson's disease.

It was a huge shock to fans and the footballing public. His doctor had noticed how much Kennedy had been perspiring long after a game of five-a-side. It was Parkinson's. Family talked of how tired he had always been. Fans talked of it explaining the lethargy that frustrated so many of them.

Whilst playing, Kennedy joked that he hated playing on the left flank at the Kemlyn Road end of Anfield because sat there was a regular who would always shout, 'Get going, you lazy sod.' Later he never used his illness as an excuse for that style but it does make him smile when he thinks of his three European Cup gongs.

The fans though have never forgotten Ray Kennedy. A testimonial at Highbury in 1991 was well attended and Liverpool supporters' groups have raised thousands of pounds to help make his life easier.

Kennedy got a standing ovation from all four corners of Anfield in 2009 when Arsenal were the visitors. Maybe the Kemlyn Road regular who would scream his frustrations at Kennedy all those years earlier was there that night and had second thoughts about his feelings for this most beautiful of footballers. Sure he might not have run around like a madman, but by god he could play.

Joey Jones

1975–1978
Appearances: 100
Goals: 3

THE punk scene and the Kop are not obvious bedfellows. In 1977, whilst The Sex Pistols were politely asking for God to save the Queen in her silver jubilee year, fans who flocked to Anfield to watch their team were very much interested in silver, but it had nothing to do with their monarch's anniversary.

By the mid-winter of 1977, as the nation were considering where to put up their royal bunting, Liverpool fans had eyes only on silverware, lots of silverware. The league championship was on, an FA Cup run was well under way and most importantly, the European Cup looked a tantalising possibility.

Liverpool Football Club were the best around. Under their monarch Bob Paisley, they had won the league the previous season and they had won the UEFA Cup. Europe's finest feared them and they housed the best players.

In goal Ray Clemence, by now England's goalkeeper. Emlyn Hughes, England's captain. Phil Neal, England's right-back. Ray Kennedy and Terry McDermott, half of England's midfield; and Kevin Keegan, England's striker and by now a superstar turning the heads of European clubs and a celebrity who transcended the game he played.

In footballing terms, Liverpool were the establishment. But then there was Joey Jones. A Welsh international left-back but a player who every time he ran out toward the Kop felt compelled to pinch himself. A dyed in the wool Liverpool fan who gave his all, Jones would be the first to say that in this team, he was the punk. Anti their establishment. He wasn't refined, he wasn't slick and he wasn't a superstar but oh how he cared, and he ran and he gave his all, and because of all that, the Kop couldn't get enough.

On one occasion, Jones was substitute. It was a European game and so under the floodlights at half-time he went out to warm up. 'I was just taking some shots at the Kop end,' Jones says, a grin never far from his face when discussing his time in red. 'As I'm running about, the Kop starts to sing, "Joey do the Pogo, Joey do the Pogo." Now the Pogo was a dance at the time. The punks did it. It basically involved jumping about like a nutter and so of course I started doing it. They liked that.'

The Kop liked lots that Joey Jones did. Talk to him now, almost 40 years on, and he is still full of wonderment that he ever made it onto the pitch at Anfield as a player. You sense he still half expects to wake up from a dream. The Kop understood that pure unadulterated joy he had for being there and they adopted him as their anti-hero. Anti in the fact that he wasn't a Kevin Keegan, all curly locks and off-field contracts; but a spit and sawdust footballer who would walk through fire for just one more game in front of them.

Tattooed, slightly manic and able to smile, this was their punk. Bob Paisley must have often wondered at the player he had signed from Wrexham for £110,000 in 1975, but here he was, in 1977, Liverpool's special year very much part of the team and very much winning things.

He even scored. A few times. The pick of them was at Anfield against Bristol City, the winner and a screamer from long range. 'I am so glad you brought that up,' laughs Jones. 'I have a Liverpool programme and the cover is a photo of me striking that one to win the game. Underneath it says, "Marksman Joey Jones scores the winner against Bristol City." Marksman! Me a marksman? I show the guys at Wrexham where I work today and they piss themselves. They've started calling me "Marksman". It was a great goal though. Kevin [Keegan] had scored, but they equalised and so I saved the day with a volley from distance that flew in at the Kop end. That was great.'

Deadly from 25 yards, Jones was by now Liverpool's established left-back. Emlyn Hughes had been moved inside to play centre-back with either Phil Thompson or Tommy Smith, and Phil Neal was at right-back. It was a very good back-four in a very good team.

So good, they had reached the quarter-finals of the European Cup and there they would face St Etienne, the French champions and the

Captain Alex
Raisbeck (middle
row, centre) and
the Liverpool
squad prior to the
1905/06 season.
The club finished
the campaign as
champions.

The great Elisha
Scott, wearing
his customary
gloves and
knee-pads holds
the fort for
Liverpool at
West Bromwich
Albion in March
1926.

Jimmy Melia poses for the cameras prior to Liverpool's return to the First Division in August 1962.

Ian St John celebrates his winning goal with Liverpool's other goalscorer Roger Hunt in a Wembley bath after the 1965 FA Cup Final win over Leeds United.

The 1965 FA Cup Final. Ron Yeats shaking hands with Bobby Collins prior to kick-off.

Emlyn Hughes AKA Crazy Horse, with his old mate Princess Anne at Wembley before the 1974 FA Cup Final.

Peter Cormack enjoying time on the ball at Ipswich Town's Portman Road in September 1975.

A sea of red and white in Rome, May 1977, and the travelling Kop show off their banner dedicated to Joey Jones.

Craig Johnston celebrates Liverpool's penalty shoot-out win over Roma in Rome with Ian Rush (left) and Sammy Lee that wins a fourth European Cup for Liverpool.

Still got it! The Kop show their appreciation for John Barnes 17 years after he left with a banner at the end of the 2013/14 season.

*Robbie Fowler celebrates
what he hoped would
be the winner with
Steven Gerrard during
the 2000/01 Uefa Cup
Final against Alaves in
Dortmund.*

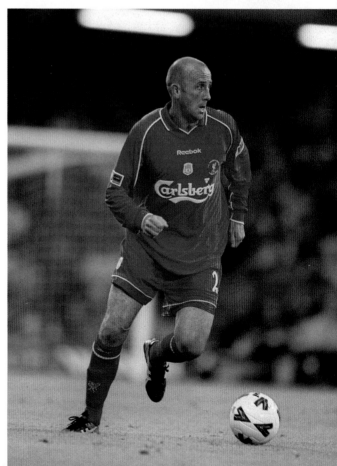

*All the time in the world!
Gary McAllister strolls
around the Cardiff
turf during the 2001
Community Shield against
Manchester United at the
Millennium Stadium.*

He Drinks Sangria! Luis Garcia does his customary 'thumb in mouth' celebration having put Liverpool 2–0 up against Chelsea in the 2006 FA Cup semi-final at Old Trafford.

Luis Suarez celebrates another goal, this time at Cardiff in the 6–3 win at the Cardiff City Stadium, March 2014.

previous season's runners-up. Liverpool lost the first leg 1–0 but that set up a special evening under the Anfield floodlights where against the odds, Paisley's men won 3–1 to send an already stir-crazy crowd on a one-way ticket to delirium.

'Oh it was special,' says Jones. 'They were a good team them. I was asked to mark a guy called Dominic Rocheteau and he was very good. A French international. I did really well against him though. I think they thought I was a weak link and he'd rip me to bits but I did all right that night. I remember the pitch was really bad. We were playing so many games that season it was quite cut-up but no matter we went through and from there, the final looked more than likely.'

It was more than likely. Having beaten Zurich Grasshoppers in the semi-final the team were off to Rome for the final. The league was won (Jones missed only three league games that season) and an FA Cup Final against Manchester United was on the horizon. This was serious, this was football on Everest, but Joey Jones so often wondered what the hell he was doing on the mountain.

The FA Cup Final was lost at Wembley on the Saturday but the team went home down but far from out ('Oh we had a good few beers on the train,' laughs Jones). A quick turn around in Liverpool and it was off to Rome. There were no big changes to routine, no fanfare. 'We flew to Italy as if it was any other match,' says Jones. 'Bob didn't really do team-talks. He had done the whole bit about the last time he was in Rome he was in a tank and that was great but he didn't go into huge tactics with me. There was never a big team-talk so why now? Just the usual thing. Wembley had been a huge blow but now we were very much back to work.'

Jones's night's work was solid. He kept the ball moving and he made those crunchingly purposeful tackles. At left-back he was often faced with marking Borussia Moenchengladbach's danger man, the Danish playmaker Allan Simonsen.

Jones did his job, nothing fancy, no marauding runs down the left-wing; but Simonsen often drifted over to the left-wing as the Welshman wasn't giving him much change. Indeed it was from the Germans' left side that the Dane scored to level the scores after Terry McDermott's earlier silky goal.

No matter, Tommy Smith rose to head a second and when Phil Neal put away a penalty, Liverpool's sea of red in the ground prepared to swell late into the Roman night.

McDermott, Smith and Neal had their European Cup goals but Jones had his banner. A huge flag that dominated the Olympic Stadium and that proudly proclaimed that:

JOEY ATE THE FROGS LEGS, MADE THE SWISS ROLL AND NOW HE'S MUNCHIN' GLADBACH!

It was a symbol of fan passion and humour that actually summed up the man that it spoke of. Jones had no idea it would be there, but on what was always going to be a special night it meant so much.

'First of all, just to walk out onto that pitch and see how many Scousers had made the journey was amazing and seemed to make things easier,' he recalls. 'Then I saw the banner and I felt ten feet tall. To have something like that, that big with my name on it, was special. The German players we faced wouldn't have had a clue who I was. They would have been briefed about the rest of the guys and how to stop them but I'm guessing, Joey Jones wasn't mentioned a lot. But there was my name on this huge banner and I felt like the best player in the world.'

With a European Cup winners' medal in his hand and the fans' scarves and flags draped around him, Jones revelled in the team's lap of honour, 'I actually wanted to be in with the fans,' says Jones. 'I remember jumping up on the fence to be closer to them and the police thought I was a supporter draped in a Union Jack flag and up to no good so they set the dogs on me!'

Of the game, Jones recalls a terrible touch he made when trying to trap the ball early on, and he recalls that Emlyn Hughes, playing at centre-back never once passed to him. 'Who could blame him?' jokes the Welshman.

Details from the game are clearer than those from after. The celebrations went long into the night with press and fans invited in to share in the European Champions' glee. Paisley stayed sober for clarity's sake but he was alone. 'We drank a lot,' says Jones. 'I was sick all over my hotel floor, all over all my things. Who cares though and anyway, I don't think I was the only one. Tommy Smith was downstairs throwing journalists he didn't like into the hotel swimming pool. I'm glad he didn't throw me in, I would have drowned.'

Jones had come to Liverpool and for all his insecurities as a footballer he had stayed afloat. Not that that stops him joking. Always armed with a smile and a quip, Jones often mocks his own game, mocks his own place in the squad and that stemmed from arriving as a raw 20-year-old fresh off the Kop. Hearing that Liverpool wanted to sign him certainly rocked his boat.

'I was fishing when I heard!' says Jones. I was in a small boat with a mate and there's my dad on the shore. I thought something had happened. I was worried. We never had a car and he's walked all that way and so we head into shore quickly, and he shouts to me to say a guy from Wrexham had been over (we never had a phone) to say Liverpool wanted me. I nearly fell off the boat! Bob Paisley was going to get in touch and so we had to give our neighbour Hazel's number as she was the only person around with a phone.'

Jones didn't catch a fish that day but he was heading to Melwood to train with men he regarded only with childlike idolatry. 'Here I am next to players whose posters are all over my bedroom wall back in Llandudno. I can't believe I am with these guys, especially Tommy Smith. He was the ultimate. Tommy helped me a lot. It had been well documented in the local papers that he was my favourite and he was great with me. They all were.'

Jones fitted in immediately. The step up in quality from Wrexham was immense but Paisley wasn't shy in picking the youngster during the 1975/76 season. Phil Neal often filled in at left-back but Jones got his chances and impressions in the crowd were immediate.

'I had played at QPR but my first game at Anfield was the following week against West Ham,' recalls Jones. 'I ran out of the tunnel, turned right and there it was. I had stood on the Kop so many times but to see it from the pitch in all its glory was just brilliant. My legs went a bit wobbly. I knew exactly where my mates stood and I knew exactly what they'd be getting up to, as not long before I was too. I ran towards them and up went my fist. The whole terrace responded and cheered and I guess we bonded from there. I'd like to think they saw the player who was going to give everything and was very much one of them. I always felt I was representing the lads off the Kop out there on the pitch.'

Fans had taken to him immediately, but Bob Paisley and his staff might have sometimes wondered how their well-oiled machine was going to cope with him. Especially faced with an irate neighbour demanding compensation for a broken window.

'We were doing a shooting session at Melwood on a Good Friday,' laughs Jones. 'It wasn't good for me. We had the balls lined up, you'd lay one off to Roy Evans and he'd lay it back for you to shoot. I hit it and off it goes, over the bar, over the wall and straight through a bungalow's window. First time that had ever happened! The club paid the damages but they weren't happy. The guy who lived there was going berserk (he must have been an Evertonian) and as it's Good Friday they have to pay more to get someone out to board it up.

'Bob wasn't happy. He had some words for me but mainly to say that I should be getting my body over the ball and not to lean back! Always coaching Bob. I was never going to get the number nine shirt after that, in fact I did well to keep the number three.'

Windows weren't the only thing getting a smashing from Jones during those early days. On the first day of November 1975, Liverpool went to Middlesbrough. They won 1–0 but finished the game with ten men when Jones was given a red card for some over-zealous defending; of himself not the goal.

'That was a bit naughty,' admits Jones. 'Today I would be taken to court. It was one of them. The guy came at me and I thought he was going to hit me, so I head butted him. John Hickton it was. I think he lost some teeth and I have never had the chance to apologise. My dad passed on some advice when I was young on the council estate, that if I ever thought someone was going to hit me, get one in first. Those words flashed before me on the pitch as he approached me and bosh, I've nutted him. Off. Bad. I shouldn't have done it and I knew that immediately.'

It wasn't all glazier bills and early baths though. Jones was doing plenty on the pitch. He wasn't the complete left-back Alec Lindsay had been, but he was certainly holding his own.

Jones laughs at his own ability but when it is suggested that Bob Paisley was not the sort of manager who bought and played dud full-backs, Jones gets more serious, even if it is just for a minute. 'I was never confident at Liverpool and if I'm honest I was still a bit in awe, even during the 1976/77 season,' he says. 'There I was playing for my boyhood heroes and I had to pinch myself that I was there playing with them. I held my own though that season. I think some of my team-mates maybe first thought I wasn't right for the team but I did my bit. I did my bit.'

He did indeed. His team were playing the biggest of games in the most iconic of stadiums and with Jones around there was always a sense of mischief, even when he was watching from the sidelines. In 1976, Liverpool went to Barcelona in the UEFA Cup. Jones was on the bench watching his fellow Welshman John Toshack score the goal to secure a famous 1–0 win that sent Liverpool home with a commanding first-leg win, but sent the home fans home with only anger and frustration in their hearts, emotions they weren't going to keep to themselves.

'We were brilliant that night,' says Jones. 'A classic away performance and we had stifled the team and frustrated the fans. I was sat at the side of the pitch. Back then there were no luxury dugouts like today with their jacuzzis and five star restaurants. During the game a few gobstoppers had been thrown at us on the bench but on the final whistle it got much, much worse.

'Down came parts of the seats, full seats and loads of the seat cushions they had at the Nou Camp. I wasn't having any of that. I picked up all these cushions and started to throw them back. I was having a whale of the time, hitting the locals, throwing them like Frisbees, bouncing them off their heads. Then I start throwing them from under my leg and from round my back. I'm having a great time when Bob grabs me by the collar. "What the fuck do you think you're doing?" he screams.

'"I'm not having them throw things at us, boss," I say.

'"They're throwing things at their players because we won Joey. Now get off, you're going to start a riot."'

Paisley had his eye on Jones. He liked his bravery and enthusiasm. In fact when he wrote a book called *My 50 Golden Reds*, Paisley included Jones, writing that, 'He always gave you the impression that if he hadn't been playing on a Saturday he would have been with his mates on the Kop every Saturday and there haven't been too many players who were more popular, either with his team-mates or with the fans. I'll always have a place in my memories for Joey because what he might have lacked in finesse he more than made up for with his personality which helped to make sure there were plenty of laughs in the dressing room when he was about.'

Paisley might have laughed but he often wondered what might happen next. When his players went off on international duty, each and every one of them would get a telegram from the manager saying, 'GOOD LUCK'. Jones would get one but his said, 'KEEP OUT OF TROUBLE'.

Jones loved playing for Wales and he loved being in the middle of the Anglo-Scot rivalry at Melwood. With Toshack he represented the Welsh dragon with pride and always left his mark on games and players, however big their reputation. When Kenny Dalglish signed in 1977, he arrived at Melwood and walked around the dressing room, introducing himself and exchanging pleasantries. He then got to Jones with whom he had had plenty of Home Nation tussles. 'Fuck off you skinny Welsh bastard,' he said before breaking out into laughter. The two became firm friends.

Dalglish has recalled how proud Jones was to play for Liverpool and Wales. When Scotland faced the Welsh in a World Cup play-off fixture at Anfield, Jones was so keen to let his Scottish team-mates know about the sort of support the Welsh would bring. 'Wait til you see it, Kenny,' Joey said. On the night of the game, Jones ran out of the Anfield tunnel and sprinted toward the Kop, his fist pumping as usual, ready to salute the land of his fathers. He looked up only to see a sea of tartan. He could only laugh.

After the glory of Rome, Jones struggled to hold down a regular spot at left-back. Emlyn Hughes would often fill in there and Jones spent much of his time on the bench. It was from there he watched Liverpool retain the European Cup at Wembley and whilst the fan in him was delighted, he knew deep down that his time at his beloved club was almost up.

'I had nothing but respect for Bob Paisley though,' says Jones. 'He was my boss, the man who made my dream come true. He was a top manager and a top footballing man. He didn't say loads and sometimes I'd have liked him to say more to me in terms of encouragement but he had this knowing way about him. He also had a fantastic team of staff around him. Ronnie Moran, Joe Fagan, Roy Evans, Reuben Bennett, Tom Saunders; each of them was brilliant and they were a team within a team. They were so ahead of their time, doing the kind of sports science stuff then, that people do now. Not that they knew they were doing it. It was just simple, basic stuff.'

Jones's last start for the club came in January 1978 at Chelsea in the FA Cup. Liverpool lost 4–2 and Jones had been given a torrid time by Chelsea's winger, Clive Walker. Having been pulled off and despondent, Jones went to put a tracksuit on. 'I was struggling to get this thing on,' Jones says with a naughty laugh. 'There I am next to Bob trying to get this thing on and to get my arms through the sleeves. When I do, I smack Bob in the face. Right in the face. I didn't mean to, but it must have looked bad. I don't know if it was that punch or Clive Walker, but I never started a game again for Liverpool.

'I was soon off and Alan Kennedy came in from Newcastle, but hadn't I had fun, hadn't I had a good time? Players brought to Liverpool from the lower leagues usually get put in the reserves for a couple of seasons and then make the first team. I started off in the first team and then went into the reserves!'

A laugh is never far away from Jones's mouth. He played the game with a laugh and the fans – staid in their quest for honours – got that this game we all go and watch must not be taken too seriously. On one occasion in a team hotel, Paisley sat around with his players and being a huge fan of quizzes took questions from the floor. 'Who was the last man to break his leg at Wembley?' asked Jones. Ooh a good one. Paisley racked his vast footballing brain and spent ages coming up with suggestions. 'Bob was saying all these obscure names from the 1950s and 1960s who he thought had broken their legs,' said Jones. 'None of them were right.

'He was getting more and more frustrated. No one else had a clue and so I got up and headed for the door. "Come on Joey," said Bob, "who the hell is it?"

'"Evel Knievel," I said and walked out. I could hear all the lads pissing themselves and apparently Bob went mad. I was right though. The daredevil had crashed jumping over buses in 1975.'

When he returned to Wrexham a package arrived from Melwood. Jones read the note that had come with it. It was from Ronnie Moran. 'You forgot your boots,' it said. Jones opened the box to find a pair of dirty, ankle high hobnailed boots with leather studs. The kind worn in the 1930s. Jones still has them.

Jones also became the proud owner of the legendary banner that celebrated his European culinary exploits in Rome, 1977. 'Two fans, Phil Downey and Jimmy Cummings (who sadly isn't with us anymore), gave me the banner years later. That was special. It was from the fans and I was very much one of them. That banner was in my garage for years but I have since given it to the club museum. I have to say I think as much of that banner as I do my winners' medal.

'I am so proud. If I am remembered for nothing else but that banner, then that will do me. I started off as a fan, then I played and now I am a fan again. Wrexham is my spiritual home, but Liverpool will always be my team, my club. Mind you I came wanting to play like Tommy Smith, but only managed to play like Tommy Cooper.'

Steve Nicol

1981–1994
Appearances: 468
Goals: 46

ALAN Hansen once called Steve Nicol the most unstreetwise
footballer in Britain. The Scottish international was alluding
to his fellow countryman's naivety; a lovable tendency for
gullibility that – in the jungle that was his Liverpool dressing room –
could get a man into strife.

Nicol is remembered by Liverpool fans fondly and much of that
stems from what they have heard, what they have read about this
amiable young footballer who came to the club to help himself and
them to trophies but who also took the brunt of his team-mates' banter
and pranks. Yes, Hansen was right, he may well have been the least
streetwise footballer around but he was also one of the most dec-
orated.

Steve Nicol won things. He won the FA Cup, three times. He won
the European Cup and he won the league championship, four times.
He won the Football Writers' Footballer of the Year, he won 27 caps
and he played in the 1986 World Cup. He won hearts too and not only
is he remembered as arguably the best full-back the club has ever had,
he is also recalled with a knowing smile.

By the mid-1980s sections of the Liverpool fans were – unlike Nicol!
– very streetwise. They were by now used to travelling all over Europe
watching their team, they knew their team and they would often drink
with the players. Stories of Nicol's ability to not only dish out the jokes,

but also be the brunt of them were nothing but endearing and the player became as popular on the terraces as he was at Melwood.

Sure the likes of Dalglish, Souness, Rush and later Molby and Barnes and Beardsley might have been the schoolboy favourites but there was – and still is – a section of supporters who valued everything the young man from Ayrshire did during his 13 years with them.

We'll get back to what he did and won on the football pitch in a bit. What about the wind-ups? Speaking from his American home in Connecticut, Nicol still laughs when we talk of life at Melwood. 'It was relentless,' he says of the jokes. 'The thing about it though is it was all good-natured, there was nothing sinister about it all.'

That was the thing about Nicol, he took it all in his stride. Getting into the best team in Europe? Let's work hard and see where we get. Taking a penalty against Roma in Rome to open a European Cup Final penalty shoot-out? Why not, give me the ball. Being wound up day after day by some of the best players in the world? That's fine, I'll give as good as I get. Well maybe not as good…

The pranks happened from the off. On one occasion early on in Nicol's time at Melwood, Bob Paisley walked into the dressing room and handed out brown envelopes to all the players, except Nicol. They were from the Inland Revenue, tax bills for the last financial year. 'Why haven't you got one, Steve?' the players asked.

'I don't know, what are they?'

'They're payment from the club for appearing in the squad photo. You were in it, you should go to Bob and ask why you're not getting paid.'

'Aye, I will.' Later Nicol took himself off to the manager's office, demanding a brown envelope. Paisley looked him up and down and said, 'You can have the fucking lot, they're tax demands.'

Nicol was then told by team-mates that a representative from Puma (who were going to endorse him) had called and that he should meet him at a service station 25 miles out of the city, on a Sunday morning. The following week, Nicol came into training boasting that he would never fall for that. Over a few drinks later though he admitted that he had indeed gone to the service station and he had taken his wife and he had waited for two hours.

Then there was the time he was told that Kenny Dalglish had an incurable disease but that he wanted the news kept quiet. Nicol tried his best, but his grief took him to Dalglish's room to console his fellow Scot, only to get short shrift and the news that he once again had been duped.

That's how it went, week after week, year after year. It hadn't helped that on one of his first trips away with the team Nicol had turned up at the team hotel with a teddy bear on top of his bag emblazoned with the words, 'I am Sad Sam, will you cuddle me and love me and make me happy?'

It was the club's Scottish contingent, all-powerful and all-seeing who particularly went for the young Nicol. 'In my early years, I drove with the Scottish lot home for an international,' Nicol recalls. 'I was with Kenny [Dalglish], Graeme [Souness] and Alan [Hansen]. I was going up to play for the under-21s, so I'm just a boy, in a car with these superstars. It was the middle of winter, there's six-foot snowdrifts along the side of the M6.

'I'm sitting in the back with Alan and I'm still a bit star star-struck. Only 12 months ago I was watching them on telly and I am just happy to be there. Taking it all in. Listening to their stories and all that. Suddenly Graeme pulls over, there's a problem with the windscreen wiper. "You're the youngest, go out and fix it." Fine by me, I get out in my T-shirt and Graeme drives off. He stops along the side of the road about 50 yards up. I run to the car and he drives off again. This went on for a while. I had frostbite on my nose!'

Nicol could be equally as chastised for what he did and said. Having finally signed a deal with Puma, Nicol received a new pair of boots. He took a size 12 and as the players used to give the youth team players new boots to wear in, Nicol went to the young goalkeeper who had the same size. The keeper takes them, pulls out the paper stuffed inside the toes, plays in them and returns them to Nicol saying how comfortable they are. 'Really, they just won't fit me,' says Nicol, unaware that the paper was there. Such was his easy going and quiet wit; his team-mates soon nicknamed him Chico, after one of the Marx brothers.

Then there's the time he weighed himself carrying two bags of shopping and screamed, 'Christ, I've put on two stone!' All red rags to Liverpool's bulls who thrived on such a faux pas. 'That last one with the groceries,' says Nicol. 'I was away with Hansen and had had a bit to drink. That's my excuse there.'

The thing is, Nicol was far from stupid. He was canny and he was horizontally laid back, a trait that served him so well at this most intense of clubs. Playing as a part-time teenager at Ayr United in Scotland, Nicol was called into the manager's office after training to be told that Liverpool, the European champions, wanted to sign him and that Bob

Paisley, a three-time European Cup winner, had been on the phone and had made an offer. 'OK', he said in his own placid way.

'OK?' came his manager's response. 'Only fucking OK?'

Nicol took the signing in his stride, he took walking into the dressing room in his stride and he certainly took the banter in his stride. He was there to learn, to get better and to ultimately play and so whilst he might have been on the end of the senior players' cutting wit, the help they gave him far outweighed the funny stuff.

'The guys were great to me,' Nicol says. 'I can talk about all the wind-ups and all the mickey taking but that was just a drop in the ocean compared to the help and advice they gave me. You got help all the time as far as the game was concerned. Hansen was the worst winding me up, but he gave me so much help on the field and they all taught me so much about how to play the game. That's why Liverpool worked. It doesn't work when it's all about belittling people and the help isn't there and it's only banter for banter's sake. Everyone was of the same ilk. The English guys and Scottish guys were always at each other but we were all pulling in the same direction.'

Some though didn't find it so easy. Ian Rush struggled to cope and later John Aldridge would too and whilst both became big figures themselves in the dressing room, Nicol immediately adapted to his surroundings, and immersed himself in what it took to become a Liverpool regular. He spent a couple of seasons in the reserves (that was the Liverpool way) he got on with everyone, and he quietly impressed the staff enough to get his chance.

This was a new era for the club. Paisley had bought a number of youngsters for very reasonable prices and he was quietly moulding a new team. European Cup or no European Cup, things needed changing and he was shedding the team's skin once again.

'That may well have been happening,' says Nicol. 'Ronnie Whelan, Bruce Grobbelaar, Ian Rush, myself, Craig Johnston, Mark Lawrenson; we'd all been brought in for different fees and spent different amounts of times in the reserves and so yes, Bob probably was building a new team but that just didn't concern me. I was too busy trying to get into the team. Paisley was obviously thinking ahead but I just wanted to improve. You're not concerned with how things look from the outside. All you want to do is impress the manager and his staff. When you walk into the European champions' training ground you also want to impress your peers. That's the concentration.'

His attitude was a breath of fresh air, albeit the photos taken of Nicol wearing a Liverpool scarf, an inane grin and a Scottish Tammy hat hadn't impressed. For Dalglish, Hansen and Souness, it caused a few issues. 'In the dressing-room us three Scots had a wee bit of credibility until Nicol signed,' wrote Kenny Dalglish in his autobiography. 'We had built up an understanding that the Scots were the Master Race. We would quote historical facts to the English players to prove it. Some of the most important inventions and discoveries in the world came from Scots, like television, the telephone, penicillin, the steam engine and tarmac.

'Their names are part of history – John Logie Baird, Alexander Graham Bell, Alexander Fleming, James Watt. Not to mention those other wonders of the world – golf and whisky. Per head of population, the Scots are the most educated race in the world. We did well defending ourselves and flying the flag of Scottish supremacy, until Nicol came. Everything we had built up, he destroyed in ten minutes because of the photograph that was taken of him when he signed.'

Steve Nicol made his first-team debut at Birmingham in the First Division in August 1982. He wouldn't get many chances under Paisley (this was his last season as manager) but he had impressed and the great man was sure he had made the right choice for an eventual replacement for Phil Neal at right-back.

On the bench that day was Craig Johnston who took the struggles that came with getting into the first team far harder than Nicol. 'Craig wore his heart on his sleeve and was down on himself a lot,' Nicol says. 'He wanted to play and made his feelings known a bit more than others. I was different. Totally. I got on with things.'

The Scot was hungry, sure, but unlike the hot-headed Australian, he would take rejection as easily as he took the gags. The following season he was overlooked by Joe Fagan for the League Cup Final replay against Everton (ironically for Johnston) but wasn't going to make the fuss that others might have. 'I was still at the stage of establishing myself,' Nicol told Tony Evans in his book on the 1983/84 season, *I Don't Know What It Is But I Love It*. 'I just accepted Joe's decision. I didn't want to come across as bigheaded. If you did, you'd be slaughtered. It didn't do to get carried away.'

Not that this stoic and relaxed attitude would altogether do. In the pre-season of that first campaign under Fagan, Nicol had very much harboured ambitions that this would be his year, the season he became a regular in the team. Those were his inner thoughts anyway, voicing them was a different thing altogether.

'During training, Ronnie Moran and Roy Evans pulled me aside and asked, "have you spoken to Joe about how much you want to play?" I hadn't. It hadn't crossed my mind. "Well you should," they both said. They were right and I think Joe realised I was ready for a chance.'

Not that it would be easy. Nicol was seen as a right-back and whilst Phil Neal was by no means above a challenge from an eager youngster, he had made the berth very much his own since arriving in Bob Paisley's first season in 1975. The former Northampton Town man (known as Zico after the great Brazilian) played 417 consecutive games between October 1976 and September 1983. He missed a couple of games then due to injury and then (having been ironically nicknamed 'Crock' by his team-mates) went on to play another 127 back-to-back fixtures. No, this man was not easily budged.

Neal got the system. Only admit to serious injury, the obvious ones. He knew that to lose your place in the team wasn't advisable and he would soldier on with knocks. Even a broken toe wasn't enough to keep him out.

What was soon very obvious to Liverpool's backroom staff was that in Nicol they had much more than a mere right-back here to bide his time until Neal's body packed in. Nicol was impressive with the ball, good in the air, could pass, cross, run and tackle. They had a footballer on their hands and so other options opened themselves up to the patient Scot.

It was in October 1983 that that ability first materialised in a match situation. Liverpool were on the plastic at Queens Park Rangers, a surface they despised and Craig Johnston had got himself booked early on. He had been sent off the week before and Fagan feared another dismissal. The game was goalless and tactically, bringing Nicol on for Johnston on the left meant more industry. Nicol was two-footed so no problem there and he could score goals. There was only seven minutes left and his effort from the edge of the box won a game the team always dreaded.

Nicol was once again impressive a week later at Anfield on the left filling in wonderfully for the injured but always industrious Ronnie Whelan. There he stayed for a while with a run of form that peaked with a goal in the 3–0 win over Everton at Anfield. Nicol, a young but green full-back bought for the future was instead a versatile and dynamic midfielder with an eye for goal and very much of the now.

He would of course go on to play several positions for the club and all of them well, but it was clear that Nicol was no Jack-of-all-trades. There was substance to his game, a fine knowledge of how it should be played and of how to put a set of tactics into practice. He was brave too. From the off, he set about getting in and amongst Graeme Souness in training. 'I'd bounce right off him,' he laughs, but the club captain was certainly a fan.

'This lad can play anywhere in the midfield or the back four,' said Souness at the time. 'He can defend, tackle, he can head the ball, he can take players on and he can score goals and not only would it not surprise me if he eventually finished up in my old position at Liverpool but also I see him as a natural captain, lifting up the trophies for them as well. His only problem is that he is so honest and nice that he is easily wound up – and that can be fatal at Anfield.'

Souness was wrong about his position, about one day skippering the team (although he did on the odd occasion) and about his niceness being fatal. Nicol strolled around life at Liverpool without seemingly a care in the world.

In May 1984, Liverpool faced Roma in the European Cup Final in Rome.

The game finished 1–1 and so went to a penalty shoot-out. Nicol had come on for Craig Johnston in the game and when it came to picking five brave souls to take the spot-kicks, he of course said yes, and agreed to go first. Amid Roman whistles and blinding flash photography, he blazed the ball over the bar.

'We had practised penalties at Melwood before we left and I was the only one who scored,' says Nicol. 'I was down to take one but we didn't have the order sorted out and it made no difference to me. There was a bit of umming and arring so I just said I will go first.

'It was odd, I was obviously gutted I missed, but I never ever thought we'd lose. We still had four to go and I just felt we would do it. That comes from being young. I made a complete arse of my penalty kick but all's well that ends well, hey?'

Nicol was a European champion, part of the set-up at the biggest club around. He got how the staff worked, he got that you had to keep your feet firmly on the ground, he got that you had to listen and learn but also that you had to think for yourself. '[The staff] didn't spend sessions shouting instructions at you,' he recalled. 'But they knew what they were doing. If you were feeling it and not putting in a hundred per cent one day, Ronnie or Roy would just come up and whisper in your ear, "We're watching you." You'd shit yourself.'

Nicol also got that despite the ribbings and those wind-ups, the team was very much together, a unit, on and off the field. '[After training] you didn't want to go back to your digs and sit there all day,' Nicol said. 'So, you went to the pub. Any excuse. There was only one rule. No mates. No outsiders. As long as you took your medicine in training the next day, you were fine.'

Nicol started 46 games the following campaign and was very much part of Fagan's final season at the club, mainly patrolling the right side of midfield. He started the European Cup Final at Heysel in Brussels but by the time the game kicked off, starting line-ups, football matches and the trophies they bring, no longer mattered. Thirty-nine people had been killed after crowd trouble and the good name of the club had been dragged through the mud.

Prior to the fateful night in Belgium, Liverpool had set about replacing Joe Fagan who had announced his retirement and the club's policy of looking within brought them to Kenny Dalglish. Only 34 years of age and still very much a player but now the man given the task of bringing the club out from Heysel's shadow and to re-build its image.

Dalglish did just that and he also re-built a team. For Nicol, Dalglish's appointment meant a more settled role at right-back, the position he was bought to fill. It also meant getting used to having a friend as the boss. 'It was seamless,' Nicol says. 'Absolutely seamless. He had so much respect in the team. He knows what he is talking about so we listened and he was still a great player and so he played. Easy. No fuss.'

Dalglish managed the transition well, even giving his friend the chance to get the abuse off his chest before he officially took over. 'He called me up and said, "If you've got anything to say, say it now because I've got the manager's job." Of course I thought it was a wind-up.

'"You're taking the piss," I said. He convinced me he had and so I got it all off my chest, called him a few names, got it out the way and we went from there. He was now my manager.'

And what a manager. Hard decisions were taken firmly with the likes of Phil Neal and Alan Kennedy making way for Nicol and Jim Beglin respectively. Chico had replaced Zico.

Jan Molby, the Danish midfielder brought in by Joe Fagan to replace Graeme Souness flourished, Steve McMahon came in from Aston Villa and the likes of Craig Johnston and Gary Gillespie became so much more than valuable squad members. The team won its first 'Double' in 1985/86 and the beam on the players' faces after the FA Cup Final victory over Everton was a world away from the tears that followed Heysel.

Nicol had enjoyed a fabulous season. The back four (or sometimes five as Dalglish often toyed with a sweeper system) was a firm foundation on which the team's success was built and now a regular at full-back, one central defender and club legend was quickly full of admiration. 'I was switched from the left side to the right of Liverpool, back four towards the end of my career, when my knee problems had taken their toll on my running, it made me feel I could light a cigar and read a newspaper to have Steve on the outside,' wrote Alan Hansen in his autobiography.

'His fitness was astonishing. Dieticians would be horrified at the amount he ate. He could eat for Britain. He and I and our families once were on a Norwegian cruise together and he probably consumed more than the rest of us put together. It was not unusual for him to go through six or eight packs of crisps in one go. But he never carried any excess weight, hardly missed a tackle and gave the impression of being able to bomb up and down that right touchline forever. Suffice it to say that after our first match together on the right, I thought, "Where have you been all my life?"'

The following season was trickier with the team in slight limbo. Rush was leaving, Dalglish was biding his time to get the players he wanted. Nicol though cared little for all the speculation about who might come to the club. 'I didn't think about stuff like that,' he says. 'It's hard enough to keep in the team, I was not going to worry about who would come in and who the boss might sign.

'Today players put their noses into so many things, but to concentrate on playing at the highest level and trying to stay the best, that was all that mattered to me. It wasn't my business. That's why we had Kenny. It wasn't what I was being paid for. I was paid to play well and do a job for those supporters. And by the way, if I went to Kenny and told him who I thought he should sign, tell him anything in fact, can you imagine what he'd say? "See you later, Stevie," and that's being polite.'

There was no need for anyone to worry. Dalglish got exactly the right people in as a new and improved, slicker and more dynamic Liverpool as born. Peter Beardsley, Ray Houghton, John Aldridge and John Barnes were seamlessly brought in and brought a new dimension to the side's thinking. Not only were the new recruits good enough to fit right in but the players already there, used to maybe a different style of football, underlined how good they were by adapting just as quickly.

'It just worked,' says Nicol. 'It clicked. We had had pre-season and trained well but it was the Arsenal game on the first day of the season that was key. You can train and play friendlies but you don't know until you play a proper game. We had Barnes, Peter and Aldo and of course were already strong but it was there at Highbury that I thought, "We're actually fucking good." I managed to score the winner, which was also nice.'

Nicol scored plenty. After the Arsenal game he scored at Coventry and then the team went to Newcastle where he got a hat-trick. At St James' Park he played on the right side of midfield. Barry Venison played at right-back wearing the number three shirt, Mark Lawrenson played at left-back wearing the number nine jersey. The team bamboozled opponents with their football as much as their shirt numbers and for Nicol the perfect day ended with him clutching the match-ball.

The goal that sealed the hat-trick was a little dink over the onrushing Newcastle keeper and had all the hallmarks of a Dalglish effort. The manager went as far as saying in his season diary that it was Nicol, 'Who stood out in an entertaining team performance,' but that was it as far as lavish praise was concerned.

Brilliance was expected by Dalglish, not celebrated. 'Whether you were his mate or not, Kenny let you know if you weren't at it,' says Nicol. 'Myself and Alan Hansen once played a pre-season game at Bristol on the Saturday. We then drove back to Liverpool, which back then was about a six-hour drive. Big Al picked me up at seven on the Sunday morning to drive to Scotland for a testimonial for an old mate of his. We didn't get back from that until midnight and then on the Monday we had Phil Neal's testimonial against Everton at Anfield.

'I was on the bench for that one but Kenny got me on. I had been almost falling asleep on the bench and so I couldn't run, I just couldn't move for the 20 minutes I was on. All that travelling, all that playing and I was gone. After the game we're in the dressing room and Kenny's straight over to me. "What the fuck was that?" he said.

'"What do you mean?" I asked.

'"If you don't want to fucking play, don't fucking play, but don't go out there and do that." It's a testimonial game and he's on me for dropping my standards. You knew though. When that happened keep your head down and your mouth shut.'

The year after the title-winning 1987/88 campaign, injuries dictated yet another new position to add to his already buoyant portfolio. At centre-half, Nicol enjoyed perhaps his best ever campaign, winning the Footballer of the Year. Hansen had missed most of the campaign but it was the slick skipper who first put Nicol's nerves to rest in his new role.

'I first played there in the January of 1988 at Aston Villa in the FA Cup,' Nicol recalls. 'Kenny walked into the dressing room and says, "You're playing centre-back." That was it. OK boss. I'm getting changed with Big Al and I'm asking all these questions. "What are we going to do and how are we going to play it?" Big Al looks up and coolly says, "Hey, just go and play."

'It went well for me during the 1988/89 season back there but I couldn't say if I had a favourite position. I just liked playing. I liked midfield, I liked the wing, I liked full-back on either side and I liked centre-back. I just liked playing. What's not to like?'

In the April of that season there was Hillsborough and a moment in the players', the club's and of course the fans' history that will never be forgotten. Nicol was playing that day and like everyone connected with the club it took its toll. That toll was most keenly felt on the manager who set about tirelessly trying to console and help the bereaved and the affected. He didn't want thanks, his plight was nothing compared to those he helped but it did have an effect on him and in 1991 he shocked everyone by resigning.

Nicol was – and is – a great friend of Dalglish but as ever, he was not going to lose too much sleep over change. And anyway, in came Graeme Souness, a man he knew all about and whilst his tenure didn't go to plan, Nicol had sympathy for the task that the new man faced. 'When I look at it now, you can see Graeme took over at the very worst time,' says Nicol. 'A bit like Moyes taking over from Ferguson. The team needed a revamp and to be honest the players Graeme signed were regarded as the best around and the ones to sign. You can't argue with points, positions in league and with facts, but you can try and step back and be a little objective and see that there were a lot of us that were past our best, and he was unfortunate that so much had to be done. Hey, we still won the FA Cup.'

That win at Wembley against Sunderland in 1992 was Nicol's last honour at the club and whilst he played on under Souness's successor Roy Evans for a bit, he eventually left for Notts County in the autumn of 1994. When asked if he felt respected by the fans, Nicol is quick to say yes. 'I felt very much appreciated. Respected by the fans? Definitely. By the team too; everyone understood that we had superstars. Souness, Rushie and Kenny were the best in Europe at one point but there was this knowledge from the crowd – and the squad – that without the rest of the players nothing could be won.

'Without the other guy it didn't happen. It was a puzzle and we all had a role. We'd be out in Liverpool in normal pubs with the punters. We got to know the guys who went to games and travelled everywhere to see us and they became close. We'd have a drink, we'd discuss the game and that gets out and that makes everyone associated with the place that bit closer. It's a massive cliché but that's the truth. We enjoyed the crowd, the game and we enjoyed each other.'

Having retired, Nicol moved to America. He played a bit for the Boston Bulldogs before the game picked up over there and soon, he was the very much respected coach of the New England Revolution and winning coach of the year accolades. Today he is a pundit on American television and whilst he thinks he will now stay over there for the rest of his days, he will always be indebted to the club and its fans.

'Oh my god,' he says emotionally. 'Listen, I owe so much to the place and to the city. My family and myself owe them so much. The person I am today is because of that place. There's so many things that are so dear to me and that only happened because I played for Liverpool. The people who worked at the club and who supported them, and of course the people who played with me, they were all wonderful and everything at the club was done properly. There was never any passing the buck. People there were responsible for their actions. You get pulled into that environment and that becomes normal. You don't actually realise how great the place is until you move on.'

For so many fans, the same could be said of Steve Nicol.

Craig Johnston

1981–1988
Appearances: 271
Goals: 40

AT Melwood, the club's training ground, Liverpool players were long treated to a bit of exercise apparatus ominously called the 'sweatbox'. It was created by Bill Shankly in the 1960s and consisted of one player, one ball, four walls and two or three minutes of physical torture.

'They timed you,' recalls Ian Callaghan, and by 'they' he means Shankly, Bob Paisley, Reuben Bennett, Joe Fagan and Ronnie Moran. 'You had to run as quick as you could, with the staff all shouting at you and you'd hit the ball against the wall, control it and run to the other boards. It was really hard work. You would come out of there and your legs really were like jelly.'

Barking loudest among the staff was Ronnie Moran. A player when Shankly arrived, Moran became the sharp end of the manager's staff. If these incredibly knowledgeable men were the boot-room, Moran was the studs, and was always on hand to make sure players, whoever they may be, were putting in the required effort.

Things like the 'sweatbox' were created by Shankly to enhance his teams' physicality and strength of character but with Moran nearby it also kept players humble. Training at Liverpool was, on the outside, simple, ball-based and no frills but whilst the players were put through their paces – even in just a competitive five-a-side game on a Friday – you would hear Moran's voice, rasping his opinions, keeping the players' feet firmly on the ground.

'You big-headed bastards,' was a particular favourite of Moran's. League championship medals were handed out on the first day of pre-season from a shoebox without ceremony and the players were left in no doubt that what they had achieved the previous season was all in the past. 'Big-headed bastards.'

It didn't matter who you were, Moran was on to you. Even Kenny Dalglish and Graeme Souness, two men with ample reason to have enlarged craniums were screamed at as they went about their business. Stay humble and stay hungry, that's what Moran ensured. One player though during Moran's long reign of terror, who needed no such treatment, was Craig Johnston.

'I was crap,' Johnston said when taking stock of his playing career. 'I had a dream to become the best player in the world, but I failed miserably. In fact, by playing for Liverpool, I was the worst player in the best team in the world... you really have no idea how crap I was.'

Self-effacing and honest, Liverpool fans will smile at Johnston's words but they might also take issue with them. Johnston was no Dalglish or Souness but the fans that grew to adore him will recall a footballer that never stopped doing what they would do if handed the red shirt, namely work their socks off.

Johnston, his long, black curls flowing in his slipstream, never stopped running, never stopped trying to prove he belonged and whilst his enthusiasm sometimes bordered on hazardous, he remained one of the most popular players among fans who cherished his eccentricities. Perhaps they offered an antidote to the humdrum of their side's constant success, but it was likely that in Johnston they were watching a player who seemed as regular and as happy to be there as they were.

Take Wembley, May 1986. Liverpool have reached the FA Cup Final, their first since 1977 and walk out under the spring sun to face Everton. It's a momentous occasion, the first all-Merseyside FA Cup Final but still these are players who have won titles (in fact they have won one just the week before), European Cups and are not easily overly dumbstruck by an occasion. Craig Johnston though (whilst his team-mates look for their loved ones as they make that walk from tunnel to pitch) is suitably overawed.

Actually overawed is a little strong, but this is the culmination in what for him as been a journey. Journey, that is such a cliché, overly used by *X-Factor* contestants but in Johnston's case it is true. He had travelled from Australia, paying his way in order to achieve his dreams of professional football and here he is about to play in what is still the biggest game in club football. He knows that millions back home will be up at all hours to watch the game and watch him. This is the realisation of a dream.

In 1985/86, Johnston enjoyed his best season in Liverpool red, offering fantastic energy and creativity on Liverpool's right side. Liverpool beat Chelsea to win the title on the last Saturday of the season and then played Norwich in the semi-final of a silly little tournament called the Screen Sports Super Cup, created for those clubs who had qualified for Europe only to be banned after the events at Heysel in May 1985.

Despite a cup final on the Saturday, Liverpool fielded a strong side and some players were playing for their Wembley place. In the first half, Johnston felt a twinge in his back, an injury that had long given him problems. 'I looked expectantly at the bench,' Johnston recalled in his autobiography, *Walk Alone*. "Get on with it," was the barked response. I didn't need telling twice. As the substitutes warmed up I lifted my game accordingly and scored a cracking header. It meant that I had found the net in every competition that season… except the FA Cup.'

Johnston played the cup final, seemingly on a mission to do just that. Liverpool were trailing at half-time to a Gary Lineker goal and were seemingly out if it. They weren't creating chances and were even arguing with each other. Bruce Grobbelaar and his left-back Jim Beglin nearly came to blows as Everton threatened to consume them. Then from nowhere came a lifeline.

As ever, it came from Ian Rush's opportunism. Latching on to a cute Jan Molby through ball he took it around Bobby Mimms' outstretched hand and nudged the ball goalwards where it crept over the line. As it did though, there was Johnston's outstretched boot, hell-bent on making the goal his own.

It was a silly move, he might have even been given offside and there was no doubt it was Rush's goal but there you had it, there you had Johnston's absolute desire to score. Earlier that day, television crews had caught images of Liverpool fans scaling walls, clinging to friends' arms through toilet windows several stories up at the old stadium, doing anything, risking everything to make sure they were present at this most historical of finals. Johnston was doing exactly the same thing. He had to be present on that score-sheet and he would risk everything to make it so.

Six minutes after Rush's equaliser, Johnston got his moment. He was being tightly marked by Everton's Pat Van Den Hauwe but such was that desire, not even a defender they called 'Psycho' could prevent him achieving all he'd ever wanted. 'I saw a space down the wing and I started to spring into it,' he recalled.

'The ball was on our left wing but Van Den Hauwe followed me all the way for 70 or so yards. By then, Jan Molby had the ball. I knew he'd try to find Kenny first, but something prompted me to make that last ten-yard dash. Instinctively I went, and it was only because I had a bigger heart that I connected with the cross. Psycho Pat didn't have the legs left in him, and it was the easiest goal I've ever scored.'

Johnston simply leaped vertically toward the sky, his feet doing a sort of scissor kick as he leapt. 'I shouted, "I did it… I did it." Ronnie [Whelan] and Rushie were the first over and whenever they see me now they scream like girls, "I did it… I did it."' Johnston had indeed done it and so had Liverpool. Another Rush goal and the FA Cup was won, the club's first Double and Johnston was at the very heart of it all.

Johnston wasn't like most footballers. Keen on photography, the writer of chart-topping songs (he wrote and produced the 'Anfield Rap'), and the designer of innovative football boots (he sold the idea and original design of the Predator boot to Adidas) Johnston was a man able to think outside of football's box but you won't hear of too many more players with such drive to get to the top of the game.

Johnston's quest to be a footballer was always an uphill one. As a boy he had got into a fight and taken a kick to the leg and from that he developed a disease called osteomyelitis that rots the bone and doctors talked of amputation; his mother signed a form allowing them to do just that. Fortunately one doctor saw a cure beyond the saw and for Johnston, whilst unable to play his beloved game for a long time, his dream was still alive.

Craig Johnston impressed at youth level in Australia and confidently wrote to Manchester United, Chelsea and Middlesbrough asking for a trial. Only Jack Charlton at Boro replied and whilst agreeing to see him play, told him that he would have to pay his own fare. His mum and dad sold the house, and their boy was waved off as he set off for England.

What a sight he must have looked as he arrived in England's north-east. In torn jeans and with bleached blond hair, Johnston, the keen surfer, was not what Jack Charlton would have called your archetypal footballer. Charlton put the old into old school and didn't mince his words when he first watched this wild-looking Aussie race around a trial match lacking any sort of finesse.

'[Charlton] went around the dressing-room bollocking everyone. "You – where are you from?" he asked me.

'"I'm from Australia, mate."

'"I'm not your mate and well… you… you kangaroo are the worst fucking footballer I have seen in my fucking life. Now fuck off."'

Johnston cried and that night phoned his parents 10,000 miles away. He wanted to tell them that it had gone badly, that the manager hated his game but on hearing his mum's excited voice, he lied and told her that Jack Charlton really rated him and was extremely excited to have him at his football club.

Johnston, for what he lacked in technique, made up for in spirit and likability. Senior players at the club, including Graeme Souness took to the young Australian and in exchange for him cleaning their cars, they gave him enough money to stay in their digs and keep him safe from Jack Charlton's prying and angry eyes.

In the meantime, Johnston watched the first team squad train from afar and then, alone in the car park would replicate what he had seen, dribbling between rubbish bins from morning until dark. 'The car park was my penance for being a useless footballer,' he later said.

Johnston, in his car park actually outlasted Charlton, who in 1977 joined Sheffield Wednesday and his successor, John Neal, noticed this strange kid running in and out of bins and enquired who exactly he was. 'Ah, that's Kangaroo,' came the reply. 'He always practises in the car park – he's crap.'

Neal was intrigued and from there, having been invited to train with the youth team, his stock grew and grew. His game became more and more refined and in January 1977, two years after being told to 'fuck off' by a World Cup winner, he was making his debut and wouldn't you know it, it was against Everton in the FA Cup.

Johnston took his chance, he played, he scored goals and soon had the biggest clubs and best managers wondering whether to take a chance. Brian Clough was the first to make his move, calling him from Benidorm to say he wanted him and explaining that this was an expensive call, but he would be back soon to seal the deal.

Forest were the reigning European champions but 20 minutes after Clough's call came another, this time from Bob Paisley. 'Aw piss off, I responded,' recalled Johnston.

'"No, it's Bob Paisley… I've heard all about you from the lads, Graeme Souness in particular. We'd like to sign you."' Liverpool got their man and for a handsome fee of £650,000. He had his big move and was heading to a club themselves on their way to their third European Cup. 'It was solely down to the four or five hours I'd spent in the car park every day.'

Paisley's interest in Johnston was understandable. Here was an exciting, young and fresh player who brought with him an air of unpredictability. Yes, he was taking the side to the top of the European tree for a third time but Liverpool would finish a disappointing fifth in the league and Paisley was aware that his was an aging team, living off its wits.

Paisley had seen first hand how slow Shankly had been to change his great team of the 1960s and how that had affected the club's hunt for trophies. Paisley wasn't going to make that same mistake and so in came a glut of new, young faces. As well as Johnston, Ian Rush was finding his feet, Bruce Grobbelaar would soon replace Ray Clemence in goal, Mark Lawrenson came from Brighton, Steve Nicol form Ayr United and Ronnie Whelan from Home Farm in Ireland.

Johnston might have got his big move and was living his boyhood dream but he was still star-struck by his surroundings. Having played a few games from off of the bench, Johnston's first start was in Tokyo in December 1981 against Brazilian side Flamengo in the World Club Championship match. He and his team-mates got a lesson from Zico and Junior and on their return he started again, this time in a Boxing Day defeat at home to Manchester City that left them 12th in the table and seemingly way out of the race for the title.

Things were hard at Liverpool. The senior players were trying to put their finger on what was going wrong, the staff were bluntly telling them to work it out for themselves quickly and the youngsters were terrified that their generation was going to be dubbed a failure. Johnston though was gaining a following on the terraces. He had come off the bench to score a vital extra-time goal to knock Arsenal out of the League Cup in December and the fans, increasingly frustrated at the football on show, took to his vitality and incessant work-rate. A winner at Old Trafford in April further raised his stock.

In fact, such was his popularity that Paisley, the winner of three European Cups had to endure a spatter of boos at Anfield during a league game against Sunderland, just days after a hard-fought European

Cup defeat in Sofia when he took off his young player for the older and safer option of David Johnson. So taken aback by the sound of boos in his ears, Paisley went to the press to explain himself, suggesting that in fact Johnston was too eager, too full of running.

'There were ten dead men out there, weary from midweek, while Craig, who played only half an hour as a substitute in Bulgaria, was fresh and more likely to cause us damage with his inexperience. It was impossible for the rest of the team to respond to a player bursting with energy and enthusiasm and keen to make an impression, as Craig is. I sent on David Johnson because he's more used to these situations, but that would be too intelligent for the few yobbos in the crowd to understand. Everyone's entitled to their opinion and I'm not labelling them all yobbos. I'm only speaking about three of four. But if any Liverpool fans think that I've got it in for Craig, they're wrong. I did it because the rest of the lads were so tired they couldn't keep up with him.'

With terrace approval, Johnston's belief in himself was growing. The club turned its fortunes around and went on an incredible run to pip Ipswich to the title. Johnston had played his part, mainly from the bench but still; he had a First Division winners' medal. Surely nothing from here on could be daunting to a man who had done so much to get his hands on one.

But Johnston remained full of self-doubt. He particularly dreaded the derby games, especially at Goodison Park. 'Because I wasn't one of the stars, I shit myself before games,' he admitted. 'It was worse before the derby. I remember being at Goodison and I was sick with worry. If you do something good, then great. But if you lose the ball, all the blues are laughing and the reds are moaning. It's the most frightening place in the world.'

Johnston would win more titles, in fact he'd win four more. He'd win two League Cups, the FA Cup and a European Cup but still, he never felt totally settled, totally sure of his place on the team-sheet. When he wrote the lyrics to the 'Anfield Rap' in 1988 he gave himself the line, 'Come on Kenny mate, give us a game'. Yes it was tongue in cheek but it summed up what he felt was a constant battle to be picked.

He was at Liverpool, playing with and against the best in the world, he was winning trophies and he was receiving plaudits from writers and fans alike. For all that though, in his mind he remained the scruffy kid, not long off the plane from Australia, trying to learn his trade alone in a Middlesbrough car park.

New team-mates had noticed that here was a player with rough edges. Alan Hansen wrote in his autobiography, *A Matter of Opinion:*

'[Johnston] operated on the right side of midfield and was super-fit and enthusiastic. But he was very individualistic – a sort of maverick, I would say – and although he was popular in the dressing room, he could be exasperating to play with. He was a little erratic when it came to reading the game, and he could be very erratic indeed with his crossing.'

Johnston was aware of his shortcomings and like at Middlesbrough, he did everything he could to rectify them. 'I was so embarrassed that I didn't meet the required standards for a Liverpool player that I had my own key cut for Melwood,' he later admitted. 'Nobody knew about it. I did everything I could to become better. One time we were training and Ronnie Moran stopped us. "What the fuck is this?" There was a set of cones in the figure of eight. He thought that kids must have broken into Melwood and had a kickabout. "Bloody kids." After training, I admitted to Ronnie that I'd been there the night before practising by doing some shuttles with the ball. "What for?" I explained I needed to work on my left foot.'

One man though never fully convinced that his hard work alone was enough, was Joe Fagan. A brilliant football man, Fagan had replaced Paisley as manager in 1983 and was a very popular manager among his players, having often been the go-between for them and whoever was boss. Fagan, a Scouser, would have two seasons in charge but his tenure was hard for Johnston, who as hard as he tried couldn't convince the manager that he was worth a regular place in the side.

Fagan had grown up under Shankly, building teams who, whilst as fit as any other around, all knew their role; all knew where and when they should be playing. Johnston's positional play and regard for tactics were not his strongest points. He wanted the ball and he wanted to surge forward, always forward. Fagan, so tactically astute, had his doubts.

Steve Nicol was used for a European Cup game in Bilbao in 1983, being far more prone to hold his position on the right. That set the tone. Johnston was upset by the decision and whilst still getting plenty of game time, those insecurities and doubts constantly plagued him. He even put in a transfer request after being left out at Coventry (a game Liverpool lost 4–0, so maybe he ought to have smugly sat back and gloated).

Johnston often contributed to fine performances. His best came in Lisbon at the Estadio da Luz against Benfica in the European Cup.

Liverpool had won the home leg 1–0 and were expected to struggle, but instead were brilliant, beating Sven-Goran Eriksson's team 4–1 with Johnston a constant threat. He put the team 2–0 up and looked more than at home among the continent's elite.

Liverpool were challenging for three trophies and just days after Benfica, took on Everton in the League Cup Final at Wembley. Fagan had just signed John Wark, the free-scoring midfielder from Ipswich to bolster his numbers, a signing that Johnston took as a slap in the face.

Johnston started against Everton but when he was substituted before extra time he let those feelings out, 'Now's your chance to get Warky on,' he barked at the manager. Wark wasn't even eligible for Wembley and it was clear, the Scot's arrival had unsettled him.

Fagan bluntly told his player, in front of 100,000 watching fans at Wembley, to 'piss off'. It was a low point for Johnston who watched the rest of the game forlornly wrapped in a blanket.

Having won the replay (Johnston played), and preparing for a league game at Watford, Fagan wrote in his diary, 'It's decision day regarding Wark. I am going to put him in midfield for Johnston. I think he may bring more stability to midfield. I am sorry to have to do it but this is the part of the job that I get paid for.'

Johnston was furious that a winning team had been changed, something he felt was never done at Liverpool but he did show maturity, keeping his emotions in check as best he could, knowing that with a European Cup Final on the horizon and Wark unable to play in it, it might serve him best to keep his head down. In public at least.

At Liverpool there was a group of fringe players who took it upon themselves to sit and moan together. A kind of substitutes' support group. They called themselves the Sour Grapes Club (SGC) and Johnston was the chairman. 'Whatever I did, it was not good enough,' Johnston later said. 'In the reserves, you're disenfranchised. If you took it personally, you'd implode. Then, when you got your chance, you tried too hard. So I started the SGC and we used to have meetings and blame everyone else. We'd get together in pubs on the Wirral. We all seemed to live there and the elite group lived in Southport. As chairman, I had to be on call for the other members. It made the dressing room more buoyant. Everyone heard about it and it became a big joke.'

Johnston certainly could laugh at himself. At Watford having been demoted to the bench in favour of Wark, Johnston forgot he had got a ticket for his friend, the comedian Stan Boardman. On being asked to warm up his day got worse with shouts from the crowd. 'Fuck off back to Oz, you long-haired bastard.' Johnston, having a very bad day and being asked to warm up again, reluctantly jogged toward the tormentor. 'Kangaroo shagger!' Johnston looked at his bench who are all laughing and pointing at the crowd. He looks up and there's Boardman smiling mischievously. 'It gave me a laugh on a bad day.'

Good days outweighed the bad ones and Johnston had his place in the European Cup Final team in Rome. Here he was very much in with the best and acceptance and a sense of belonging were all he ever really wanted. After his match-winning performance against Benfica, Johnston had gone for a drink with a few of the players in a nearby bar. Not only had the beer tasted better then any beer he'd ever had, he was lifted when a group of fans came in and noticed their heroes.

'Wow,' said one to another. 'There's Craig Johnston and Kenny Dalglish.' It was a simple moment but to Johnston it was everything. 'They'd said my name in the same sentence as Kenny's,' he recalled. 'I'll never forget that.'

Johnston very much played his part in Rome both on and off the pitch. It was Johnston, having got into the music of Chris Rea in Middlesbrough who had put his team-mates onto his song, 'I Don't Know What It Is (But I Love It)', and it was that song that, led by Johnston, David Hodgson and Graeme Souness (all formerly of Boro) the team sang as they walked out into the intensity of the Roman evening.

'I had given Chris Rea's album a hiding to such an extent that all the players knew the song off by heart,' Johnston recalls. 'One of us would sing a verse, and the rest would come in with the chorus, clapping and chanting.' The team was – perhaps even worryingly – relaxed prior to kick-off and the Roma team must have wondered who had come to their most intimidating of grounds. 'If we'd let the tension get to us, we'd have been a beaten team from the off,' said Johnston. 'Singing Chris Rea and acting as though we didn't have a care in the world was our way of dealing with it.'

Another way of dealing with it was playing with the calm assurance of simply the best team in Europe and after the first ever penalty shoot-out in a European Cup Final the trophy was won for a fourth time. The victorious team were taken by their sponsors to a villa in the Roman hills where champagne and Chris Rea lyrics flowed in equal measure. Johnston was a European Cup winner. Not bad for a surfer from Down Under.

Things with the manager didn't get easier though. Souness had left for Italy and Fagan now had the likes of Jan Molby and Paul Walsh as attacking options as well as a much-used John Wark. Johnston was the fall guy. He could still laugh at the situation as he did when Stan Boardman gave him a golden bench the night Ian Rush got the Golden Boot.

His humour was running out though and soon he went to the papers who gleefully soaked up his tales of woe. 'I DON'T LIKE YOU MR. FAGAN' yelled a *Sunday Mirror* headline and with Fagan telling reporters that he felt it was time the player left, it seemed inevitable he would leave at the end of the 1984/85 campaign.

Johnston's plight though was the least of the club and football's problems that summer after the disaster at Heysel that saw 39 people killed prior to the European Cup Final against Juventus. Fagan was going to retire anyway but instead of finishing on a high he returned to Liverpool in tears.

Fagan retired and in came Kenny Dalglish, a man who had long admired the work Johnston put in to better himself. That was as a team-mate, now he was his manager and that admiration breathed new life into Johnston's Liverpool career. Johnston played 61 games in the Double season, netting ten goals. This was a happy man. The depression and insecurities were lifted for what was his pinnacle in red.

Not that he didn't value his place on the field or recognise that giving it up too easily was always a dangerous game to play. Prior to a vital game at Leicester for the penultimate league game of the season, Johnston had woken up with terrible back spasms. He could hardly walk, let alone get to the team bus taking them to Filbert Street.

Ronnie Moran was phoned by Johnston's wife and told the news. He could see a specialist after the game and for now he was to stay in bed. 'Stuff that,' said Johnston. 'Somehow or other I would get off the floor, struggle down to Leicester and retain my place in the side.' He did just that. It wasn't as far to go as Australia to England but it was just as symbolic. Johnston had treatment on the back, played in a 2–0 win and a few days later helped Liverpool win the title with a 1–0 win at Chelsea.

The following two seasons were harder. Still a regular in 1986/87 the back was causing more problems and when Dalglish began to build a new team without Ian Rush, the arrival of Ray Houghton signalled the end of Johnston's time at Liverpool.

He got off the bench for the defeat to Wimbledon in the 1988 FA Cup Final but that was to be his last appearance. Earlier in the season,

Johnston's sister had had an accident in North Africa and was in a coma. He had got her back to Australia and that spring took the decision to retire from the English game to help care for her. Some thought it was a ploy to engineer a move to another club or just a dramatic way of saying goodbye. It wasn't. It was simply time to go home.

The club though were never far from Johnston's thoughts and less than a year later as he was surfing on a board decked out in Liverpool colours, he was called to the shore to be told that Liverpool fans had died whilst watching the FA Cup semi-final at Hillsborough. Johnston was on the first available flight back to Liverpool.

There he met with fans and relatives of the dead and injured. He also met Dalglish who told him he realised now that Johnston had had a tragedy and how thankful he was that he had come now that the club were having theirs.

Johnston has gone on to have other adventures away from football but he will long be remembered with a fond smile by the fans that flocked to Anfield and beyond to watch his eager exploits, for it seemed that Johnston – this funny, talented, boisterous Australian – was only ever trying to please them. He was after all, just like them. A normal guy doing his best.

'While football is a glamorous business,' he later wrote, 'this world is full of self-effacing people, anonymous types who do what they can for others, and nobody stands up at three o'clock on a Saturday afternoon and gives them a round of applause. They're humble folk but heroes in their own right. Those who have spent our lives in the limelight have lots to learn from them.'

John Aldridge

1987–1989
Appearances: 104
Goals: 63

ALDRIDGE. There's something about the name. A commentator's dream. It must be the syllables. Try it. Ald-Ridge! There is no doubt that something glorious has just been finished. Ald-Ridge! Its very sound suggests a wonderful ending to something special. Barnes… Beardsley… back to Barnes… Ald-Ridge! The name is footballing punctuation. The perfect finish to a glorious sentence.

As for the man who owns the name, that's exactly what he did. A lot. He finished things. A fantastic footballer of course and capable of fine link-up play but John Aldridge had a wonderful knack for a brilliant finish.

Even the end to his two-and-a-half-year career at Liverpool; what a beautiful finish. It's mid-September 1989 and the visitors to Anfield are Crystal Palace, newly promoted and hungry to make an impact on the country's biggest teams. John Aldridge hasn't been able to make an impact on Kenny Dalglish's team-sheet and so before the game, he has agreed to join Real Sociedad in Spain.

He sits on the bench and watches Liverpool, his team, the team he took so much pleasure watching as a young man. But this is different. This is harder. He wants to be out there. He needs to play. Goal after goal goes in. It's 3–0 at half-time. It's 5–0 after an hour and the Kop are revelling in destruction. Usually Aldridge would be too, but this is different. He needs to play and so he knows this is his last time in his Liverpool kit.

On 67 minutes, Ronnie Whelan breaks from midfield and is brought down in the box. Dalglish, not a man necessarily directed by sentiment, ushers Aldridge from his tracksuit and not only onto the pitch but on to take the penalty… at the Kop end. He does just that, the ball is in the bottom right hand corner and a raised arm to the terrace on which he so often stood says it all. What a beautiful finish.

The fans will have flocked out of the ground that night, all smiles. A 9–0 win will do that for a set of supporters. Eight different goalscorers too. Back on top of the league. Plenty to smile about. Soon though it would have hit them. That was his last game. Sure they had an enviable squad that would go on to win the club's 18th league title come May, but that was John Aldridge's last game. For a moment those smiles were frowns and memories of his fantastic time in red will have run through their minds.

If goals make fans happy, then John Aldridge was laughing gas; 63 in 104 games. Prolific is a word tagged on to the toes of careers but that's what Aldridge was. A striker's striker who would arrive in an opposition penalty box, make himself very much at home and in and hour and a half, would help himself to their things. He wasn't into weaving pretty patterns, he had others behind him in the team who could get on with such trivial things but, when they were all done with such trickery, just stick it in that box and let Aldridge do the rest.

'Aldo wasn't a natural footballer, but he was a natural finisher,' recalled John Barnes, his provider in chief. 'Think about it, he wasn't tall, but he scored lots of headed goals, he wasn't really that quick, but he got on the end of crosses and through balls because of his determination and intelligence. John's timing was phenomenal. He was usually picked last in the five-a-sides, but everyone knew he was the club's premier finisher, and without him the team wouldn't have been anywhere near as effective.'

Effective! Calling the team that Barnes and Aldridge played in effective is like calling the Great Barrier Reef a fish tank. Quick, artistic, tough, brilliant. Theirs was among the club's finest but when Aldridge arrived in the winter of 1987, there was only doubt. Even the most ardent of fan was worried just how much of an effect the loss of Ian Rush would have on the team.

It was a strange time. Rush had been sold to Juventus in the summer of 1986. His goals had won Liverpool the Double but he was then immediately loaned back to the club for one more season. He continued to score but that only made things harder for the fans he was leaving. With every Rush strike they pined for him a little more.

Some even took steps to stop the move. The 'Rushie Must Stay' campaign had hopeful fans sincerely believing and hoping that Juventus had kept the receipt and might return their goods but to no avail. He was going. And how do you replace perfection?

This was the atmosphere any new striker was walking into. For months, newspapers had speculated and guessed at whom Dalglish would choose. It became a race between the red tops to bring the exclusive news; who would be filling Rush's boots?

Alan Smith at Leicester was mentioned, Michael Laudrup at Juventus too. Brian McClair at Celtic was an idea, as was Chelsea's Kerry Dixon. Dalglish though had long had his clever eyes on Oxford. Aldridge had scored against Liverpool in one of Dalglish's first league games as manager and his record in a fine Oxford team was excellent.

The papers loved it. Not only was the story breaking about who would replace Liverpool's number nine, but here was a player who even looked like the departing striker. Much was made of Aldridge supposedly being Rush's doppelganger but soon the comparisons wouldn't be concerned with haircuts and facial hair. Could Aldridge score goals with the proficiency of Ian Rush? That's what fans were wondering.

Aldridge made his move to Liverpool in late January 1987 in a deal worth £750,000. The day he signed, he arrived without the moustache – maybe as a way of deflecting the Rush associations. He was photographed standing on the Kop, a Liverpool scarf around his neck, looking out on a view that for so long he had enjoyed as a fan. This was a great moment but he was already hiding something from his new boss.

'Gathering dust in a newspaper archive is a picture of my first day as a professional at Anfield,' Aldridge wrote in his autobiography. 'In it, I look pleased, but in trying to keep the photographer happy, the smile is hurting the muscles in my face. I am holding both the FA Cup and the league championship trophy; the honours Liverpool had won the previous season. Take a closer look and you can see two plasters on my right hand. There is evidence of bruising. As my hand was not in a plaster cast, few people would have known it was broken.'

Aldridge had finished a party thrown by his wife to celebrate his big move but after a few too many drinks, the striker's fist found its way through a window, only to discover a brick wall behind it. It wasn't the sort of thing you told Kenny Dalglish on arrival at the biggest club in England. 'I gave the obligatory interviews, posed for the cameras, and nervously sipped water from a bottle. Then Ron Yeats showed up – Big Ron Yeats, the captain of the Liverpool team when they won the FA Cup in 1965.

'"All right, John, how are you?" he said, grabbing my right hand and shaking it with enthusiasm. The pain shot though my body ending up in my feet. On another day, a normal day, I might have fainted.'

Instead of collapsing Aldridge told the press how it felt to replace a legend. 'I'd settle right now on being just half the player Rushie was at Anfield,' he said. 'And if people give me that kind of recognition when my Liverpool career is over, I'll remember it as the greatest compliment of my life. Obviously I'd love to be as good as he is, but I can't get anywhere near him. Nobody can. Granted there is a similarity in the way we look, but that is where the similarity ends.'

Actually, he was wrong. There were other similarities too. When Ian Rush arrived at Liverpool in 1980, the shy youngster struggled to cope with the alpha males in the Liverpool dressing room, a place where any misdemeanour, however small, was picked up by the likes of Kenny Dalglish and Graeme Souness and used against you.

Rush, this most lethal of strikers wasn't so lethal when it came to dealing with his dressing room comrades. He was nicknamed E.T. because he spent so much time phoning home and his peers wondered if he would fit in. Soon he would of course but that initial period at the club was undoubtedly hard.

Aldridge felt the same. He talked to the press like a star-struck fan, about being elated to be there etc, etc, but Aldridge was no groupie and when his first days at the club turned out to be harder than expected, he wasn't afraid to have a word. Here he was at the cub of his dreams, training with players he had long admired from afar, but instead of soaking up their vast knowledge he was deflecting jokes and wind-ups. 'I found some players keen to take the mick out of me, which caused much irritation at the time,' Aldridge recalled. 'You couldn't do anything wrong without somebody taking the opportunity to laugh and belittle you; and, because I was so vulnerable and therefore inclined to bite back, it seemed as though the more I complained the worse it got.

'Craig Johnston tried to make me look stupid after training at Melwood one day and I had to put him straight. After that, I think the lads respected me a bit and I got on well with everyone from then on.' Not that getting into the starting XI was as easy. Aldridge made his full debut at Anfield a month after his arrival, and he scored the winner against Southampton but still, this was Liverpool, not Oxford and a pat on the back was about as good as it got for such contributions.

Aldridge, much to his frustration was mostly a sub – if that – and was wondering what he had been signed for. Dalglish though was biding his time. The manager was in no hurry to unleash new players. His board had generously made big funds available over the Christmas of 1986, but Dalglish knew who he wanted, and they weren't yet all available. He wouldn't be hurried, even if it meant that Everton pipped the club to the title (which they did).

Aldridge came in but Dalglish wanted others; then and only then would things change. Until then, the new striker could settle in, get a feel for the place, and become a Liverpool player. That was easier said than done. Newspaper reports over the summer complained that the club had made the wrong choice in recruiting Aldridge. The player himself performed badly on a close-season tour to Israel whilst playing up front with the manager himself.

For his manager though, the Rush years had finished (for now) and the summer's transfer activity was done in earnest. He called his striker, put his mind at rest, informing him he was now the main man; he signed Peter Beardsley and John Barnes, got back to training and then, at Highbury in August 1987, unleashed hell.

Aldridge had been born in 1958, in Garston, Liverpool. Expelled from school, Aldridge relied on the gift of his father's gab to get back in, but trouble was never far from the streetwise youngster. Football though offered him discipline. Aldridge and his mates played behind his house on a small concrete slab, perfect for a bit of three-a-side.

Watching became every bit as exciting and essential as playing and with his father a Red, Aldridge made his way to Anfield with a box to stand on for the first time in January 1967. Roger Hunt caught the young man's eye and he later cited his 'obsession' with scoring goals on those days watching his hero.

As a teenager, and a fine player, Aldridge got a trial at Liverpool, scoring a goal and hoping that soon all his dreams would come true. 'You've done very well, but we can't take you on at the moment,' said Tom Saunders, one of the club's coaches. Aldridge was devastated but his dad persevered and wrote a letter telling them to have another look.

They agreed and once again the youngster did well, actually better than well. He scored five goals in a 6–3 win. 'If I'd farted that day it would have smelt of a rose garden,' he later said.

Nothing. Aldridge, despondent but hungry went onto play for South Liverpool, Newport County and then Oxford before finally getting the dream move and now at Arsenal, he was taking the field for a new season that crackled with new possibilities.

Travelling fans packed out Arsenal's Clock End on a scorching August afternoon. Arsenal fans too sought any view possible with a few brave souls getting onto the North Bank roof. Any start to the season excites fans but at Liverpool on that famous old bank of terracing at Highbury, something special was happening. Aldridge (the 'tache back), Barnes, Beardsley, a new silver kit; things were fresh. Ian Rush was missed but not grieved over.

The three new attackers combined brilliantly for Aldridge to score a fine header to open the scoring and a late Steve Nicol goal ensured the points. From there Liverpool had lift off. Teams were brushed aside; attack after attack and in Aldridge here was a player absolutely at ease with the responsibility of scoring goals.

He managed to score in each of the first nine games. Yes, plenty were penalties but this was a focal point for everything the team was trying to achieve. 'Oh Johnny, Johnny! Johnny, Johnny, Johnny, Johnny Aldridge', screamed an adoring set of fans.

Early front-runners Queens Park Rangers (front-runners only because Liverpool had had to postpone early home games due to a faulty sewer in the Kop) came to Anfield and were beaten 4–0. Rush, having a week off in Serie A, came home to watch. He was impressed.

'I always felt that John was the main man to take over from me,' Rush said. 'He is scoring goals at a faster rate than I ever did, and Liverpool look a better side than they did last year. There are not many strikers around like John, and by playing with wingers they have so many more options this season.' Rush was right. Comparisons between the departed and the new are inevitable but in this case they were lazy. Dalglish hadn't looked to replace Rush; he had looked to replace an old system. Rush had long thrived on passing from the centre of the park, from Dalglish himself or later Jan Molby and the Welshman was a genius at playing off the shoulder of the defender.

Aldridge could do the same but he was just as apt at playing alone up front, something he did a lot with Beardsley dropping into deeper positions. Often it was Barnes who was closest to Aldridge and with the industrious Ray Houghton soon joining on the right hand side of the midfield, the team had a wonderful balance to it.

You could see they were all having the time of their lives, but none more so than John Aldridge. 'The 1987/88 season is one of my favourite subjects,' he later said. 'If you catch me in a bad mood, turn the conversation to the events of that period of my life and you can guarantee I'll cheer up.'

Look at footage of Everton's visit to Anfield on the first day of November 1987. The blue half of the city had enjoyed a 1–0 win at the same ground just four days earlier. They had heard much about this brilliant new side and would have relished busting what they saw as mere urban myths about their rivals' form. Liverpool, in front of the live television cameras, were keen to re-establish them.

Aldridge didn't score that day but his face when Steve McMahon did tells you everything you need to know about his desire and his passion. Face screwed up in delight, fists clenched and eyes as wide as the Charity Shield, he is as obsessed as the punters going wild with him.

Aldridge's memorable goals (he scored 29 in all competitions) include a far post sliding effort against Arsenal that had the Kop go wild at its opportunism after fine work from McMahon. Then there was the less talked about deftness to his game, perfectly shown off in the scintillating 5–0 win over Nottingham Forest at Anfield. Here Peter Beardsley dropping into his own half, dropped the shoulder, made space and dissected the centre-halves to find an onrushing Aldridge whose dink over Steve Sutton belied talk of a mere goal-poacher.

The best though, once again against Nottingham Forest but this time at Hillsborough in the FA Cup semi-final, summed up everything these three new players brought to the team. Beardsley expertly lays off a long pass to Barnes. Barnes lays it back to Beardsley who has already moved into a wider position before brilliantly playing the ball back into space behind him for Barnes to attack.

Forest's defenders, as captivated as everyone, have drifted towards the magic, leaving Aldridge one-on-one in the box. Barnes swings the ball in and on the volley, Aldridge provides that finish.

It was magical stuff but football being a cruel mistress it ended with no such glory. Aldridge's last contribution to this, his favourite season was a penalty at Wembley against Wimbledon in the FA Cup Final. Aldridge hadn't missed from 12 yards for Liverpool, and so when the team were awarded a dubious penalty it seemed obvious that they would equalise Lawrie Sanchez's first-half goal.

Aldridge had only become the team's penalty taker because he'd needed the toilet. On a pre-season tour, he was relieving himself in a dressing-room cubicle when Dalglish announced that Peter Beardsley would be taking the spot-kicks. During the game, Liverpool were awarded a penalty, Beardsley stepped up but Aldridge, oblivious to his manager's wishes, took matters in his own hands, dispatched the ball and never looked back.

Nine months later, here he was facing Wimbledon's Dave Beasant in the FA Cup but despite a well-struck penalty, the big keeper had done his homework and pushed the ball wide. Aldridge dropped to his knees. Liverpool's chances of another Double were gone. It was a hard end to the best of seasons, but for Aldridge, things were about to get even harder.

Aldridge was enjoying a summer's game of snooker at his home in Calderstones. The radio was on and as he addressed a tricky blue on the green baize, the newsreader said the words that left him thinking perhaps his Liverpool career needed snookers. His club were re-signing Ian Rush. 'I knew Ian's return would hasten my departure from Anfield,' admitted Aldridge. 'Footballers might occasionally be paranoid and insecure but they can smell a threat to their place in the team in a gale-force wind.'

Rush hadn't settled into life in Italy. More was made of his so-called failings in Serie A than was strictly true but in the summer of 1988, the football clubs of Europe were made aware that he was a striker for sale. Colin Harvey at Everton was keen, Bayern Munich in Germany wondered if he might swap pasta for bratwurst. Even Alex Ferguson made very real enquiries at Manchester United. Rush was considering his next move when the phone went. 'Rushie, it's me, Kenny. You're coming home tomorrow.' With that he was once again a Liverpool player.

Aldridge, upset and concerned, was not a man to sulk. Rush was welcomed home by ecstatic fans and old team-mates alike but Aldridge, whilst not naïve enough to think this wasn't a problem, also knew that his game suited the team's system better than the old master's.

Dalglish wasn't indulging himself with old friends. This wasn't jobs for the boys. A young manager, Dalglish had learnt from his playing days under Paisley and his staff that a great team never stands still.

Rush had become available, he was a proven goalscorer and so he had made his move.

Rush arrived back not fully fit and the tempo of the English game – all bustle compared to Italy's cageyness – would take getting used to again. So would the fact that for the first time, alongside him in the Liverpool squad was a player just as skilled at finding the back of the net.

The opening game of the season was at Charlton. Rush was on the bench. Aldridge scored a hat-trick. He had already scored an overhead kick in the Charity Shield against Wimbledon at Wembley. He clearly wasn't going to sit back an admire Rush's return.

Dalglish didn't see things in black and white. Rush's arrival was just as worrying for Peter Beardsley and the Scot had ideas that he could play Aldridge and Rush together and that's what he often did. The two goalscorers got on. They had been in touch whilst Rush was in Turin, the Welshman calling him in England after hearing that Aldridge had been in trouble with the law for an incident involving an irate barmaid, some spilt orange juice, two nightclub bouncers and too many beers. 'Mr Aldridge, this is Liverpool CID,' said a strange voice down the phone.

'Hi Rushie,' said Aldridge. Rush was better at scoring goals than he was at pranks.

Liverpool weren't at their fluid best but they were picking up results, often with all three forwards playing. Rush's first goal back at Anfield came in November against Middlesbrough. Rush got the first but Aldridge and Beardsley also chipped in for a 3–0 win.

Rush's fitness concerns though meant he endured long lay-offs and so it was Aldridge and Beardsley who played up front in a run-in that almost won yet another Double.

Liverpool had lost 3–1 on New Year's Day at Old Trafford but then came an unbeaten streak that saw Arsenal's lead at the top of the First Division scythed down and Aldridge went on a run that saw him score in 11 straight games. Liverpool were very much back in it, and for all his summer worries, so was Aldridge.

Aldridge's 21 goals in 35 league games had taken the club to the brink and on the last night of the most emotional of seasons, Liverpool needed only to stop Arsenal winning by two goals at Anfield to win the title. With only seconds remaining Arsenal did just that. The old stadium hasn't witnessed many moments like it. A place synonymous with the home team's glory, here was audible silence. The away fans went crazy of course but from the Kop, a ripple of applause that transformed into the most sportsmanlike appreciation for not only what they had witnessed but their team's efforts under the most trying of circumstances.

'At times like that you don't really know how to handle it,' recalled Aldridge. 'My immediate reaction was to slump to the ground in genuine shock. David O'Leary, my Republic of Ireland team-mate, tried to console me but I ushered him away. I was far too upset to talk to anyone.'

This was a footballing disaster. A word used to describe defeats, but a word that now, in the spring of 1989 had no place in a sporting context. On 15 April, Liverpool had once again gone to Hillsborough to face Nottingham Forest in the FA Cup semi-final. Six minutes into this game, the referee stopped the game and with that whistle, a light went out in English football. 96 fans were killed at Hillsborough. 96 people who got up and went to watch their beloved team, and who didn't come home.

Football was of course secondary and Aldridge wondered if it could ever be uppermost in his mind again. He considered retirement but he did play again, whether football ever meant the same is less certain. 'Every year when you wake up on the day of the anniversary, straightaway you think about what happened and then you relive it,' he said on the eve of the tragedy's 25th anniversary.

'The day comes back every year and then you go to the service and they don't get easier to attend. I don't care what anyone says.' Aldridge and his team-mates joined their manager at the victims' funerals, something that affected Aldridge. These were his people. This was his city and for so long he too had stood on the nation's terraces watching this club.

'Once you sit down just after 3pm at the anniversary service, and they start reading out the names, it is like someone gets a knife out and puts it in you. The time it takes to read out the 96 names with the bell ringing in between is cutting. It gets you and it is very sensitive and poignant. That for me is the hardest part of the service.

'If I wasn't a footballer, I would have been at the semi-final as a fan. So I am one of the lucky ones and there are a lot of lucky ones. There is probably a little bit of guilt. Those fans came to see us, so I can see where people are coming from when they ask if I feel a bit guilty. I don't think you get totally over something like that. Life has changed and we know a lot more now than we did 25 years ago, but people should have been counselled – that goes for players and the management.

'It changed me a little bit in ways I don't want to talk about; having to go through what we did and do what we had to do, all the funerals, was really hard on your body, but it was absolutely the right thing to do.

'It's not about us though, the families are the real heroes… When you think about what they have been through for the past 25 years, it puts everything in perspective. They are truly special people.'

Aldridge and the football club did a lot of soul searching in those days and weeks after Hillsborough. Soon though, football started back again. Aldridge scored twice against Nottingham Forest in the replayed semi-final. He also had tongues wagging when he rubbed the top of Brian Laws's head, who had just scored a decisive own goal. It didn't go down well. 'My only defence is that I was so determined to win the game I lost the ability to think straight. It was so unlike me and I regretted the incident immediately,' Aldridge wrote. 'Three days later, Liverpool played Forest at Anfield in a First Division fixture. Before the game, I approached Brian as he came off the coach and offered an apology. His reaction was short and firm and totally unexpected.'

That reaction consisted of two words and so during that league game, and having left Laws on the turf, Aldridge once again rubbed his head. 'This time I was pleased with my intervention.'

The FA Cup Final against Everton was always going to be the most emotional of days and it was. Aldridge grabbed his only ever goal against Everton for Liverpool in the fourth minute but was denied an FA Cup Final winner by a late Stuart McCall equaliser and watched from the bench as his replacement, Ian Rush scored two goals to win the cup.

And that set the tone. Rush started the following season with Peter Beardsley and Aldridge knew that this time, chances to prove himself wouldn't come. A move had to happen and he took the courageous and ultimately very successful step of going to play in Spain.

As the final whistle went after the demolition of Crystal Palace, Aldridge ran to his Kop. Off came the shirt and off came the boots and into the crowd they went. 'I wouldn't describe it as an altogether happy memory for me because I was leaving the club I loved – and the club I had always dreamt of playing for – but to get the chance to score at the Kop end in my last game was special,' recalled Aldridge.

'It was a very poignant moment for me. Everyone knew I didn't want to leave. I'd have stayed there for the rest of my career if I could and I told Kenny I wouldn't go if he'd give me a chance. But he made it clear that Ian Rush and Peter Beardsley were his preferred front two and so, with a World Cup coming up the following summer, I realised I couldn't hang around and just sit on the bench.

'I remember when we got the penalty against Palace and the Kop suddenly started singing my name. They clearly wanted me to come on to take it and I was a bit surprised when Kenny went along with their wishes. If I had to leave the club then this was the best way to do it, scoring a goal at the Kop end and having the crowd show their appreciation for what I had given the club over the years. At the end of the game I was all over the place emotionally and it's really difficult to put into words exactly how I was feeling at that time. It was a real mix of emotions, that's for sure.'

Having retired from the game, Aldridge today is very much part of the furniture at Anfield. He works for Radio City and makes no excuses for being a huge fan. In Istanbul in 2005, with the game at the business end of the penalty shoot-out, Milan's Andrei Shevchenko strode forward, having to score to keep his team in it. Liverpool were on the brink of their miracle. 'He's a good player him,' said Aldridge. 'He'll definitely score.' The rest is history and Aldridge was screaming as loudly as anybody.

Being from Liverpool is by no means a guarantee of any sort of hero-worship on the terraces. The fans want to see more than the recipe for Scouse in your kit bag. In Aldridge they immediately saw that this was a man who understood and felt what they felt.

At the 1994 World Cup whilst waiting to get on as a substitute for the Republic of Ireland he was held up by the fourth official. He let his tormentor have it in the most Liverpudlian of ways. Tony Evans, the author of several fine books on Liverpool, recalls watching it and feeling closer to a former player than ever.

'Forget all the goals, forget that he's a Kopite who played like it when he wore a red shirt, this was his moment. With his entry as a substitute for Ireland delayed by an over-officious flunky, Aldo gave him a piece of his mind, which was beamed across the world by a dozy television director. The expletive-ridden rant in the thickest Scouse was one of the great comedy moments of all time. A whole generation of kids across the world were traumatised. I know he wasn't playing for Liverpool at the time but what you've got to understand is that Aldo will always be one of us. Fact.'

John Barnes

1987–1997
Appearances: 407
Goals: 108

J OHN Barnes gave Liverpool Football Club ten brilliant years but
for the first three weeks of this first season, Barnes's cult among
the fans was built on mythology. In the summer of 1987 a collapsed
sewer at the Kop end meant that Kenny Dalglish's team would play
their first three games of the new campaign on the road.

A travelling fan would return to Liverpool like a latter day
Christopher Columbus in faded denim and Adidas trainers, a smile
on his face, new chants on his lips and stories of greatness newly
discovered. For he had sailed to north London, he had been to Coventry
and he had travelled to West Ham. If Columbus had found the West
Indies, our intrepid explorer had seen John Barnes, a footballer who
himself hailed from the Caribbean and now with each swivel of Barnes's
hips, the travelling fan told of a brave new world.

Less travelled fans listened to stories of a new Liverpool but how
much of it could they believe? Was Peter Beardsley really an inventive
and skilful number seven in the mould of Kenny himself? Was John
Aldridge really making Ian Rush's arrivederci more than bearable? Was
Barry Venison playing like Phil Neal? Did the team really look good in
a silver kit? And Barnes? Was he really that good, and that committed?

The latter had been questioned ever since it was reported that
Dalglish was keen on the Watford man. The Liverpool board had made
funds available to the manager over the Christmas of 1986. The cheque
from Juventus for £3.2 million had cleared, Rush was still on loan but

new players could now be bought. Dalglish wouldn't be rushed but he did have an idea who he wanted.

In December 1986, Liverpool went to Watford and were beaten 2–0. Barnes scored the second goal, a brilliant solo effort that had *The Times* drooling:

'Barnes, who was a delight, danced past Gillespie and sprinted from the halfway line to the edge of the Liverpool penalty area where, alone with his thoughts, he hesitated as three defenders converged on him. The solution to his problem was a wicked low drive into the bottom right hand corner of the net, so precise it might have been directed by a computer.'

Enquiries and then offers were made, the player notified and an unofficial deal agreed upon. Barnes would stay until the end of the season and then make his move. The papers though saw it differently. Liverpool wanted him they said, but Barnes was stalling they said. He was holding out for a move to Arsenal, Tottenham or better still Italy's Serie A.

Liverpool fans flicked through the back pages and some took umbrage. Players Liverpool wanted didn't think about it or hold out for, god forbid, better offers. They got up there and they held up a scarf for the photographers and they touched the This is Anfield sign. No, to some Barnes wasn't right at all.

The whispers and false reports must have been frustrating? 'Not at all, because I knew I was coming,' says Barnes from his home on the Wirral. 'Simple as that. All the reports were false and whilst that was a bit annoying as some fans thought I was stalling, I knew the deal was done and that I was coming. Like now, people get things wrong in the press. Watford and Graham Taylor had recognised I was going to move on and Liverpool had made their move in January.

'I was going to stay at Watford until the end of the season and that was fine and Liverpool being a club that did everything in-house, that stayed quiet. Some fans thought I had a bad attitude and that because I hadn't come immediately they thought that I had snubbed them. It wasn't true of course. I knew 100% I was going. Liverpool were happy, Watford were happy, I was happy. Some fans weren't but I hoped I could win them over.'

And that's what he did. Those games away from home were brilliant performances by the team and in Barnes, they had a focal point, a player who would hold the ball, beat opponents, and cause general havoc. In the second game at FA Cup holders, Coventry, the team were mesmerising. Liverpool won 4–1; attack after attack from all angles. Whelan and McMahon stood firm in midfield whilst others from full-backs to centre-backs weaved their magic.

Talk among football's chattering classes had been that the club would not be able to replace Ian Rush, however many new players came in. After the Coventry win, *The Times* correspondent wrote, 'I have news for the non-believers; Liverpool are dead, long live Liverpool.'

Barnes was being talked about. Those fans who had made the trips away, talked of Peter Thompson, Steve Heighway, even Billy Liddell. Men who hugged Liverpool's left-wing with grace and wonderment. Those who hadn't been on the road listened to the stories and they longed to see for themselves.

And they came in their thousands. The first game at Anfield against Oxford in mid-September was a lockout, queues forming at the Kop by noon. Fans who had seen him play couldn't wait for others to be enlightened too; fans who hadn't seen him couldn't wait to see what the fuss was about.

He had already set up Aldridge's opener with a pinpoint cross from the left before, in the 37th minute, he curled in a free kick from 25 yards that sent the crowd crazy. Peter Hucker in Oxford's goal was the only man standing still as the ball spun in his net. 'Johnny Barnes, Johnny Barnes', screamed the crowd. Myth had just become reality.

'That damaged sewer actually helped me I think,' says Barnes. 'There was that slight mistrust of me after all the false transfer rumours and so to be able to go away for a few games, play well and win, people came back to Liverpool saying I was doing alright. If I had played my first game at Anfield and struggled a bit under the pressure, they might have got on my back. By the time I got there and I scored, things were great.'

It seems ridiculous to think there was ever a time or a fan who didn't trust John Barnes but with every cross, every dribble and every goal, that mistrust melted away. Even those most set in their ways, the old timers still unsure of anyone who wasn't Billy Liddell had to revise their thoughts.

'I have a great story about that,' says Barnes. 'My friend used to sit at Anfield in the Main Stand. Behind him were two old guys, two Scousers, very much from the old school. Both of them would talk about how they didn't want black players in their team. Both talked about how black people couldn't hack it and were no good in the cold. All that stuff. They certainly didn't trust me but then I set up Aldo's goal against Oxford that first time at Anfield and then I curl a free kick into the top corner. The crowd goes crazy and when everything has calmed down, one old man turns to the other and says, "He's not as black as I thought."'

Barnes hadn't come to Liverpool on a crusade. He wasn't there to change people or to solve any of Britain's prejudices. He loved football. He had grown up idolising the West Germany team that won the World Cup in 1974. Liverpool to him were iconic. He was there to play.

The issue of race though was never far from the conversation after Barnes's arrival. Neither Merseyside club had ever signed a black player. Howard Gayle had flirted with the team in the early 1980s but that nut was a hard one to crack. Barnes's arrival had people talking, wondering how the city and its people would react.

Dalglish cared little for such tittle-tattle. He himself was a protestant Rangers fan as a boy but had played and excelled at Celtic. Crossing divides meant little to him and neither did talk of race. 'At Liverpool we are not concerned with race, creed, or the colour of a person's skin,' Dalglish wrote in his season diary.

But, the talk didn't go away. National Front graffiti was cleaned from a wall outside Anfield (the club were always suspicious about how and why it got there) and onlookers were keen for signs that Liverpool fans themselves would show a resentment for their new player.

Nick Hornby in his seminal book, *Fever Pitch,* that intellectualised what it is to be an Arsenal fan, wrote that on the opening day of that 1987/88 season at Highbury, Liverpool fans threw bananas onto the pitch as way of protest. Nothing was further from the truth. The only skin on the pitch that day was the skinning Barnes gave the Arsenal full-back to set up Liverpool's first goal. 'Johnny Barnes, Johnny Barnes, Johnny Barnes', sang the crowd.

Of course there had been a racist element to Liverpool's crowd. Racism on the terraces in Britain in the 1980s is well documented and no club was immune. Barnes's signing wasn't meant to be anything other than a strong addition to Liverpool's squad, but of course his presence altered things. Barnes wasn't there to cure Merseyside of racism though, and instead he set about playing, relaxing into his new city and hypnotising his public with a football.

In February Liverpool went to Goodison Park for an FA Cup tie. Ironically, on impulse, Barnes had his head severely shaved that morning and then faced the sort of abuse used by skinheads, as every time he got the ball the sound of monkey chants sullied the occasion. Barnes though played on, as if buoyed by what he has always classed as laughable ignorance. He played a one-two with Beardsley and sent a wonderful curling cross, so accurate the diminutive Ray Houghton didn't need to leap to head Liverpool into the next round.

The game though will long be remembered for what remains an iconic image. A banana thrown from the crowd is nonchalantly back-heeled from the playing surface in a gesture by Barnes that only lifted him higher above the hate around him.

Even today he flicks the memory away with calm authority. He knows that had he been excelling in an Everton shirt, Liverpool fans might have been armed with the fruit and the chants. That's why he knows his presence on a football pitch had no deep impact. He had after all seen it all before and today, over two decades later, he is still asked to comment and discuss racism in the game.

'People say I broke down barriers playing at Liverpool, but I don't agree,' says Barnes. 'If I had been a crap footballer, then I'm not breaking anything down, it's not even talked about. By being good, the perception of me has changed but not of black people in general. Barack Obama, Beyonce, they are not changing people's perception of black people; they are changing the perception of themselves.

'Until we change perceptions of a normal black guy walking down the street in Brixton, then nothing will change. I don't like the idea of sporting role models just for the sake of being black. I like black intellectual role models because the perception is black people will be fast, will be skilful footballers, or they will box. I didn't break down any barriers because look where we still are today. It's not just football though. Look at journalism. A lot is written about racism in football and what football must do but if you go to a press conference, you won't see many black faces in the press seats.

'Liverpool against Everton was the match at the time in England. There was no game more high profile in the country and so for an incident like the banana one to happen got a major reaction. For me it was nothing new, I had had it at Millwall, West Ham, and Chelsea all my young life but now it was getting a lot of attention. It was reported on and of course the photo was printed again and again.'

The skill Barnes showed when addressing that errant banana at Goodison was emblematic of what he did to footballs all season. Barnes, having aced his premier performance at Anfield, went on and took the breath away. The team did, but there was Barnes on the left, drifting in, swaying out, flicking and dribbling and making the oldest of fans fall back in love with the game.

Barnes said later that that season everything he tried, every trick, every pass, every shot came off. His comment suggests there was a bit of luck involved; like Van Gogh laughing at how every stroke of his brush seemed to get his sunflowers just where he wanted them. Maybe genius is hard to explain, especially if you are the genius.

Barnes was individually fantastic but he knew this was about the team. Steve Nicol said earlier in this book that despite a good pre-season and decent friendlies, he didn't know just how good this team was until they played at Arsenal that August. Barnes though is having none of it. Maybe it was because he was new to the club, but he knew and he knew immediately.

'The players already there were brilliant,' says Barnes. 'Everyone talks about the new signings but you have to remember that the guys in the squad were the best around. Whelan, Nicol, Hansen, McMahon, Grobbelaar. They were incredible and instead of six months, maybe even a season to gel, it just clicked from the off. The first week in training just felt like we had all been playing together all our lives. That was huge credit to Kenny. He saw players, good players and he thought about how they would work together. It clicked. Maybe it wasn't all designed, only Kenny knows but every Liverpool player felt like they had played with the others all their career.'

There was no fancy system, no fancy formation, 4–4–2 with Barnes joining the attack and giving dynamic width and Houghton on the right, able to do more of his work infield. Beardsley floating off Aldridge who often played alone as a target man. The full-backs were encouraged to get up high, and the centre-halves were very much playmakers.

Gary Ablett who finished the season playing left-back behind Barnes used to say that if he needed a rest he would pass to Barnes who would then hold it for a few minutes to give him and others a breather. Steve Nicol who played much of the season at left-back prior to Ablett was equally as grateful.

'Playing behind Barnsie was a dream,' he says. 'For a full-back knowing you could pass it forward and it was going to stick, knowing you could then bomb past him and get forward was fantastic. It was freedom. I had Ronnie Moran screaming at me to get back but otherwise freedom. The team had freedom. All we did was go out and play. It was wonderful.'

It seems Barnes's was often used by his team-mates. Such was his ability to take a pass and keep the ball, some may have over-relied on him. 'Earlier in my career, the first thing I thought of doing when I had the ball at the back was to play it to the feet of Kenny Dalglish,' said Alan Hansen. 'When I played with John, he was the one who became my favourite passing target. If anything, I gave him too much of the ball – it was an easy option for me. It got to the stage where John became tired of it, and deliberately took up positions in which he knew I couldn't reach him. Instead of showing for the ball, to be played to his feet, he would occasionally turn and start running away from me. He might have moved only five or six yards, but that was enough to make it difficult – if not impossible – for me to bring him into the play. I said to him, "You've worked out how not to get the ball from me, haven't you?"

'He smiled. "Too right I have," he replied.'

This book isn't necessarily about greatness but there is plenty of it about. Barnes was immediately a Liverpool great. His cult may have lay in those early mythical days and in the way he coolly took to his work at Liverpool, but oh there was greatness.

In October 1987, First Division leaders Queens Park Rangers came to Anfield and were swept away 4–0 (the third such scoreline in a row). Craig Johnston opened the scoring and Aldridge got his customary goal but then it became the John Barnes show. His first goal was a wonderful show of one-touch football; a one-two with Aldridge and a great finish high into the net. The second was Barnes at his breathtaking best. As he won the ball in the centre-circle, the Kop were chanting, 'Easy, Easy', and Barnes was making it look just that. He slalomed through the Rangers defence and slipped the ball past David Seaman in goal. It was his favourite goal for Liverpool. Dalglish called it the best he'd ever seen at Anfield.

Like Liverpool's attacks, the superlatives kept coming. Sir Tom Finney said that a player like Barnes comes around only once in a lifetime. Bob Paisley was equally as impressed. 'The supporters have taken to him instantly,' said the former boss. 'The award of a free kick to Liverpool is now a major event at Anfield. There is an excited chatter about the place as he strolls forward in his casual way. His accuracy with a dead ball is another great bonus for us. He has already scored some great goals and seems to revel in the pressure that comes with constantly growing expectations of what he might do.'

The mere sight of Barnes was beautiful. He was in peak condition; the tighter shorts worn at the time were under as much strain around his thighs as the defenders that he tormented every week. The sight of him contorting his body, both feet off the floor, generating whip on a cross in the way tennis players flick a wrist to create topspin was one of the era's most spectacular.

He had a way about him. He was that type of footballer that grown men would watch and release strange sounds as replacements for the words that were failing them. 'OOOAWOOOF'.

He glided when others walked. Even the football boots he wore seemed more exotic. Diadora to the usual Adidas or Puma. Italian flair over German efficiency.

With the title all but won and an FA Cup Final spot theirs, Liverpool played Nottingham Forest at Anfield. Clough's young team were one of Liverpool's closest rivals that season. Liverpool had only just beaten them in the semi-final of the cup. Barnes had been brilliant at Hillsborough that day.

Forest's right-back Steve Chettle had been silly enough to tell the press how easily he'd cope with the winger. 'I'LL HAVE BARNES ON TOAST', ran a headline. Barnes was too clued up about the ways of the world to believe Chettle had said exactly that, but he was fired up and played brilliantly, winning a penalty and setting up Aldridge's second goal.

At Anfield though on a spring evening in April, Barnes's brilliance was very much part of a team. A team that that night completely purred. 'That 5–0 win was the closest thing I ever got to perfection on a pitch,' says Barnes. 'The team were that good. I have played in great performances for 30 minutes and then we have gone quiet and then good for another ten but to do it for 90 against a top team, because they were very good, was incredible. I was so proud to be part of that team that night because it was so perfect. Even when we went 4–0 up, no one was showing off, no one was trying to be flash, no one exaggerated anything because as well as being brilliant we were a very humble side. No one was looking for individual merits. It was very pure. It was all about the team.'

It was also enough for people to consider if this was indeed the best team Liverpool ever had. The side that took the 1978/79 title in such style was compared with Dalglish's men and Alan Hansen who played in both sides thinks the seventies lot edges it, but he would. That team's defence was just brilliant, conceding only 16 goals all season.

For Barnes, what his team lacked in '78/79s efficiency they made up for with style. 'I think they were a stronger team than us as in they were more consistent, they won games, not with the flair that we had but they got the job done. We were very expansive, but Bob Paisley's team knew how not to lose. I think we entertained more and could play wonderful football. Theirs was very strong and organised. I don't think they would have lost to Wimbledon in 1988 or Arsenal by two goals in 1989.'

Ah yes, the bad times. Barnes's Liverpool in the late 1980s had to endure two defeats that cost them the Double in 1988 and 1989. Wimbledon won the FA Cup Final at Wembley and Arsenal the final league game by the improbable two goals they needed at Anfield. Barnes actually took the latter especially badly and felt he was at fault as in the last minute, when instead of keeping the ball and running down the clock, he tried to beat his former team-mate Kevin Richardson but lost the ball, Arsenal attacked and Michael Thomas went upfield to score.

It was the rarest of blips. The following season, Barnes scored 28 goals, won a second Football Writers' Player of the Year award and was once again, for the third season in a row, the country's most exciting talent. His hat-trick in the last game of the season at Coventry was pure excitement. He had power and finesse and could finish as well as any centre-forward.

AC Milan's great team under Arrigo Sacchi won back-to-back European Cups in 1989 and 1990. That side contained Dutch steel and flair in Frank Rijkaard, Marco van Basten and Ruud Gullit. All three were considered the best in the world at the time, with the latter two certainly the most iconic attackers.

Barnes though – unable to test himself on the same scene thanks to the ban on English clubs – was showing traces of both men. The pure strength of Gullit and the goalscoring ability of van Basten. He was that good.

England fans were never fully convinced, wrongly suggesting he wasn't the same player for the country. Barnes was the same player; it was that he was in a different team, playing a different way. Some even booed him after the 1990 World Cup, insinuating he wasn't one of the heroes that reached the semi-final in Turin.

To others though, with Scouse passports he was the main man. A young Steven Gerrard recuperating at home after a garden fork had penetrated his shoe and pierced a toe – sat on his sofa every day and watched videos of Barnes's goals. Each one studied, memorised, dreams forming in his young head of when it might be his turn.

Barnes had come to the city and fallen for its charm as much as it had fallen for his. Some fans nicknamed him Tarmac (the black Heighway) when he joined. The players called him Digger after Digger Barnes from *Dallas*. Barnes liked the dressing room and they liked him. 'It was easy for me to settle,' he says. 'I was straight into the side and playing. I think Aldo might have struggled with all the banter at first because he came in earlier and wasn't playing.

'I came in the summer and went straight into the first team and didn't have a problem with any of that. I liked the dressing room, I liked the guys and because training and results were going so well I had no problems.'

At one Christmas fancy dress party, the players were dismayed at seeing a guest turn up dressed in the white gown and pointy hat of the Ku Klux Klan. Their worries turned to laughter when the hat came off to reveal it was Barnes.

'I would do that again,' he says. 'Wearing a KKK suit ridicules the racists and the bigots. I wasn't endorsing the KKK, of course I wasn't, but I was making fun of them. Things like that can cause a fuss and they shouldn't. I felt for Prince Harry when he wore a Nazi outfit a few years back and got a lot of stick for it. He wasn't wearing it because he was supporting Hitler, he was wearing it to ridicule them and what is wrong with that?'

Barnes struggled under Graeme Souness. He openly criticised some of the Scotsman's methods and having ruptured an Achilles tendon playing for England in 1992, his match time and form were patchy.

Souness left in 1994 and it was under Roy Evans that Barnes – like Ian Callaghan had before him and Steven Gerrard has done since – reinvented himself, moving inside into a central berth and instead of beating men with pace and skill, he opened teams up with a fine range of short and long passing.

'It was forced on me,' Barnes says. 'When I lost my Achilles, the doctors thought I wouldn't ever play again. They didn't tell me that but it's what they thought, I have since found out. So, I couldn't run and I realised I had to become a holding midfielder. I had always liked to pass the ball and out on the left wing I would play one touch, short, sharp passes so that wasn't new to me. I could intercept things and got used to the positional stuff.

'What was good was a very talented group of new, young players were coming through. Steve McManaman, Jamie Redknapp, good players and so I could play second fiddle, no not second fiddle because I had a big part to play and the team was all-important, but I was happy to allow them to do what they wanted.'

Sometimes though, Barnes just stepped from the young mens' shadows and underlined who was still the boss. At Blackburn in October 1994, Barnes unleashed an overhead kick that belied any talk of old age. Robbie Fowler, the young star of the side was awestruck. 'I don't think I've ever seen a more talented player in training,' said Fowler. 'There were things he could do that you used to stand and applaud. Sometimes, his presence alone would win matches for Liverpool, because he could dominate the opposition. He never gave the ball away, and in training he could do absolutely anything.'

Jamie Carragher, who made his debut for Liverpool in Barnes's last season, has since said he was among the best players he ever played with, albeit he has bemoaned the fact that Barnes was the one player who could escape the wrath of Ronnie Moran. 'If I ever put Barnes through but he miscontrolled, Ronnie would blame the weight of my pass,' said Carragher.

With Barnes in midfield, Liverpool won the League Cup in 1995 but whilst their style and form was excellent, the Premier League wasn't won and with the young players appearing on magazine covers and enjoying the spoils that came with being a pro footballer, they were soon nicknamed the Spice Boys.

'It was unkind,' says Barnes. 'These were players who worked so hard, but they didn't win the trophies. If they had won and Manchester United had lost then Beckham and Giggs would have been called Spice Boys. It was cruel and unkind but that's football.'

Barnes left Liverpool in 1997. Ten years he had been there. Ten years he had been the club's most talented entity, the player who would set you on your way to the match with a skip in your step. There was such grace about his play. During that seminal 1987/88 season, a film crew shot a game Liverpool played on a wet and muddy day at Manchester City in the FA Cup.

It captured much of Barnes's game at close quarters and showed it in slow motion. It was perfect. Barnes for all his power and his skill is best watched in slow motion. You see the balance, the poise, the eyes wide open, the peripheral vision. A master at work.

For the first three weeks of his Liverpool career that talent for the majority of Liverpool fans was purely word of mouth. A legend that became beautiful reality. Now, three decades since he arrived, all fans have left is the stories of one of their finest. The legend will never fade.

Robbie Fowler

1993–2001 & 2006–2007
Appearances: 369
Goal: 183

G ARY McAllister tells a great story about Robbie Fowler. One that sums up the striker perfectly. Its setting is Dortmund, the UEFA Cup Final, May 2001. McAllister is placing the ball for a corner. The score is 3–3 and things are getting tense. 'The Liverpool subs were warming up,' says McAllister. 'I'm putting the ball into the quadrant and a huge dildo comes flying onto the pitch next to us.

'Robbie went over to it, flicked it up with his left foot and volleyed it straight back into the crowd. I was in hysterics. The lads in the crowd must have been doing a bit of shopping in the more adult of Dortmund's shops. Typical Robbie though. Most would have shied away from it, but he had to have the last laugh.'

That was the thing about Robbie Fowler, that was the appeal. Sure he scored goals with stunning ease and regularity, sure he was proud to pull on Liverpool's red and sure he so wanted to make the club a renewed success, but none of that was as important or endearing as how he liked to do it all with a laugh.

Maybe it was because Fowler started to play and score in the new Premier League era when the game began to take itself far too seriously, but fans, as well as drooling at his impish skills, took to this local lad who became the perfect antidote to all that.

Robbie Fowler was of course labelled a scally by the press. From Toxteth, young and with a glint in his eye, the easy stereotype suggested that if he wasn't scoring you goals, he'd be outside looking after your car. It is true though, the fans from the very off had an affiliation with Fowler. The papers could fill their boots with talk of goalscoring street urchins; but the only thing Fowler was robbing was fans' hearts.

And how those fans needed to fall in love again. Liverpool Football Club in 1993, when Fowler first took to the field for them were neither here nor there. The managerial tenure of Graeme Souness had been nowhere near as wonderful as his playing days and the club lacked direction and the old guard were clinging on without much fizz.

Bruce Grobbelaar and Ronnie Whelan, stalwarts of glorious days gone by were now struggling to influence whilst big money signings such as Paul Stewart and Nigel Clough clearly weren't long-term solutions. Liverpool had won the FA Cup in 1992 but since then they had been beaten by Bolton in the same competition. Soon, Bristol City would inflict the same embarrassment.

They'd finished sixth in the table in the inaugural season of the new Premier League and Souness was struggling to bridge the gap between the older players and a brighter future. Add to that the gigantic error in giving the *Sun* newspaper an exclusive story about a heart operation he had in 1992, and he had lost – irreparably for some – the respect and love of the fans.

In September of 1993, Liverpool went to Fulham in the League Cup and their fans weren't exactly skipping along the River Thames in anticipation of the night's work. Four days earlier they had seen their team lose at Goodison Park, a third straight defeat. Glum times indeed.

A look at the team-sheet at Craven Cottage though and spirits will have been raised – only slightly – but such was the sporadic nature of raised spirits at Anfield, anything would do. On the team-sheet wearing number 23 was the name Robbie Fowler. The more learned amongst the supporters will have heard it before on the football grapevine for this was the young boy from the city who had been banging in goals at all levels for a number of years.

Immediately Fowler was darting around, making this happen, lifting gloom. Shoulders that had been slumped were now upright and keen. Frowns were replaced with eager grins. Youthful exuberance will do that. Having had a hand in two goals, Fowler made his own mark on the score-sheet with an expertly taken half-volley. Yes it was only a League Cup win at Fulham but in the fans' minds, the tiny green shoots of hope were the best they'd had in a while.

Liverpool had been struggling to score goals and the 12,000 crowd for the second leg against Fulham at Anfield spoke again of apathy in need of urgent treatment. Once again it was Fowler to the rescue. The youngster scored all five goals in a 5–0 win to firmly announce his arrival, and the sparse crowd could boast they were present at the birth of a hero.

Fowler walked into the dressing room elated; Ronnie Moran said he should have had six. A telling-off from Moran. He'd arrived all right. This deserved a celebration. Fowler went to the local chippy near his mum's and got his favourite, special fried rice with barbecue sauce and a can of Irn-Bru.

Robert Bernard Fowler was born in April, 1975. The youngster though had bad asthma and a problem with his hips. For his parents it was a case of not, 'how many goals will he score when he grows up', but how well will he walk? The condition cleared up of course and the young man got on with learning about life and football on the streets of Toxteth.

It was an inner-city childhood full of scrapes with parental authority; a childhood spent climbing things (Fowler liked to climb things), playing with his mates and of course learning to master a football. Fowler was happy-go-lucky. Toxteth was home, it was where he and his friends lived and laughed. To others though it had become synonymous with trouble and uprising.

In the summer of 1981, social unrest was brewing in most of England's cities. One Friday in July, a young, black man being chased on his bike by police fell to the ground and was helped by a group of friends who multiplied and fought with the authorities for hours. The following day riot police were dispatched and trouble ensued, raging into the night. It is said that Willie Whitelaw, Margaret Thatcher's Home Secretary, was called at 2am and asked by Merseyside's Chief Constable if his force could use CS gas on the crowd, something the police had never done before on the British mainland. Whitelaw gave his consent and rolled over back to sleep.

That was the thing. Areas such as Toxteth were very much afterthoughts, minor annoyances to the government in Westminster. Unemployment was up in Toxteth, 21,000 registered out of work. The rioters were both black and white youths and the MP for the area, Richard Crawshaw, stated that the trouble had erupted from a genuine belief among the young that the police were 'not even-handed'.

Thatcher herself took a break from her busy schedule to visit Toxteth, as the trouble had gone on for weeks. She walked around a city she cared little for and was dumbstruck by what she felt was a lack of motive for social unrest. 'The housing there was by no means the worst in the city,' she said. 'I had been told that some of the young people got into trouble through boredom and not having enough to do. But you had only to look at the grounds around those houses with the grass untended, some of it waist high, and the litter, to see that this was false analysis. They had plenty of constructive things to do if they wanted. Instead, I asked myself how people could live in such circumstances without trying to clear up the mess.'

It summed up her and her government's feeling that this was a city that should be left alone to clear up its own mess. For the young Fowler, it was strange to see his streets on the television and whilst protected from the trouble by his mum, he was oblivious to what outsiders felt. This was home.

'At the end of it all, Mrs Thatcher said she felt for those poor shopkeepers, and they planted a few trees down on Princes Road, and called it a garden city,' wrote Fowler in his autobiography. 'Nothing much changed, expect that Toxteth was now twinned in people's minds with the Lebanon. But it's funny, I lived there right in the middle of it all, and I didn't notice anything different. I didn't even know about the place being this infamous ghetto until I was much older, when I kept getting the same reaction whenever I said where I was from. Even now, people can look at you like you've got two heads if you say you're from Toxteth.'

Fifteen years after the riots, life for Fowler had changed. Life for footballers had changed. The Premier League and life post-Gazza's tears in 1990 had shifted the sands. Higher wages, new-found fame and 'cover-boy' lifestyles were now a footballer's lot. It was a far cry from the perception of Toxteth. The mid-1990s was all about Cool Britannia and Britpop and riding that hedonistic wave were pro footballers.

Magazines such as *Loaded* wanted footballers on their cover. Paul Gascoigne was the don of the mid-90s footballer, as players were suddenly the nation's rock stars, as infamous for the antics they got up to and the glamorous girls they dated as the goals they scored.

Liverpool, by now was a team of talented young bucks. Fowler was brilliant, and with Steve McManaman, Jamie Redknapp, Jason McAteer, Phil Babb and David James in the team, the squad had teenage girls' hearts racing and nightclub owners' cash-tills ringing.

Much was made of their antics. David James misses training so he can model in Milan for Armani. Jamie Redknapp is dating the pretty girl from girl band Eternal. The whole team wearing cream suits to the FA Cup Final in May 1996 ('They looked like ice-cream salesmen,' noted Steven Gerrard).

The problem was though for all the team's brilliance, neither the league nor the cup was won and so came the label that haunted the team; that of, 'the Spice Boys'.

Outsiders scoffed but for Gerrard, a youngster at the club finding his feet, these guys were inspirational. 'I never considered the label offensive,' Gerrard said. 'I was steaming to be a Spice Boy. Let me be in your team! Let me be your mate!

'The image was false anyway. Nobody used to say, "Oh we're the Spice Boys. Let's all go off for modelling assignments." No chance. The Spice label was a media creation. They worked their bollocks off. None of "the Spice Boys" took the piss in training. None of them eased off. That wouldn't happen.'

Labelling Robbie Fowler a Spice Boy was odd. The Spice Girls were very much a man-made band, put together with clear thoughts and motives. Manufactured. Fowler wasn't like that at all. He had burst on the scene as a teenager just wanting to score and when the chances came his way there was no thought, just natural action. No, Fowler wasn't Spice Girl or Boy, he was AC/DC thrashing their guitars in a garage and coming up with a sound that just worked.

It had always been so. Robbie Fowler the schoolboy footballer was actually Robert Ryder as he had his mother's name back then. He had scored goal after goal at schoolboy level, scouts everywhere were keen but Fowler and his family were in no rush. As a player he would never panic in the penalty box and here he was, not yet shaving and keeping the likes of Kenny Dalglish at Liverpool guessing.

As a young man he had fallen for Everton and hoped to play for them some day but then, at the 1989 FA Cup Final whilst outwardly commiserating with his family at their 3–2 defeat, he pondered on Ian Rush's two goals. He knew Liverpool wanted to sign him and were probably best equipped to help his career and he allowed his mind to drift to matching Rush's exploits. Shortly after, Kenny Dalglish drove the teenager back to his Toxteth estate in his Mercedes. 'You can imagine how good it was when all my mates were there to see them.' The boy's head had been turned.

Soon, as a Liverpool player in the youth team, senior players would go to youth games to see the player everyone was talking about. Reserve football was a stepping-stone this kid had no need for; Graeme Souness was going to play him. He scored 18 goals in that first season and that was despite a broken leg that kept him out of most of the action.

By now Roy Evans had taken over the manager's job and there was a sense of new beginnings with a tint of old methods. Evans was very much born from Shankly's boot-room and was very much part of the club. Whereas Souness had tried to change things too quickly, the polite and considered Evans would go back to basics.

Fowler, McManaman, Rob Jones, David James, and Jamie Redknapp were all keen and Ian Rush and John Barnes were the perfect players to guide them. Fowler was brilliant. He scored 25 league goals, three of them coming in four hectic minutes at Anfield for the quickest hat-trick in Premier League history.

Liverpool won the League Cup to get among the honours but more importantly and more excitingly even for the fans there was a young, fresh squad able to play the game in the manner to which they were accustomed. This was football at a fast pace. Good passing, good movement and at the end of it, Robbie Fowler.

If the 31 goals he scored in the 1994/95 season were good, the following year would be even better. Once again, he terrorised defences but had started the season slightly unsure of his place in the team. Ian Rush, an institution at the club and the perfect mentor for Fowler, had been his partner but Evans had spent £8.5 million on Nottingham Forest's Stan Collymore and started the new signing with the old master for the first game of the season.

Fowler though was as bright as the bleached blond hair he came back from his holidays with and wouldn't sulk. He scored a belter at Tottenham the following week and went on to cement his place as the most exciting young striker in England, maybe Europe.

In October at Old Trafford he upstaged Eric Cantona with two goals in a game that welcomed the Frenchman back from his long ban. The first goal, instinctive power and a keenness for angles that left Peter Schmeichel on his backside. The second, strength to bounce away Gary Neville, composure and the most delicate of lobs that left Peter Schmeichel on his backside.

There were also the goals against Aston Villa. One in the league after a sumptuous turn against Steve Staunton followed by a left foot shot that managed to fly into the Kop end goal with both power and grace. The other was in the FA Cup semi-final at Old Trafford, controlled on his thigh and smashed into the far corner with thunderous ease.

One, against Manchester City was perfect. The ball was played across the 18-yard line, Fowler dropped the shoulder, sold one defender, cut inside another and passed the ball into the bottom corner. His goals against Newcastle in the famous 4–3 win and the celebration that saw him fly headlong into the Kop net to be with his beloved ball are as memorable as the match itself.

Fowler scored all sorts of goals but even the tap-ins he made look beautiful. There was something in the way he struck the ball; it was soft but strong all at once. He longed to score goals but it seemed that he didn't feel the need to hurt the ball when doing it. He'd often pass it in and has a striker ever hit the side netting in the goal as much as Robbie Fowler?

He could head the ball, volley the ball and take chances so early that goalkeepers – coached to set themselves before a shot is struck – were still getting themselves together whilst the sound of the ball on the netting indicated that they shouldn't bother.

'When I left,' wrote Ian Rush, 'I felt I was leaving the Liverpool strike force in good hands.' Rush had not only helped Fowler understand and perfect the art of goalscoring, he had been revitalised by the young man's vigour. Rush was a one hand in the air kind of man when it came to celebrating his goals. Now here he was, sliding head first along the grass with Fowler like an old man losing himself at a rave.

Fowler had that effect on people. His approach to the game was about joy. Yes he would train hard and take on advice but there was a naturalness about his game that put springs into steps. Ian McCulloch, the lead singer of Echo and the Bunnymen, all rock and roll moodiness, lights up when talking about Fowler's ability. 'Some people have nervous ticks,' he says. 'Robbie Fowler just scores goals, and it's mega.'

1996/97 was the closest Fowler got to winning the league with Liverpool but once again, for the third season in a row he managed to break the 30-goal mark. One of them was probably the best he ever scored. It happened in the Cup Winners' Cup in Norway against Bergen when he flicked a Stig Inge Bjornebye header over his head with his heel and smashed it in. Brilliant.

The fans had their hero. The same, 'clap, clap, clap' chant afforded to Ian St John and Kenny Dalglish greeted his every move. He was now called 'God' by those same fans but there were some who had less biblical thoughts about him. Having scored after just 23 seconds, against Middlesbrough at Anfield, cheekily he celebrated by pointing to an imaginary watch on his wrist and it didn't go down well. Emerson, Boro's Brazilian midfielder supposedly wore a T-shirt under his shirt the next time he faced Liverpool that read, 'Fuck off Fowler'. He didn't score to unveil it and anyway, Fowler would have only laughed.

He liked a joke but they could go too far. His actions at Stamford Bridge in 1997 when he questionred Graeme Le Saux's sexuality was silly; a schoolboy error and one he very much regretted. He knew that things could often get out of hand.

One other such prank happened in Russia after a UEFA Cup tie against Spartak Vladikavkaz in September 1995. On the flight home, having taken his trainers off before a sleep he went to put them back on to find they had been cut into pieces. He went to his bag for another pair and the bag had been cut up too and yes, so had the spare trainers.

Fowler wanted revenge and would indiscriminately seek it out. His first port of call was Neil Ruddock, the proud owner of a pair of new Italian leather shoes, a present from his wife. Fowler got hold of them and took to them with scissors but so incensed was Ruddock that he hit the young striker and cut his lip. 'There was a trail of blood going from the tarmac right into the baggage reclaim,' recalled Fowler. 'I didn't go down though, contrary to some of the stories that were told afterwards. Maybe I should repeat that: I didn't go down!'

Later, a young Steven Gerrard had his trainers cut to pieces and was desperate to find out who the culprit was. Robbie Fowler swore on the life of his daughter that it wasn't him. Gerrard only realised later that at the time, Fowler didn't have a daughter.

Incidents were now following Fowler around, adding to his allure among fans. There was the penalty he won at Arsenal in 1997 that he pleaded with the referee wasn't the correct decision. There he stood apologising to David Seaman in goal, and asking team-mates if – despite a title race being at stake – he should pass the spot kick back to rectify things. Fans at the Clock End were screaming for him to just stick it in but Seaman saved it, only for McAteer to knock in the rebound. Some wondered if he had missed on purpose. 'It was a soft penalty,' recalls Neil Ruddock, 'but I just think his brain was scrambled at the time and he didn't know what to do. Deep down being the cocky little Scouser he is, he'd have wanted to score.'

Fowler was merely playing as he would have as a kid. It's what made him so appealing. 'I have never been a cheat, never thrown myself to the floor at any time, and I have never agreed with this idea in the game now that if you can commit a defender and get him to touch you, then you go down. I've always had a different idea, that if you can commit a defender, then shoot, even if it is a little old-fashioned.'

The act of sportsmanship didn't go unnoticed by football's bigwigs and Fowler got a letter direct from Sepp Blatter at FIFA applauding his actions and how much it helped the integrity of the game. Fowler was amazed. 'The President of FIFA was writing to me, telling me what a role model I was!' he later laughed.

Not that the authorities were always so keen. The day after his correspondence with Mr Blatter, he got a bill from UEFA for £900 after he was punished for revealing a T-shirt that season in a Cup Winners' Cup tie at Anfield that supported the 500 sacked Liverpool Dockers. Both he and Steve McManaman had been privately making donations to the Dockers and were keen to get publicity for their plight. He took his rap on the knuckles but with every moment like that, his cult status and stock rose and rose.

There was something about goal celebrations and Robbie Fowler. The watch against Middlesbrough, the Dockers T-shirt; in 2006, playing for Manchester City he scored a vital goal against Manchester United and held up all five fingers to the away support to indicate Liverpool's five European Cups.

His most notorious incident came after a goal against Everton at Anfield in 1999 when, having scored a penalty, he ran to the away fans and pretended to snort the touchline in answer to the rumours that had been rampaging their way around the city and the game that Fowler had a cocaine habit. Fowler had endured chants from Evertonians, and so here he was, giving it straight back. He got a four-match ban and a £32,000 fine for his troubles but you'd bet that given the chance, he'd do it again.

When he went to Everton as a Manchester City player he once again scored against his tormenters and ran from the Gwladys Street End all the way to his travelling fans smacking his head again and again. He had been called a smack head all night, now he was doing just that. He got booked but again, you sense his streetwise nature loved every minute of it.

Fowler had left Liverpool in December 2001 under a cloud. He had badly injured his knee against Everton in 1997 and then had more problems with his fitness, and whilst still able to show off that natural ability, they affected his game and mobility. Liverpool fans though never stopped loving him.

Under Gerard Houllier, Liverpool were rebuilt into a trophy-winning squad and in the 2000/01 season they went on an amazing cup run. Make that cup runs, they won the treble. They also came third in the league and qualified for the Champions League for the first time since the competition they so dominated in the 1970s and 1980s was rebranded.

Fowler was by now not the main man in the squad but he was vital to the team's progress. Sami Hyypia and Stèphane Henchoz and been signed at centre-back, Markus Babbel at right-back, Didi Hamann and Gary McAllister in midfield. Youngsters such as Emile Heskey, Danny Murphy and of course Jamie Carragher and Steven Gerrard were hungry and desperate to be the generation that brought success back to the club.

There was also another young man who scored goals in the team. Michael Owen had burst onto the scene aged just 17. He had scored goal after goal and he had a burst of pace that will have made Fowler's horse (called Some Horse) blush. He had become the nation's sweetheart and great hope with an amazing effort against Argentina in the 1998 World Cup and was so often picked ahead of Fowler by Houllier.

The crowd though knew where their hearts lay. Owen with every goal he scored must have wondered why he couldn't get the same acclaim, share the same love with the fans as his team-mate Fowler. It wasn't just that Fowler was a local lad, whilst Owen came from Chester. That wasn't it. Fowler had an edge that Owen lacked. Owen was a worker, he put in the hours, he had ambitions to be the best, and he wanted to score for England as much as he did for Liverpool.

Fowler was more organic. He just happened. Fowler might have been ambitious but the fans could see themselves in him. Get the ball and hit it; no need for coaching manuals here thank you.

Both scored goals that famous season. Owen's two efforts at Cardiff to beat Arsenal in the FA Cup Final were cherished and glorious. Fowler's cracker against Birmingham to help win the League Cup might not have been as Roy of the Rovers but it reminded the fans of the love they had for their hero.

That was both domestic cups won but Liverpool also made inroads in Europe and took on Spanish side Alaves in Dortmund in the final.

Fowler – having dispatched with the sex toys – got on the field in the second half and looked to have won it when he put the side 4–3 up with 15 minutes left. The Spaniards scored a last-gasp equaliser but no matter; the game was won with a 'golden goal' in the 117th minute of extra time.

It was glorious. Game after game in the run-in brought drama and excitement. Fowler might not have been the talent that had arrived in the team in the mid-1990s but he was just as cherished. His overhead lob at Charlton just days after the UEFA Cup Final was everything those supporters had come to love. The ball drops in the penalty area and that usually brings on a panic. A ball bouncing in the box can make the calmest of footballers go weak at the knees but not Fowler. Like all great scorers that loose ball brings serenity and he can think about what he wants to do, in this case, hook it over his head into the net.

Fowler's days though were numbered. His relationship with Gerard Houllier wasn't great. The manager often made him captain as Jamie Redknapp was injured but the Frenchman was certainly keener on the Owen/Heskey duo to lead his attack.

That relationship was strained but nothing compared to that between Fowler and Houllier's assistant, Phil Thompson. Two Scousers at work, there was no love lost back then and the situation was made worse at Melwood one day when Thompson was retrieving some balls from the goal. A shot flew past his nose, narrowly missing that most unmissable of targets. 'You meant that,' hissed Thompson at Fowler standing outside the area. 'If I'd meant it, I'd have hit you,' said Fowler. He had a point.

The beginning of the 2001/02 season and Fowler's days were numbered, a fact that was made clearer when he took a strange voicemail from his team-mate Gary McAllister. The veteran midfielder was asking 'Robbie' if he was interested in coming to Liverpool as Houllier was interested in taking him. Fowler was confused and confronted McAllister who wasn't going to lie; he had meant to call Robbie Keane. Fowler could laugh but soon he was off to high-spending Leeds for £12 million.

It seemed odd seeing Fowler in Leeds colours and just as weird later when he went to Manchester City. It was even weirder to think of another set of fans adoring him. City fans especially took to him and loved to sing, 'We all live in a Robbie Fowler house,' when it was reported that their player had become one of the richest men in football with investments in the property market.

Not that Fowler disappeared. He and Steve McManaman were very much at Anfield the night in 2005 when Chelsea were beaten in the semi-final of the Champions League. The team celebrated in a bar on Albert Docks and it was there that he got into the manager Rafa Benitez's ear that he should come back. The Spaniard would have to get used to that. Soon both Steven Gerrard and Jamie Carragher were at him to bring 'God' back too.

This was no Scouse love-in though. Both Carragher and Gerrard were too ambitious, too keen to win trophies to talk a manager into bringing a mate in. In Fowler they saw an addition to the squad. They were European champions and so of course had great players but Fowler brought something that is hard to come by; goals.

The day he signed, Fowler told the press that it felt like Christmas morning. He wasn't the only one excited. 'I walked through the door and Paula, the lovely girl on the reception at Anfield, who I've known for a long time, almost broke down in tears. That almost set me off too,' said Fowler.

Fowler scored goals. His face at heading in at the back post against Fulham to open his Anfield account was that of the boy who had scored five against the same opponents 12 years earlier. He added 11 more in his second spell that ended in 2007 to take his tally to 163, making him Liverpool's fifth-highest goalscorer.

The thing is, stats and figures don't suit Fowler. Stats and figures are for the number crunchers, accountants. Fowler was no accountant. His goals brought wins and glory and happiness to the fans, who today still love him. 'The Kop has had other heroes since Fowler left,' says former team-mate Gary McAllister. 'None are like Robbie though. Fernando Torres? Luis Suarez? The fans adored them both but come back in 25 years and see whose name they are singing. It will be Fowler's.'

Not bad for a boy from Toxteth, that part of the country dismissed by Margaret Thatcher for lethargy and trouble. What would she know though?

Jamie Carragher

1997–2013
Appearances: 737
Goals: 5

WHAT does it take to be a Cult Hero? This book has offered many explanations from appearing on an iconic album cover to throwing-up in a Roman hotel room. Yes, they can vary but it seems that Jamie Carragher has just about tried them all.

Playing very well and helping the team win trophies is always nice. Carragher did that. Giving your all and playing a lot of games can be a bonus too. Carragher gave more than everything and did it 737 times (a figure only bettered by Ian Callaghan's 857 games).

Converting from the blue of Everton to every bit the Liverpudlian augurs well in the popularity stakes on the Kop too. Carragher came from a line of blues, but today has a season ticket in Anfield's Main Stand with his son, who trains with Liverpool's younger teams. Yes, he's very much a red.

Considering a 'Bootle revenge mission' on a player who broke your leg might also appeal to some fans' more basic instincts. Lucas Neill had broken Carragher's leg in a game at Blackburn and can count himself fortunate that he didn't have Scouse retribution inflicted on him when Carragher's friends spotted him shortly after in a local shopping centre.

Choosing Liverpool over England will always go down well. In 2007, Carragher opted to concentrate on his club football. Calling a Radio Station from your car to have words with the presenter who has just called you a 'bottler' for doing so adds another layer to the cake of popularity. Carragher did just that.

Throwing things at flash cockneys. That will go down well too. Carragher, having been pelted with 50p pieces at Highbury in 2002, chose to retaliate in kind. 'Have some of that you cheeky bastards,' he thought as he threw a coin back before taking an early bath for his generosity.

Having a dad who becomes instantly recognisable at Liverpool games home and away, in England and abroad and who brings a Johnny Cash classic to the Kop's already considerable songbook. That's what happened. It was Carragher's dad, Phil, who had the coach ferrying him around Europe during the 2004/05 season first play, Cash's 'Ring of Fire'. You can still hear the introduction to the song aired today.

Throw in a bad dose of searing cramp in a Champions League Final and you have a player who the fans didn't just watch and admire, but they also respect and see is every bit as impassioned by their club as they are. Have you ever had cramp? Bad cramp? It really hurts. You might have had it in bed in the middle of the night. Not nice is it? Now imagine that pain when you're also trying to stop Andrei Shevchenko, Hernan Crespo and Kaka getting in next to you. Yep, Jamie Carragher did a lot.

Cult Heroes can often differ from the more recognisable, glamorous legend in their midst. Albert Stubbins was never as slick as Billy Liddell. Ian St John was far grittier than Roger Hunt. Craig Johnston lacked any of Kenny Dalglish's panache. Carragher's tenure in red coincided with Steven Gerrard's, one of the best players ever to play for Liverpool, a man and a captain who so often dragged the team up by its heels, slapped it about a bit and pushed it on toward glory. He would get into most fans' all-time XI and of course he comes from the city he plays for. Carragher is a different kind of hero, his job was to neither score the goals that won trophies nor to lift them. Instead he put himself on the line, he blocked and he destroyed opponents, be it their attacks or their morale.

He could play too, better than he is given credit for, doing the simple things well and allowing those in front of him to get on with their jobs whilst he cajoled and organised his backline. Gerrard was very much the modern hero, the Roy of the Rovers type. The poster boy. What so many of Liverpool's fans – themselves not enamoured by the flash and the glitzy – loved about Carragher was the honest way he played. Nothing fancy, just stick a pair of shin pads on, pull up your socks, tie up your black football boots (no multi-colours here thank you), get out there and give every last thing you've got.

Gerrard also flirted with leaving. There were reasons of course; the thought crossed his mind that other clubs might satiate his desire for honours, whilst he wondered if the club might actually want to cash in. He didn't go anywhere of course but he did have to re-win some love.

Carragher might joke that it was only because no one ever came in for him that he didn't consider leaving, but whilst he will have impressed managers, he was a player so engrained in his surroundings, that it would be a waste of a phone call or a fax to even enquire about taking him.

Contract talks when it came to negotiation time were always easy with Carragher. The equivalent of a tap-in for player and club. 'One conversation,' he wrote in his autobiography. 'Quick agreement, sign the contract. Get on with football. Simple.'

And that was Jamie Carragher. Simple. Tough, uncompromising and strong, but simple. Fans like that. 'I'd always think of myself as a supporter who is lucky enough to be playing,' he says. 'I don't take myself too seriously, I'm just a normal lad without airs and graces. Just a normal lad, a local lad, who is fortunate enough to live their dreams.'

Stories are aplenty of Carragher's ability to, well to be normal. One was about a wallet. A journalist asked Carragher if he had ever bought anything outlandish since he had become a footballer. Was there anything he had bought that stood him out from his crowd? A wallet. The journalist was confused. A wallet?

Carragher had gone out with his friends for a drink. It was his round and when he went to the bar to buy the drinks he took a wallet out from his pocket and pulled out his cash. His friends' eyebrows rose as one. It wasn't a particularly expensive wallet. Not Italian. Not kangaroo leather. A wallet. Money though is carried in pockets. That wallet never saw action again.

Jamie Carragher, born and raised in Bootle. The first six weeks of his life were spent in the Alder Hey hospital with a condition known as gastroschisis. His bowels were outside his stomach and he endured operations that today have left him without a belly button.

A fighter from the start, Carragher grew strong and with a dad who lived for football, his tutoring in the game came in the amateur leagues of the city in which his dad ran teams. This was football at its most primal. Carragher talks of the venues he would go to watch – Stuart Road in Bootle or Buckly Hill in Sefton – and how he fell for a game he would one day call his livelihood.

'I was mesmerised, not only by the football but by the whole culture that accompanied it: the togetherness, the banter, the aggression, the celebrations in victory, the despair and conflict in defeat. I was eased into this world, then locked into it.'

Like his father, Carragher was in love with Everton. He would go along to Goodison, taking in the sounds, and the smells and the swear words. Graeme Sharp, that fine Scottish centre-forward was his hero and when invited to play at Liverpool's School of Excellence, he came wearing his Everton kit.

Dalglish the Liverpool manager nicknamed him Sharpy. He was impressed with the youngster. One day he would manage him. 'The fact he brazenly strolled in wearing his Everton strip said a lot about the young Carra's character,' wrote Dalglish in the foreword to Carragher's autobiography. 'He showed no inhibitions, regardless of his surroundings. It's a positive attribute he's taken into his adult career. Whether he was playing a five-a-side aged eleven or excelling in the San Siro or Nou Camp in the Champions League, he's never changed. I love seeing that sense of dedication, professionalism and pride in the people of Liverpool, which is why the city became my adopted home after I moved from Scotland. Nobody epitomises these qualities more than Carra.'

Carragher did try life with his boyhood idols but the budding professional footballer in him realised that the set-up at Anfield would suit him far more and so it was red, not blue that became the colour of his work. He was a vital part of the 1996 FA Youth Cup winning team that included a free-scoring Michael Owen and the fact that it was West Ham they beat in the final – a team that included future England stars, Frank Lampard, Rio Ferdinand and Joe Cole – said much of Carragher's excellence. The following season he made his first team debut.

The first of his 737 appearances came in a League Cup defeat at Middlesbrough in January 1997. He came off the bench that night as he did three days later at Anfield in a 0–0 draw against West Ham. It was a week later that he made his first start, filling in for the more flamboyant but injured Patrick Berger.

This was by no means a nothing game. Liverpool were harbouring serious ambitions to win the Premier League. A win would see them top the table. No, this was not an end of season jaunt to give youngsters a bit of experience. Manager Roy Evans needed wins and he turned to Carragher, to play in central midfield. The team included five Scousers

– Carragher, Dominic Matteo, Jason McAteer, Steve McManaman and Robbie Fowler – and the crowd took to their seats wondering, just wondering if this might be their year. Carragher took to the field full of verve. Too much. He was booked in the first twenty seconds. 'I fouled Andy Townsend in the first few seconds,' he recalls. 'I think it was a bit of nerves on my part. I flew into him. Left my mark!'

He went on and did more than that. With Aston Villa frustrating Liverpool, the home side won a second half corner at the Kop end and Carragher headed in the first of his five goals for the club. It hardly opened the floodgates in terms of Carragher goals, but it did awaken the fans to an eager new buck, who one day would go to any length to help win games.

Did Carragher feel that being from the city helped not only in his popularity at Anfield but also the time and patience afforded him? 'The supporters love to see a local player come in and do well but it is the do well bit that counts,' he says. 'Maybe you do get a bit of leeway to start with as those fans want to see you excel. As a local lad you can try and get into things, but don't take your time. Any player at Liverpool hasn't got the luxury of finding their way.

'They have to get going fast because play badly and you won't play many times more. You have to hit the ground running. That's what Robbie did, Stevie McManaman, Stevie Gerrard, myself, we did well to start with and went on to have great careers with the club.

'As you establish yourself, every player has a bad game, you are still learning your trade but you are doing so under the full scrutiny of the fans and the press who look closely at how kids – especially local kids – are doing at the big clubs. That's what makes it more difficult.

'Every young player has a bad time, and you have to come through that because the demand at Liverpool is so big. The ones who do come out of those blips will go far.'

On the field – and especially under the management of Gerard Houllier, Carragher became a regular in the team, mostly playing at either right-back or left-back but occasionally in central midfield or his preferred spot at the centre of the defence.

On the pitch then, he was learning his trade in the full glare of the footballing community. Off it he was prone to forget that now, as a fully-fledged member of one of England's biggest sporting institutions, eyes from elsewhere would also be on him. After their Christmas party in 1998, Carragher found himself of the front page of the *News of the*

World, pictured drunk and in a compromising position with a stripper that might have looked more festive had he been holding some mistletoe over her head.

He was young, but people look to use such actions to bash footballers with. 'I made a few mistakes but I was young,' Carragher says. 'I wasn't used to the scrutiny and the attention. I was doing what lads everywhere do aged 19 or 20. When you're in the public eye you soon realise you have to act differently. I got that.'

The fans got that here was a player that thought like them, he certainly talked like them and if the paper was to be believed he relaxed like many of them. He was basically young, learning the ropes, trying to get by. There would be teething problems on the pitch and some might doubt his quality in those early years, but most just got him. They always would.

And soon he got them. Carragher had enjoyed possibly his finest game for the club in January 1999 but the team had lost 2–1 at Manchester United in the cup, thanks to two late goals. Carragher was as gutted as he ever had been on a football field and so he headed to his old local where he grew up hoping to see some sympathetic faces. Instead he faced laughter from Evertonians. He got the laughter, that was to be expected but as he left the pub, he realised his past was very much behind him. He was a red.

Under Houllier, Carragher grew in stature and confidence. He would crunch into bigger names with bigger reputations. He had great positional sense and would look to play simple passes. Houllier – in his most iconic season of 2000/01 – used Carragher predominantly at left-back. Markus Babbel, a German international had come in at right-back, and Sami Hyypia and Stephane Henchoz were very much a centrally defensive partnership and so it was left-back for Carragher. No fuss, no worries. Just solid performances.

He was no flying, overlapping type. He was though perfect in Houllier's back-line. Babbel would offer more going forward and so Carragher could at times become a third central defender. Two footed and comfortable on the ball, Carragher was central to the team that won all three trophies and played in 58 games of a titanic season.

Carragher scored a fantastic penalty in the League Cup shoot-out against Birmingham. Right in the top corner. The fifth penalty too. The pressure well and truly on. This was a player competing though for some recognition. Some fans felt he wasn't good enough. Jon Arne Riise was signed in the summer of 2001, a gung-ho forward-thinking full-back. Those fans were pleased, looking for more dynamism, a player who they might notice more. Riise with his red hair and big lungs fitted the bill.

'I don't go on the websites or anything but I believe there's murder there after a game if we have got beaten,' recalled Carragher. 'But I'm not kidding people, if the team were to get beaten then I know I'd be one of the first to get criticised!'

Carragher simply moved to right-back and played 53 more games the following season, including 16 in the Champions League where he began to learn about defending against Europe's top teams and their different systems.

Former team-mates will tell you of Carragher's sponge-like ability to absorb all things football. Stats and facts, or ways of playing; he soaks it up. A love of the game born on the fields of Bootle as a boy, his desire to learn and better himself was a striking and endearing feature. You can imagine that at half-time during his last ever game for Liverpool, had his manager Brendan Rodgers suggested he do something different he would have listened, given his opinion and then put the manager's wishes into perfect practice. He was no yes man of course, but he was a team-player.

Because Carragher was asked to play different positions in his career, the word, 'utility' has often been used to describe him. Players aren't enamoured by the word. Being said to be versatile can be laced with snobbish inclinations. Like Steve Nicol before him, being able to play in several positions and play them well was only an indication of his ability as a footballer. He certainly wasn't bothered when asked to play left, right or centre.

'I was playing, that was enough for me,' Carragher says. 'I would play long bouts in one position so I wasn't being shifted about game-by-game and I didn't look at it too much. I knew what my best position was but I was playing for Liverpool in my early 20s and so why would I be frustrated? I was always in the team when fit and I might have had the ability to play a few positions but it wasn't going to bother me. We were winning, I was playing at Barcelona and keeping clean sheets, we won trophies. It was great.'

Steven Gerrard, himself now an integral part of the squad and no stranger to being moved around in his younger days, was always impressed by Carragher's ability to just get on with the job. 'I love Carra,' he said. 'So do managers. He'll play anywhere across the back, no problem. Carra's best at centre-half, but he never complained when Gerard shoved him in at left-back for the Treble season. A true pro, Carra just knuckled down. He got YT boys to ping balls at him on the left, time after time. He almost wore a hole in his left boot. Practice, dawn till dusk, turned Carra into a brilliant two-footed defender.'

But new players did come, especially full-backs. Vegard Heggem, Babbel, Riise, later Abel Xavier. Carragher though played and played. 'I just took that as a challenge,' he says. 'I understood how big clubs worked and never panicked. A lot of new faces did come but I kept my place on merit. You have to show character and whilst some people might have thought I was finished when a new player came in, I never did. You have to keep proving yourself. It wasn't until Kenny came back and I was nearing the end that I got dropped from the team and even then I got back in so I can be proud.'

One player close to coming was Lucas Neill, the Australian right-back who broke Carragher's leg in a game at Ewood Park. It would have been an awkward dressing room had he made the move. There was animosity between Carragher and Neill and friends of the injured party, feeling the tackle was purposeful, were keen to seek retribution. A few of them saw Neill at the Trafford Centre in Manchester. They called Carragher asking him to give the green light on some revenge but, like a merciful Roman emperor, he kept his thumb up. Hail Carragher, the merciful!

Shortly after Carragher's leg had healed, Liverpool replaced Houllier with Rafa Benitez. It was an exciting new chapter for the club and for the player. Benitez, this most studious of coaches had watched clips of Carragher. He was a centre-half and that's where he would play.

He played brilliantly. Sami Hyypia, a fine and popular defender became an even better player, thanks largely to Carragher's ability to organise and at times barrack anyone whose standards dropped. His heart was very much on his sleeve and team-mates who caught him at the wrong moment knew about it.

Alvaro Arbeloa got a tongue lashing at West Bromwich Albion and Pepe Reina recalls a few-run ins with the centre-half. One in particular started on the pitch and continued in the dressing room, only finishing later that night with apologetic texts from both sides.

It had all started when Carragher wanted Pepe to kick it long but instead, Reina looked to keep it short and the ball ended up being lost for a throw-in. 'He went crazy with me, screaming at me telling me I should have just cleared it, and I was screaming back at him,' Reina later said.

'"You really think you're Beckenbauer and you're always trying to play short passes when you should just empty it," he shouted at me.

'"If I know one thing it's that your definitely not Beckenbauer, but just give me a bit of support when I've got the ball so we can try and play instead of just kicking it down the pitch," I responded.'

Soon they were friends, but Reina's words in the row summed up how some fans thought of Carragher, especially in his early years. They mistook a no-nonsense style for a lack of talent and flair. Spoilt by the likes of Alan Hansen who floated above the Anfield turf, those fans might have wondered about Carragher at centre-half but it was here that he excelled and won hearts and minds.

The road to Istanbul. It sounds like an old Bob Hope movie but instead it was the prelude to Liverpool's most iconic victory. The 2004/05 Champions League was won amid such dramatic and never to be forgotten scenes in Turkey's capital that it can be easy to forget the moments that took the club there. Carragher's role was immense and secured his heroic status.

Firstly there was his pure ability. He was simply brilliant in defence. His dramatic blocks and cramped interventions are one thing but Carragher proved himself a defender totally comfortable with the art of goal stopping. The blocks were great of course but what was so impressive was his general positional and organisational play, as good as any centre-half around, and all done against some of the best strikers in world football.

In the group stages, Carragher faced Monaco's Emmanuel Adebayor; in the knockout stages he went up against Bayer Leverkusen's Dimitar Berbatov, Juventus's Zlatan Ibrahimovic and Alessandro del Piero, Chelsea's Didier Drogba and then in the final, Andrei Shevchenko and Hernan Crespo. Not bad for a mere utility man.

Carragher's own role in Steven Gerrard's iconic and decisive goal against Olympiakos should not be forgotten. It was Carragher who picked up the ball deep and instead of just throwing it into the box, he drove forward and picked out Neil Mellor whose cushioned header sat perfectly for Gerrard's right foot to inflict the damage.

At Juventus, Carragher – captain in Gerrard's absence – was awesome in his defensive duties and helped keep a clean sheet that put Liverpool into the semi-final against Chelsea. Oh, the semi-final against Chelsea.

It was the most powerful of Liverpool nights; the best atmosphere Carragher ever experienced but it was a game played with fear.

'That was the most intense game we ever played,' recalls Carragher. 'It was the fact that every game we played against them in Europe was so keenly fought and tight. Both the 2005 and 2007 games were terrifying. Because of away goals they were so nerve-wracking and on each occasion, had they scored at Anfield we would have lost. As a defender you're thinking, we can't make one mistake here. We just can't. You focus all right but it is so draining.

'Eidur Gudjohnsen's effort in 2005 was the one. I was on the line but not quite sure of my angles as it flew past me. I might have got a touch on it and sent it in but luckily it flew past me and the post. Everything stands still for a second as he pulls his foot back. No way back had he scored. So tense.'

Luis Garcia's early goal was enough to send Liverpool to the Champions League Final. It was emotional but Carragher recognised there was work to be done. He didn't want to travel home from Europe's borders with Asia, a plucky loser. At half-time, 3–0 down, the word close to everyone's lips sounded very much like pluck.

'If someone had said to me then, "This will finish 3–0", I would have taken it,' says Carragher. 'That sounds mad now that we won, but at the time I just wanted to stop the rot. I really was thinking that this could finish six.'

Instead it was turned around in six. Six minutes in which Liverpool found fairy dust in their boots and caused the most magical of turnarounds. Carragher played the second half on the right-side of three centre-backs. It was his most lauded display. Carragher actually started to move forward with the ball, and his presence around the penalty area lead to the foul on Gerrard that won the penalty that amazingly brought Liverpool level. But then there were the tackles and the blocks and the cramp.

'That's my job,' Carragher recalls with his usual modesty. 'Block things, tackle. Strikers have to score goals and we defenders have to stop them. To me a last-ditch tackle or a clean sheet is like a goal.' That night Carragher was Ian Rush!

As for the pain, it was the Liverpool physio who was on the end of a late Carragher tongue-lashing. 'I stretched to stop a Serginho cross and my groin and calves tightened with cramp. I was splayed out on the turf in pain. Our physio is being all nice and polite and waiting to be invited onto the pitch by the ref and I'm swearing. "Fucking get on, forget the fucking ref."'

The game went to penalties. Carragher was keen to take one but Benitez had him down – due to the cramp – for one in any sudden-death scenario. It wasn't necessary of course. Pure joy had come to the fans, the club and the players after Jerzy Dudek's save from Shevchenko's penalty. It had been Carragher getting in his keeper's ear, demanding he put the Milan players off. Carragher would often bark at Dudek but the amiable keeper could take it, would shrug it off. Carragher wanted the big Pole to be less nice, go crazy. 'Don't worry about them. You don't know them do you? Put them off lad,' he said.

When that last penalty was saved, Carragher was off, sprinting toward his keeper, the cramp gone, the blood pumping through his veins. He checked and realised where he wanted to be. Among the people. Whilst Dudek lay at the bottom of a player mountain, Carragher had run to the fans, he amazingly found family but it was right that this player so immersed in what it is to be a football fan should celebrate with people who had got to Turkey by any means necessary. Weeks later Carragher got married. The wedding's guest of honour? The European Cup. For Carragher, that is very bling.

From Istanbul and with Liverpool now very much back within Europe's elite, Carragher was consistently playing at the highest of levels and winning admiring looks from football people all over the continent. Carragher sensed a sea change among the fans. 'I was a squad player first, then a first team player winning things with Houllier,' he says.

'Then under Rafa I became one of the main players and vice-captain. I was 26, close to my prime and was playing for England. I was in Champions League finals. It was steady progression. Some burst on to the scene at a very young age, players like Robbie [Fowler] and Michael [Owen] but they can have their best years before they're 23. I was a slow burner. From 2005 to 2009 I had four very good years and yes, sensed that the fans were very much on my side.'

Those who picked the England team were less sure of that form. Carragher didn't expect to be the first name on England's team-sheet; imagine him being so presumptuous? He has said that if he were manager he'd pick John Terry and Rio Ferdinand too but to not get in when one of them was injured, that was too much and so in 2007, he retired from the international scene.

Fans liked that. We're Not English, We Are Scouse is a mantra at Anfield, and by concentrating on the club that he had admitted always meant more to him, was another feather in Carragher's popularity cap. Add to that that he phoned Talksport's Adrian Durham on air who had suggested he was a 'bottler' for retiring and suggested the radio man come to Melwood and say that and you can see why fans (on this occasion of all clubs) take to him.

The FA Cup was won in 2006; another Champions League Final reached in 2007 and a serious push for the title made in 2009. Carragher was a lynchpin in the dressing room and at the club. Carragher was proud to be there, proud of the responsibility that went with his position as so much more than a mere player. 'Steven and I were in our prime, we had had Istanbul and so we were lauded as the big personalities at the club. We were consistently at the club and doing well so a lot was made of how we came through the ranks. It works both ways though. Ask a fan do they want the club to buy a superstar or give a kid a go, most would say buy a superstar wouldn't they?

'Having said that, I always maintain that Liverpool have had some unbelievable players from abroad, but if you look at the last twenty odd years, the best players have been the local lads. When we've won the competitions, it's often been the local lads that made the difference. Look at Michael in Cardiff, Stevie in Istanbul and then Cardiff, Robbie in Dortmund.'

In the darker days of The Tom Hicks and George Gillett era, there were gripes that Carragher (and Gerrard) might have used that influence in a more positive way to combat the American duo. Some even felt he hadn't helped Benitez's cause prior to the Spaniard being sacked in 2010 but to suggest that the player ever had anything other than the club's well-being at heart is plain wrong. He was arguably the club's most selfless player of all-time.

Kenny Dalglish had dropped Carragher on his return as manager but Carragher rolled those long sleeves up and worked his way back into the team. Once again, he had earned his place on the team-sheet. He retired under Brendan Rodgers in 2013, a fixture in the defence and well on top of his game.

There was no big fanfare. He got to pick the playlist at Anfield for before the game and at half-time. A bit of Bruce Springsteen, The Beatles, Oasis, Simon and Garfunkel and The Killers. Good, solid stuff. The fans sang 'We All Dream of a Team of Carraghers' whilst he no doubt cringed at the attention. 'Can you imagine a team of Carraghers,' he once joked. 'The game would finish 0–0 for sure!'

The fans will have left Anfield that day reminiscing about the tackles, the own goals, the coins being thrown, the cramps, the audible swearing and the trophies. Dave Kirby, a writer in Liverpool and a supporter who has watched the team since the 1960s was well aware of what was ending. 'It's very poignant losing a player like Jamie,' he said at the time. 'Football's about heart and soul and in Jamie Carragher us fans have had a player who would run through brick walls for us.

'You used to relate to the players. There was passion, a local identity, the people that played were people who got us, the fans. Jamie is a throwback to all that. Football is losing its edge and its soul and in Jamie going we're losing a little bit more. He's a man of the people and that is rare these days.'

Gary McAllister

2000–2002
Appearances: 87
Goals: 9

G ARY McAllister made Liverpool fans sing. Sure there were eyebrows raised in the summer of 2000 when he arrived aged 35 from Coventry City, but very quickly there was also song. 'Gary Mac, Gary Mac, Gary, Gary Mac. He's got no hair but we don't care, Gary, Gary Mac.' His age and his follicle challenges seemed to be never far from the conversation, but soon they sang and sang.

'That seemed to be the theme, my hair, or lack of it,' says McAllister today. 'When I signed, one guy who edited one of the fanzines wrote a thing asking what the hell [Gerard] Houllier was doing. "Why's he bought this bald, thirty-something guy? If he plays a dozen games I'll show my arse at Woolworths," he said.'

It's not known whether that editor ever did grace the High Street with his embarrassed rear-end but with time, goals, assists and a number of trophies, McAllister had become a star and how those fans sang:

'Oh Gary Macca, Gary, Gary Macca,
Gary Macca, Gary, Gary Mac
Oh we love yer baldy 'ead (Oh we love yer baldy 'ead)
Yer Baldy 'ead (Yer Baldy 'ead)
You're Gary Mac, (You're Gary Mac)
Oh Gary Macca, Gary Gary Macca, Gary Macca, Gary Gary Mac
Oh we loved yer derby goal
Oh we loved yer Barca pen

Oh we loved yer Spurs peno
Oh we loved yer Coventry goal
Oh we loved yer Bradford goal
Oh we loved yer Dortmund pen
Oh we love your sweet right foot
Oh we got you on a free
Oh we went and won all 3
Oh Gary Macca, Gary Gary Macca, Gary Macca, Gary Gary Mac.'

Sung to the tune of 'Alouette', such was the impact he had in his short space of time at the club, you can still hear it sung today. Look at the list of reasons, he's loved, is it any wonder?

His derby goal; that 35-yard free kick that won a crucial game at Goodison Park. His Barcelona penalty; a cool finish to send Liverpool through to their first European final in 16 years. His Spurs penalty; another great strike at the Kop end. His Coventry goal; a fantastic curling free kick at his old club. His Bradford goal; another swerving effort in the run-in to the campaign. His Dortmund pen; a spot-kick on the way to UEFA Cup glory. His sweet right foot; the weapon that made all the above possible. He was free and the team won all three; underlining McAllister's place in the team and his impact on its quest for glory.

Player and club were a perfect match, both helping the other and today both very much in one another's affections. It was just so easy. McAllister looked good in Liverpool red, he looked like he was born to wear it, and the big frustration for adoring fans was that he hadn't done so for longer. 'It's a tragedy for Liverpool they didn't sign him ten years earlier,' says Jamie Carragher. 'I'm sure the club would have won a lot more trophies during that time.'

McAllister instead had forged a wonderful career, firstly at Leicester City, then famously at Leeds where – with a midfield of himself, Gary Speed, David Batty and Gordon Strachan – he won the league title in 1991/92. He then went to Coventry to play under Strachan and impressed again with his range of passing and eye for goal. Skills that surely would have lit up even the best of Liverpool's teams.

'I am not going to say Liverpool were my team as a boy, because they weren't but growing up they were the team that played the game the way I liked to play it,' says McAllister. 'When football became serious in my life, Liverpool were the team and Hansen, Souness and Kenny

[Dalglish] were the top players. They played the game in the style that appealed to me.

'They were the best in Europe. That's a big deal. Think of the greats today who we regard as the best in Europe and these guys were right up there. Their brand of football was very continental, very fast, very modern. I'd have loved to have had a go with them. It would have been nice, to play with Steve McMahon or Ronnie Whelan. I wanted to play like that, in their pomp.'

For Dalglish, McAllister's admiration was mutual. 'I have only just discovered that when he was manager at Blackburn, he tried to sign myself, Gary Speed and David Batty for £12 million,' says McAllister. 'He might have gone for Strachan too but he was already about 48!'

Instead of playing for Liverpool, McAllister relished playing against them and always loved coming to a ground he regards as very special. 'Anfield is unique,' he says. 'It's as simple as that and you feel it, even where you're an opponent visiting the place. I loved it when I played there. It sizzled at Anfield. The drive in to the ground, the terraced blocks, the tradition. The "This is Anfield" sign is simple but there is nobody else who has got anything like that. I love it. The Kop was incredible, magical, but I especially loved the pitch. It was fast. Well watered to make it fast. It was firm. The ball fizzed around. We were playing with an Adidas Tango ball back then and that was fast and so the games were always so enjoyable.

Didn't win much but I loved that arena. You'd look around and you often thought, have they got more players? This isn't right. Hansen and Lawrenson were driving forward, the full-backs were getting high up the pitch and it seemed every player was geared toward the attack. Even Brucie in goal!

'I remember at Leeds, sitting down and talking to Strachs [Strachan] about those great Liverpool teams. He told me that at Manchester United, Ron Atkinson would give Mark Hughes and Norman Whiteside the job of man-marking Hansen and Lawrenson to stop Liverpool building from the back. Imagine that?'

What McAllister couldn't have imagined as he approached his 36th birthday was that he would be part of a successful Liverpool team. He had enjoyed a fabulous season at Coventry, scoring 13 goals from midfield but still, Liverpool? No chance.

Coventry had stalled over a new contract and Aston Villa were very keen but when McAllister took a call from his agent Struan Marshall to say Gerard Houllier had been on the phone, McAllister had eyes only for Anfield. Since 1999, the French manager had been on a huge recruitment drive at the club, moulding it into his team, making every department stronger.

Emile Heskey up front had come in from Leicester. Stephane Henchoz and Sami Hyypia were brought in at centre-back (two players who according to Steven Gerrard would spill blood for a clean sheet). Dietmar Hamann came in at midfield. Vladimir Smicer provided some skilful width and Markus Babbel was an international right-back of high pedigree. Liverpool had just missed out on the Champions League spots in 2000, but that summer final steps were taken to ensure this was a side capable of bigger and better things.

To some the most controversial signing was that of Nick Barmby from Everton. Crossing Stanley Park is never an easy stroll and it was Barmby's transfer that had most tongues wagging. The England international though was in his prime, known quality and at the peak of his powers. When McAllister was revealed as a new member of the squad, people – both at the club and beyond – questioned what the manager was up to.

'I was not alone in the dressing-room in wondering what the hell Gerard was doing,' wrote Steven Gerrard in his autobiography. 'He seemed an odd buy. OK, he was once a terrific midfielder for Leeds United and Scotland, but McAllister was now thirty-five, his best days surely behind him. His arrival was of particular concern to me. Would he limit my appearances? "It's a bit of a strange signing," I remarked to the lads when Gerard wasn't around. "Isn't McAllister over the hill? I've seen him play for Coventry recently and yeah, he's good, but why have we signed him?" No one came up with an answer. The word from above was that McAllister had been brought in as cover. I rang my agent, Struan Marshall, who knew McAllister well. "Stru, what's all this about?" I asked.

'"Don't worry Stevie," replied Struan, "Gary Mac will be brilliant for Liverpool, and for you as well. Listen to him. Learn from him."

'"Fuck off Stru," I said. "McAllister can fucking well learn from me!" How wrong I was.'

Gerrard's hot-headedness was exactly why Houllier wanted McAllister. The Liverpool squad was full of brilliant youngsters, just stepping from potential to quality but the manager wanted older players around them, to guide and to shape their games. The average age of the squad in 2000 was just 25 and that wouldn't do.

When he arrived, Houllier had Paul Ince, 'the guv'nor' and all that, a player the youngsters respected but one the manager felt wasn't right for his club. Houllier wanted experienced players but they had to be his experienced players. Ince left, in came McAllister.

Such was his keenness to join, McAllister sent his agent in to negotiate the contract with strict instructions; don't let wage demands ruin this. 'I wasn't going to ask for 50 quid a week but I didn't want wages to be an issue,' he says. 'I wanted to play for this club and win trophies and there was a chance of that at Liverpool. The negotiations were never going to be a problem. Anything realistic was going to be enough to come to Anfield.'

Houllier, the season before, had sent Carragher out to face Coventry with the task of man-marking McAllister and actually singled the Scottish international out as a weakness in the side. 'You're running on petrol, he's running on diesel,' he told his young player but like Bill Shankly, decades earlier telling a young Kevin Keegan that Bobby Moore was useless, this had to be a psychological ploy. Houllier was indeed a fan and the influence McAllister would have on the squad turned out to be huge.

'It proved to be one of the most astute purchases Houllier ever made,' wrote Carragher in his autobiography. 'There couldn't have been a finer role-model for any young player. Some older heads when they offer advice can sound too preachy and make you want to switch off rather than listen. Gary Mac wasn't like that. When he had something to tell you, it always made sense. I'm sure the two years many of us spent working with him had a huge influence on all our careers.'

That was McAllister's brief from Houllier. Come in, play and perform of course but also guide and educate. He was there to have an effect on others but quickly reiterates just how much those players affected him too. Look at McAllister's face during games that season. His smile and his pure effervescence stemmed from a man lifted by the exuberance of his youthful surroundings.

'I loved every minute of it,' he says. 'Every second I was there inspired me. To see Stevie, Michael [Owen], Sami Hyypia, the German guys, Robbie [Fowler] and Carra; to see them at work and learning the game couldn't be anything other than inspiring. I'd look around that dressing room before a game and think, "We must have a chance here." It would have been a crime had that squad not won trophies. It had so much going for it.'

Those players will have looked at McAllister and been equally as refuelled with confidence but he had had to earn that respect. Sure he arrived with pedigree, a championship medal and a load of international caps but McAllister was no fool, he knew he had to prove that physically he was still a player.

At the end of the 1999/2000 season, with a move away from Coventry imminent, McAllister went to work. The move to Liverpool was very much on the cards and he wanted to be ready. 'I worked very hard,' he says. 'First impressions at football clubs are massive and people doubted if I could still run. They knew I could pass to someone in the same coloured shirt but could I run? How would I do with the pre-season running?

'I made a conscious decision to get in and make a big impression. Footballers look and they make a judgment and that judgment can stick. You can see if a new player is intense and what their intentions are, and I tried to get into the top three or four runners right away. I had trained when Liverpool were keen, so was two or three weeks ahead of the others. I hit the ground running, literally and people thought, oh this guy can still run. I felt I had to. I wanted to win respect and win the young guys over.'

One guy he certainly impressed was Gerrard, the young player at the club so destined for greatness but who could still so benefit from those able to pass on wisdom. 'Meeting this intelligent Scot was an important moment in my career,' he wrote in his autobiography. 'As a midfielder and a man, Gary Mac was special. He strolled into the dressing room at Melwood and immediately went around all the players introducing himself. That was class. We knew who Gary bloody McAllister was, but that gesture showed his modesty. We liked that. He also had the medals, the caps and poise that trigger instant respect. It felt like football royalty breezing into Melwood. Should I bow?

'Gary was never destined for the ressies. No chance. Almost immediately, he was a fixture in the first team, directing operations like a general at battle, turning the game Liverpool's way with his vision and touch. What a player.'

For McAllister too, walking in and seeing this young man – already an England international – fine-tuning his game was hugely impressive. To offer advice whilst training every day with him, gave McAllister's legs as much new strength as all that pre-season work he'd put in. 'There was a connection between me and Stevie, straight away,' recalls McAllister.

'We shared the same agent so we had met a couple of times and you sensed early on that he wanted to learn, that he had respect for what I had done. He is the same today. He has a huge respect for ex-players, for his peers and for the game. He wants to take things from these people and I know he is quick to pass things on to the young players at Liverpool. He loved hearing stories from me about Cantona, Strachan, Ally McCoist. He was a sponge for football and you could see he was getting better and better and better.

'I took so much from him too though, and from Carra. They both lived the club and they were both fiercely protective of the club. You got that they were thinking, "This is my club. If you're in then come on. It isn't alright to just be a Liverpool player, come on let's not slack, let's do this, don't just come here and get a last pay-day," and that came from those guys, despite their young age.'

Much was being made at the time in the press about Gerrard's tendency to spray a long pass. Sure they looked great when they come off, but what about when they didn't? Gerrard's 'Hollywood passing' became an issue. The young player, always introspective searched for answers. The staff pointed out that he should pick his passes better. Fair enough but it was McAllister, on the team bus that he sought deeper advice.

'On away trips, I timed my run to the bus so I could sit next to McAllister, absorbing advice,' Gerrard wrote later. 'Every journey was like a lesson, with me as the awestruck pupil. "How are you?" Gary asked.

'"Fine, fine," I replied.

'"Macca, why am I choosing to play a long pass instead of a short one, or vice versa? I can't get my selection right."

'"Don't be worrying," said Gary, "you're still young. It'll come. If you give the ball away, keep your next pass short. Only a long pass if you know it will definitely get there."'

In September 2001, Gerrard was sent off for a bad tackle on Aston Villa's George Boateng. It was nasty challenge. Gerrard knew, but confirmation from McAllister who told him he was out of order and that he had to curb his enthusiasm when it came to winning back the ball was always going to make him listen. 'Tackling is not just about throwing everything into it, there's an art to it,' McAllister said to Gerrard. 'Learn when to tackle, how to tackle, how hard.'

Gerrard from there was never so gung-ho. McAllister was making an impression on and off the pitch. The first few months of the 2000/01 campaign and the side ticked along nicely. McAllister was by no means a bit part player but an integral part of Houllier's midfield. This wasn't a team with expansive width. Mostly it was McAllister with Hamann in the centre of the midfield and Gerrard and Murphy right and left. Almost a 4–2–2–2 formation favoured by the likes of Brazil.

'We could play that way or we could play in almost a diamond formation,' says McAllister. 'I was older and when you are my age you want to be infield because you're not going to run a line, or burst past someone. Stevie and Danny could do that but I could get past people with a pass and getting it back the other side.

'Width could be given by Babbel and Carra joining in. Emile liked to get wide too and cut in so it worked. We had Vlad [Vladimir Smicer] too for width if needs be. He was the most talented there, skill wise. The manager, the press and the fans never quite saw the best of Vlad because my god he could play. It was quite frustrating. No matter though, the manager had plenty of options.'

Houllier though was to realise that with options can come problems. In football they are called, 'Good problems to have', but they are still problems. The question of whether to play Michael Owen or Robbie Fowler was a constant one to be answered and McAllister, looking on in with one eye on his own future coaching possibilities, saw that choosing between the two wasn't as easy as it was for the fans.

Owen was the boy wonder. Houllier liked the clinical edge he brought to the team. Fowler was more about instinct. Not as coachable and for a manager like Houllier, that stung. For the fans, it was the edge that would always be more appealing and Fowler was very much their man.

'Michael was so adept at getting on the end of things and he still had his pace which made him so hard to defend against,' says McAllister. 'Robbie was a remarkable player though. The injuries he had had were bad and they clearly affected him but on the good days, the days when things weren't flaring up and he was at it, he was just electric. Some of the things he could do. That early hit of his. Oh he was good. He was just such a great lad and you could see why the fans loved him.'

Owen though was the main man as far as the manager was concerned. Emile Heskey had cost Houllier a lot of money. He was playing. Houllier liked a focal point and it was Owen's game, all buzz and anticipation that best suited Heskey's busy strength. Fowler was all about dropping deep, ghosting around the box, less purposeful than Owen but more pleasing to a fan's eye.

'Michael knew that he was never going to be as popular as Robbie,' says McAllister. 'But he didn't let it get him down. To be fair, no one was as popular as Robbie and you could argue, no one has been since. Michael could just get on with things.'

Goals flowed in a team that found making opportunities very easy. After Christmas, still in Europe and surging through both domestic competitions, the word 'Treble' began to surface among the more optimistic fans and story-driven hacks.

In February, the team lived on thin ice. They lost 1–0 at home to Roma in the UEFA Cup but went through 2–1 on aggregate and were grateful to an indecisive referee who at the Kop end, having given the Italians a penalty, decided that a corner would be a better idea. (Bill Shankly would have seen that as sweet revenge for 1965 in Milan.)

A few days later, the League Cup was won in Cardiff after a penalty shoot-out settled a game against Birmingham that the Midlanders might easily have won. This though was now the tone for the rest of the season. Game after game was huge. March going into April saw Liverpool beat Manchester United at Anfield on the Saturday, hold Barcelona to a draw at the Nou Camp on the Thursday in the UEFA Cup semi-final and then beat Wycombe Wanderers in the FA Cup semi-final at Villa Park on the Sunday. It was relentless and it was everything a footballer and a fan could ever want.

'There were no days off and to be frank, we didn't want them,' says McAllister. 'It was game after game after game and so training was very light. It was more about recovery. Footballers love that. Less work in training suits us. The thing was we were so enjoying each other's company. There was always laughter in the pool or in the massage rooms, it was brilliant. Everyone wanted to be involved and no one wanted to be anywhere else. We travelled a lot and even that wasn't a chore. We had great momentum and a player will feed off that.'

Within that run of games and fuelling that momentum like coal into a steam engine, were the welcome but unexpected goals of Gary McAllister. In mid-April, Liverpool won at Everton thanks to a wonderfully inventive McAllister free kick and from there, the suddenly prolific Scot scored in the next three games. A cult and song were born.

'The goal at Goodison stands out for me and was so important,' says McAllister. 'I was very much enjoying my football and feeling confident and so had a go.' The game was heading for an exciting 2–2 draw when Liverpool won a free kick 35 yards out, towards their left flank. Hyypia and Henchoz went forward expecting a last-gasp cross in the hope they might get on the end of it. It didn't come.

'A bit earlier I had a free kick from a similar position and noticed how their keeper, Paul Gerrard had come early to claim it,' says McAllister. 'He had got a big cheer and I think with the game coming to an end he wanted to get that cheer again. I placed the ball and could sense that he was edging to his left, preparing himself to come and get it.

'It was Carra, who was standing just behind me who could see what was happening. "Fucking hell Macca, [McAllister gives a brilliant impression of Carragher here], it's on here la', have a go." He was coaxing me into it. I'm glad he did. That was a special moment. To go to that corner of the ground with our fans going mental was the best feeling. It felt like something special was happening. It felt exciting.'

Not everyone shared McAllister's enthusiasm. Liverpool had gone to Barcelona a few weeks earlier and got a hard-fought 0–0 draw. It wasn't pretty but it was very effective. Johan Cruyff had bemoaned the tactics that saw Liverpool play with two very rigid banks of four. The local newspaper had a picture of Houllier the next day beside the words, 'Murderer of Football'.

McAllister had only played the last seven minutes from the bench but he had no sympathy with Barcelona's somewhat snobbish attitude. 'Houllier did what he felt was right that night and I agreed with him. That pitch at the Nou Camp is huge. Immaculate and huge. They want to play the way they want to play on it and we had to stop them doing that by making the pitch much smaller. That's what we did. Plenty of teams, including Arsenal and Chelsea have gone there and done the same thing since and in the end it was very much the right tactic.'

McAllister scored the vital penalty to win the return leg at Anfield on a special night at the old place to set up a UEFA Cup Final. It was yet another showpiece day for the team and the fans, but looking back, McAllister can admit that the more cautious side to Houllier's management might have cost the club a real tilt at the big one, the league.

'His forte was in organisation,' says McAllister. 'Gerard was a protector of zero. He allowed flair in the team but was more concerned with how you stop the opposition and close off their options when they have the ball. It worked and you could argue Rafa was the same. Both won trophies but I think that outlook stopped either of them winning the league. To win a title and to be the top team in a country you have to be arrogant and think whatever you do, we will do more. You have to be alpha. I think Brendan Rodgers has that now; I think he wants to send his team out with the approach that this Liverpool team will be relentless and we will attack. The Liverpool way.'

The Liverpool way is also to win things and that May, they went on a spree that still brings the biggest of grins to the gruffest of fans. In Cardiff Arsenal were beaten in the FA Cup Final by two late Michael Owen goals, despite being second best for 80 minutes. Days later they went to Dortmund for a memorable occasion, beating Alaves of Spain with a late and dramatic golden-goal in extra time. McAllister scored a penalty that night and swung in the tantalising cross that was headed in by Alaves's Delfi Geli. 'That was amazing,' he says. 'All the players celebrated with me like I'd scored but I'm sure that Didi [Hamann] and Markus [Babbel] ran back to the halfway line to kick-off and play the last five minutes not realising that was it. Typical German efficiency.'

McAllister was a master of those crosses. In Cardiff his arrival onto the pitch on the hour mark shifted the sands. Arsenal were running rampant but McAllister managed to slow the tempo down, giving his team a foothold in a game that had hitherto passed them by. With seven minutes left, he addressed a free kick out near the left flank with accuracy the only thing on his mind.

'It so frustrates me today when I see players trying to get exact whip on crosses and therefore over-hitting it or not beating the first man,' McAllister says. 'There wasn't long left, we were losing, why go for a high degree of difficulty? I want to get it in there; I want to work the Arsenal defence. I flung it in there where the keeper couldn't come and it broke for Michael. We were murdered on the day but at the end we had the legs and actually for all their brilliance we could have won by three or four.'

The last game of the season was at Charlton, a 4–0 win securing the club a Champions League spot and now finally allowed to celebrate the season they had given the club and the fans, they, 'Sang all the way home from South London,' according to McAllister.

Whilst far from McAllister's swansong, those celebrations were to be his last big hoorah for the club and he had less impact on the pitch the following season. Not that he was fussed. 'The brief was still there,' he recalls. 'The contract had been extended early in the first year and I didn't have any acceptance that I was just there to be a sub. I trained hard and wanted to play but because of what the club had done for me and the moments I had had the previous year, I wasn't going to sulk about anything.'

McAllister had come in and he had lifted the club and the fans. It was a brief encounter but it was special. Like two lovers enjoying the most intense of short flings, McAllister and Liverpool might have given each other so much more had circumstances been different but actually this passionate liaison was so wonderful, neither would change it.

For the fans, he was a Liverpool man; he responded to their affections, they responded to just how happy he was to play for them. On the last game of the season, Ipswich were beaten 5–0 at Anfield and the players did their customary lap of honour. It was known that for McAllister, this would be his last time on that pitch as a player and once again the fans sang. As he approached the Kop, the chant went up. 'What a waste of money, what a waste of money'. McAllister walked from the pitch laughing. It was perfect.

Luis Garcia

2004–2007
Appearances: 121
Goals: 30

T HERE really is nothing like it. If you're near it, you can hear it. Swoooosh! If you aren't you can see it; a bulge, like a fisherman landing the most prized of salmon. The ball has hit the net. It's what the people are there for.

Some cultures advocate dream catchers. Nets they hang over their beds so that while they sleep, dreams will be dreams, and not nightmares.

Football fans have nets too and when the ball hits them; well then dreams and nightmares are made.

For Liverpool fans, with Luis Garcia around, the ball and the net were joined in matrimony on plenty of occasions, lifting their dreams to new heights, especially in 2005, on the way to that most amazing of nights in Istanbul. But, the Spaniard's most famous moment – the one the grandchildren of fans there will be hearing about – was a goal, a wonderful life-changing goal, but the net, well the net had no part to play in it.

For Liverpool and their supporters, that goal against Chelsea in the Champions League semi-final second leg ushered in a dream they hadn't dare to dream; another final in Europe's premier competition. For Chelsea and their nouveau-riche status, it was a nightmare. Their manager, Jose Mourinho refused to comprehend it. He would rather talk of the spirit world. That seemed easier to believe in. The ghost goal. Haunting whether you wore red, or you wore blue.

For those in the former, it is still just that, a goal and a time that still haunts them. Beautifully. Luis Garcia nicks in, in front of John Terry, flicks the ball with his left foot toward goal and it hangs over the goal line before William Gallas kicks it away from his net, hoping to have saved the day. He hasn't. The referee's assistant has seen enough. The referee has seen enough. 1–0 Liverpool. Garcia is under his team-mates whilst the stadium rocks to its wonderful foundations.

Mention Luis Garcia today to a Liverpool fan and there it is; a haunting smile, their eyes are glazed over, and they are at Anfield that night, they are walking across a seemingly endless wasteland to get to the Ataturk Stadium in Istanbul, they are welcoming the players back into their city. The home of the European champions.

Songs will take those fans back to that place too. Johnny Cash's 'Ring of Fire', Ritchie Valens' 'La Bamba', The Beatles' 'In My Life'. The latter wasn't sung on the terraces, but it became synonymous (thanks to Sky TV and YouTube) with Istanbul and that spring of 2005. There is a tired melancholy to it. Fans were drained after a rollercoaster of a ride and John Lennon's words seem apt.

One of those verses begins, 'Though I know I'll never lose affection; For people and things that went before'. And there you have it. Luis Garcia was by no means the best player the fans had ever seen. He wasn't even the best player in that team, but his actions, his goals, his demeanour; they all made the fans happy and for him, they have never lost affection.

Halfway through the first half of Liverpool's return to the Champions League in the September of 2014, against Bulgarian side, Ludogorets. The game is 0–0. There is a lull and then the fans are back in headier days. Then the song goes up. Another song. Luis Garcia's song. Still sung. Still making people smile. The ghost goal. Still haunting people. Luis Garcia, the player that went before but one that will never lose affection.

Luis Garcia
He drinks Sangria
He came from Barca
To bring us joy
He's five foot seven
He's football heaven
So please don't take our Luis away

'I felt very welcome as soon as I arrived and felt that connection with the fans,' says Luis Garcia, on the phone from Madrid. 'I remember first hearing the song the fans still sing about me. I was warming up with Jon Arne Riise and Jon says, "Listen Luis, this song is about you." I listened and I was on the pitch laughing. I have a picture somewhere of that very moment. I loved it. To hear your name sung like that from the crowd is so special, and I can't explain why they sing it now, years and years since I left, but that makes me so happy.'

It's a song that takes a fan back on that road to Istanbul. A road littered with memories. Steven Gerrard's strike in the qualifying round against AK Graza in Austria, frustration at the group stage against Deportivo La Coruna and among the yachts of Monaco. Gerrard's strike against Olympiakos, worth more than all of those gold-plated yachts put together.

Jamie Carragher and Sami Hyypia shutting out Juventus in Turin, aided admirably by Igor Biscan. Eidur Gudjohnsen's miss at the Kop end in the semi-final that had roars of delight replace hearts in the mouths of players and fans alike. Plenty more. We could be here all night.

And then there's Luis Garcia. His input alone is a wonderful tale to tell. It was in the knockout stages that the little man came to life. League football was never really his thing. Knockout football seemed to appeal to his sense of derring-do. All or nothing. Vamos!

In the Round of 16 stage, Garcia scored after 15 minutes in a 3–1 win against Bayer Leverkusen. He then scored again, twice in a 3–1 win in Germany in what is often overlooked but remains one of the club's best displays away from home in Europe. Manager Rafa Benitez thought so. 'The other teams in the competition will watch our game tonight and will start to say, "Be careful, they won't be easy opponents."'

Next came Juventus. Twenty years had passed since the disaster at Heysel and here were the two teams drawn against each other in the same competition. It was a sombre occasion. Fans from both clubs approached the Anfield Road end where the Italians were standing. They brought with them a banner that read, Memoria e Amicizia; In Memory and Friendship.

Some Juventus fans turn their back; a reminder of just how deep the hurt still runs. Some though applaud the Kop's mosaic that repeats the calling for Amicizia. The Pope has recently died. There is a minute's silence. There is a sombre mood in the air.

Then it is gone! Luis Garcia flicks on a near post corner, Sami Hyypia scores at the back post. Then, 15 minutes later running from deep, the Spaniard hits the most delicious of half-volleys up and over Gianluigi Buffon and in to the goal. That is the moment. The crowd goes mad. Sudden belief. Sudden and unexpected belief that something stupid might be about to happen.

And his goal against Chelsea. Garcia burst into the box after great approach play from Gerrard and Milan Baros, in a blur of red. The game was only minutes old, but the ground had been rocking for what seemed like hours, when with Baros and the Chelsea keeper Petr Cech both floored, he put Liverpool into the final of the Champions League. Yes there was still around 90 minutes of football to play, but that's what that goal did. It put Liverpool into the final of the Champions League.

'It was such an amazing evening,' says Garcia. 'To score against Chelsea so early was key. They were a great team but very tactical. Mourinho would have drilled them all with a game plan, but we upset that with my goal and suddenly everything was very different.

'We were so up for it. When we played Chelsea we always wanted to press them like crazy. Really get into them and stop them getting that rhythm going. I must say, it was so much easier to press them that night because of the noise our fans made. I'm sure it affected Chelsea's players but with that noise behind us; well I know it helped me when it came to working off the ball."

Later that night, fans would stop what they were doing to say it again. 'We're in the final of the Champions League.' That night in a bar in town, by the docks, the always studious Benitez was learning something new; the words to the Luis Garcia song. The heavyweight preparations for AC Milan could wait for one night. Garcia's goal. Garcia's ghost goal. It had certainly lifted the spirits.

Maybe it was the beers that flowed, but Benitez was in no doubt about Garcia's goal. The Spaniard and Jose Mourinho were not the cuddly types. Liverpool vs Chelsea had become the country's grudge match. Mourinho had lost the game but he had the ghost goal as a hook on which to place his disappointment. In his mind, he hadn't lost. It was easier that way. Benitez smiled. Liverpool were booking hotels in Turkey.

'It was a goal, of that I am certain,' said Benitez. 'My secretary, Sheila, told me as much after the game. She had been sitting in the section for club employees, roughly level with the goal line at the Kop end. It crossed the line, she said. I have no reason to doubt her. She was always incredibly reliable.'

Luis Garcia had arrived from Barcelona for £6 million in the summer of 2004. The club had gone Spanish with Rafa Benitez investing in Xabi Alonso, Garcia, Josemi and Antonio Nunez. Garcia had scored some goals. 'Vamos!' he would usually shout in his mother tongue. Now in early May, with a Scouse volcano erupting around his goal against Chelsea, he ran to those fans and he once again shouted; 'Come on', he screamed. He was one of them.

'I worked with Rafa at Tenerife and he tried to sign me again when he was working at Valencia,' recalls Garcia. 'As soon as Rafa got the job at Liverpool he called me. I was at Barcelona and enjoying it there. My family were settled but when he called me and said, "Hi Luis, how are you?" I knew what was coming. He was going to ask me to sign. He said he was building a new, stronger team, a team that he wanted to be strong in Europe over the coming years and that he'd like me to sign.

'He told me how great the city was, how the fans were among the best in the world and that I would have a genuine chance to win trophies. I asked for time to think about it and I spoke with Barcelona who said they wanted to keep me and that they too had ambitious plans. They were signing Samuel Eto'o and Ludovic Giuly among other big names so I didn't know what to do.

'Rafa though called me again; he was very keen and said I had to make my mind up as he needed to make plans and so that day I decided to make the move. Rafa was so eager and I respected him, I knew him and off I went.'

Let's not gloss over this though. For all of Garcia's boyish charm and memory-making goals, things were not always easy. Fans could be as frustrated with the impish Spaniard as they were delighted. Liverpool finished fifth the season they won the Champions League.

Jamie Carragher certainly wasn't sure at times. 'Garcia sometimes couldn't cope with the demands of English football,' he said. 'His contribution would sum up Benitez's first season: fantastic in Europe, but infuriatingly inconsistent in the league.

'Luis and I had a love-hate relationship on the park, just like he had with the fans. I'd always be shouting at him for losing the ball with one of his backheels or flicks, but then he'd volley one in from 30 yards (as he did against Juventus) and it was like all the indiscretions of the previous eight months could be forgiven. When I think of him now,

I remember a player who contributed as much as any to winning my Champions League medal.

Carragher was spot on. Liverpool were woeful at Southampton, Birmingham and Crystal Palace. Garcia was a microcosm for the side. Able to be bullied, too lightweight, when they were bad, both were very bad. A fan can recall all this with a smile though. Those backheels and flicks Carragher talks of, they could be so frustrating and tired fans would let Garcia know about it, but in the end, like Carragher says, he as much as anyone helped win them their Champions League medal.

'It's true, I did find the Premier League hard; especially that first season,' says Garcia. 'I once heard that Rio Ferdinand was supposed to have come in hard and kicked me in the back of my ankles in one of my early games. He then was supposed to have said, "Welcome to the Premier League." That isn't true. He didn't say anything.

'It was so physical, so fast, and you have to be very, very strong. I wasn't that type of player. I was quick, I liked to move around people, get the ball, give the ball. Maybe I wasn't used to the fight that is sometimes required. I was light too. Only 67kg. I got in the gym to bulk up enough. It didn't work! Some of these defenders weighed 20kg more than me. I tried to find solutions, tried to be cleverer with the ball so that I could balance out those weight and strength issues.'

Garcia did improve somewhat in his second season, but those flicks, simply part of his repertoire wouldn't go away. The team improved, they were European champions so of course they did, but inconsistency still reared its head. Premier Leagues weren't going to be won. Frustration often boiled over. Its target? Luis Garcia.

'I want the fans to understand I am trying, that if something I do doesn't work, if I give the ball away, it's not because I don't care,' he told *The Times* newspaper in 2006. 'Every play I do is because it's the best thing I can think of at that moment, and, as a player, you've normally got to follow your instinct. It's not because I want to show off.'

Garcia though was adamant; this was his game, how he played it. He wasn't being lazy when he tried a flick, he wasn't trying to look flash, it was what he knew, a way of opening teams up. 'I liked to try something different but yes I did hear the fans when they were frustrated and whilst it was sometimes tough and I hated to lose, it was just part of being a footballer. I understand what it is like to be a fan, I understand they get angry and I felt the same. My game was about trying things, harder things, trying to make things happen from nowhere.'

It was strange. Here was a manager, Rafa Benitez, Mr Pragmatic; buying, selecting and standing by a player who by no means plays the game as laid out on any manager's clipboard or iPad. Benitez had managed Garcia at Tenerife. They had enjoyed relative success together. At Liverpool, Garcia became Benitez's guilty pleasure. A chocolate éclair placed within a balanced diet.

'You have to accept Luis for what he is,' Benitez said of him. 'When he played for me at Tenerife, I tried to change him, but you have to say OK, he does what he does and provides different things. I have kept trying to remind him – many times – that when he takes the risks he does, he should do it closer to the opposition box. He can give possession away and that can anger the fans. But he also does different things that excite them and he scores goals. I tried to change him in Spain, and he scored 16 goals for me, so you have to accept what he does. Luis is capable of the best and is also capable of the worst.' But no matter, the best was capable of winning you football matches and the worst; well let the others deal with the worst.

Carragher, the manager, fans; you couldn't stay angry at Garcia for long. He had this way about him. The thumb sucking goal celebration was one thing – a strange childlike add on – but he came to Liverpool and immersed himself in the place. He hardly spoke English on arrival, but got the hang of it quickly. He strolled around town, smiling at those who recognised him in his civvies.

Maybe it was his Catalonian background that made him get his new home, a place eager to stand out and be different from the country in which it exists. He liked to play guitar, something in the city of Liverpool every bit as noteworthy as kicking a football.

Garcia would walk into guitar shops. 'I play English stuff,' he says. 'Not Spanish. I like to play things like Lenny Kravitz and when I was in Liverpool I really got into The Killers. In the city, music is nearly as big as the football and I learnt a few Beatles songs on my guitar. I was in charge of the music in the dressing-room and my choices were always popular.'

Always? 'Well unless Carra walked in, then he would moan. Carra was always complaining. I saw him recently and told him he was always angry, always moaning!'

Garcia was endearing. He turned up to the Christmas party in 2005, dressed as a pimp. Hat, cane, the lot. It worked. He was, after all, Benitez's extravagance. Pick Garcia. Pimp My Team.

Garcia took on the criticism when it came. He had said he wasn't going to change but that wasn't strictly true. 'I'm trying to close that big gap between the best of me and the worst,' he said in 2006. 'I think I'm doing better in my second season. If I'm playing it's because the boss thinks my best is greater than my worst, that the best things I do can change something and the worst is not so bad he cannot have it on the pitch. But sometimes people make me feel it is. People like a player who doesn't lose the ball and also like a player who does something that's nice to see, but how many players do both? [Zinedine] Zidane... not many others. That's why you need different players, someone like Xabi [Alonso] who can keep the ball, and someone like me who sometimes loses it because I'm trying the more difficult pass.'

It was quite bullish stuff from Garcia, a player who had struggled more with the physical side of the Premier League. In Europe though, Garcia was potent, and perfect for Benitez who liked to talk about attacking, 'between the lines'. Not quite a winger, and not an all-out Number 10, Garcia certainly got in between those lines. A modern inside-forward. His goal against Juventus is the perfect example of a player menacingly getting between centre-back and full-back and beyond the midfield. Benitez and those lines. He must have been drooling that night as Garcia got firmly in between them.

'That was a special night and a big game for our team,' says Garcia. 'If you look at that Juventus side, it was packed full of great players. Zlatan Ibrahimovic, Fabio Cannavaro, Lilian Thuram, Pavel Nedved, Alessandro Del Piero. Great players. They had reached the final two years before and were second only to AC Milan in that season's competition when it came to quality.

'We weren't expected to get through, but to go 2–0 up was incredible. We let in a late goal but we had been so dominant, created so much that we felt, maybe we can live with these teams. My goal was of course one of the highlights of my whole career.

'Don't forget the game in Turin either. We couldn't concede over there and we had to be very strong, very resolute, and very tactical. That was as impressive as any of the big wins in 2005.'

In the business end of that Champions League run in 2005, Garcia was deployed on the right of a three in a 4–2–3–1. He had freedom to roam but there was a responsibility to support the right-back, Steve Finnan. This was paramount in Benitez's mind in Istanbul, and Garcia was asked to work hard to nullify Paolo Maldini at left-back.

The problem was that Benitez's attack-minded formation needed Harry Kewell to be fully fit and fully sharp. He was neither. By accommodating the Australian, Gerrard was withdrawn to a deeper, less effective role. There he and Xabi Alonso struggled to get a grip of the game. Andrea Pirlo, the deep-lying playmaker, who Benitez had hoped to take advantage of with Kewell's presence, instead bossed it. Kaka had too much space and three first-half goals spoke volumes for a system gone wrong.

Kewell hadn't lasted the half and was replaced with Vladimir Smicer. It was, however, Didi Hamann's arrival onto the field that changed things, especially for Garcia, who was – with Smicer now manning that right-hand side – pushed forward to support Milan Baros and play with Gerrard as a double-pronged thorn in the Italians' side.

'I liked to play off a striker,' says Garcia. 'I felt at my best centrally, looking for space between the midfield and the defenders. I felt I could make problems and could draw central defenders forward. In Istanbul, we had to take control of that area. Pirlo was too influential and Kaka had too much space. The changes we made stopped all that.'

All three are in the box when Gerrard heads the ball in to make people wonder. Garcia is in the box with Baros when Smicer makes people believe and the move that wins the penalty at 3–2 that makes people go ballistic is a perfect example of deeper players, playing off a pivotal striker and causing all manner of panic.

It's tiring just writing about those moments. The heart begins to quicken, there is a faint, and irrational worry that it won't happen; that Milan will hold on and win. When that penalty was given, Garcia, like the fans there and back at home, briefly lost his head. He grabbed the ball with all the impetuous confidence of a drunken teenager, and went to put it on the spot.

Xabi Alonso was on the penalties. It had been decided. Garcia was somewhere else though. He was having it. 'I so wanted to take it,' laughs Garcia, amused by his certainty that he'd score. 'I was just so confident. Carra came over to me though and politely suggested that Xabi was having it.'

Carragher had been remonstrating with the referee for Milan's Gennaro Gattuso to be sent off for his foul on Gerrard. Soon though, from the corner of his wide eyes, he noticed Garcia. Soon his wrath was moved on. 'I must have looked a like a man possessed, lashing out at everyone,' Carragher said later. 'Benitez decided who'd take penalties before the game, and Xabi had been given the nod. For whatever reason, Luis grabbed the ball and was ready to assume responsibility.

'"Fuck off Luis, this is Xabi's," I said.

'I was saving him from himself. Had he taken it and missed, Benitez – and the rest of us – would never have forgiven him.'

Garcia had – like his team-mates – asked a barrage of questions of Milan and such was their mad ten minutes of complacency, they hadn't got one right. Now though, the game was about guts, hitting physical walls but somehow climbing them. Garcia's role was vital. He kept stretching the Milan rearguard and might have scored a winner, but it was his willingness to dig in, play an uglier English game of battle-hardened grit that so impressed. At one point he even threw himself at a ball heading for goal.

The game deadlocked, incredibly deadlocked, somehow deadlocked; it went to penalties. Garcia wasn't among the five penalty takers. 'Of course I was still confident and wanted one,' recalls Garcia. 'I went over to Rafa and I said, "Give me one, I want to take one." He didn't even look at me! Watch the footage. I am in his ear, saying, "I want to take a penalty." He doesn't look at me once, he just said, "No, no, no, you have had cramp." I was arguing saying it is not a free-kick, I just have to kick the ball, I want to take one. Nothing. He did say I would have a sixth one though.'

Benitez played the percentages there but Garcia's role in the famous win must not be underestimated. Not only because of the five goals he scored on the way to Istanbul but also because of the graft he put in, especially at 3–3.

All that effort though, all that hard running and muscle cramp, it all disappeared the moment Dudek saved Shevchenko's weak spot-kick. Suddenly legs are rejuvenated and happiness overruns fatigue. 'Yes, watch us,' says Garcia. 'We all go mad.

'A few minutes before and all our legs are struggling. Carra and myself had bad cramps but we are suddenly sprinting all over the place. For another hour we are jumping about, doing our lap of honour, running, celebrating. Adrenalin kicks in I guess. We went back to the hotel eventually though and were all exhausted. It was about three in the morning.

'Of course we then had the parade in Liverpool the following day and were all still so excited, very tired but exhausted. It was a party but a tired one.'

Luis Garcia and Liverpool had taken the fans somewhere unheralded in terms of excitement and glory. Nothing could or would match 2005, but Garcia wasn't finished when it came to wonder-moments. In the semi-final of the FA Cup in 2006, Garcia once more popped up against Chelsea and scored what turned out to be another winning goal, this time at Old Trafford.

'That was a great afternoon,' he recalls. 'That goal was a case of quickly assessing the situation. I received the ball and was surrounded by five Chelsea players. My instinct was to try to beat them and get closer to their goal but in an instant I knew I had John Terry closing me down and knew I would be outpaced or muscled off the ball. The ball sat up and so I hit it and it sailed in to the net.'

Unlike 2005 though, there would be no glorious final for Garcia. Just weeks before the Cardiff match, Liverpool played their opponents, West Ham, in the league in East London. Garcia got into an altercation, just minutes after coming on as a substitute and was shown a red card. Suspension. No cup final.

'I couldn't believe it,' says Garcia. 'I didn't even know. I was in the shower and one of the staff came in to say sorry; sorry that I would miss the final. "What?" I said.

'"You miss the final, Luis," they said.

'"No, I miss two games right?" I said because that's what it is in Spain.

'"No, it's three."

'I was devastated. I am not a very good fan. I watched the last twenty minutes of the Chelsea semi-final at Anfield in 2005. That was the hardest. I was just holding Rafa's assistant, Pako Ayestaran, clinging to him when Eidur Gudjohnsen had his chance. I am not great at watching and so Cardiff was so hard.'

Garcia also had to watch the run to the Athens Champions League Final in 2007. A cruciate ligament injury had curtailed his season and his Liverpool career, and he was sold to Atletico Madrid later that summer. Soon after leaving, Garcia felt inclined to write the fans a letter of gratitude. It is quite common practice now but back then, Garcia's actions were new and clearly heartfelt.

'A football club isn't just made up of players, coaches and directors,' he wrote. 'More than anything else it's the supporters who make a club, and that perhaps is the ingredient which best distinguishes Liverpool Football Club from every other team. The supporters.'

Seven years on, Garcia returned to Anfield to play in a memorial game to mark the 25th anniversary of Hillsborough. He took in the club's atmosphere, reacquainted himself with old faces, sights, and of course songs. This was a club he helped make smile again. 'He came from Barca to bring us joy.'

Whilst writing this book, plenty of people would suggest who must be in it, their cult hero. Eyebrows were raised at some of course. Universally though, fans suggested Luis Garcia. And every time they had that same smile on their face. The feeling is of course mutual.

'Oh I can't explain in English what Liverpool Football Club means to me,' says Garcia. 'I keep in touch with my team-mates and I love to get back to Anfield when I can. I always will. When I was up there last, I walked into a bar and the barman immediately asked if I wanted Sangria. I get sent pictures of the Spanish drink sent to me via Twitter all the time. It makes me laugh. I am so pleased that I will be involved with this marvellous place for the rest of my life.'

And for the record, Luis Garcia does drink Sangria but he thinks he is a bit over 5ft 7. 'Closer to 5ft 8,' he says with a laugh. On the Kop, he'll always be a giant.

Dirk Kuyt

2006–2012
Appearances: 285
Goals: 71

AN early spring Sunday afternoon at Anfield. The referee's final whistle fills the afternoon sky like the sweet silver song of a lark, and there is a roar. Manchester United have been beaten with consummate ease. Dirk Kuyt clutches the match ball for he has scored all three Liverpool goals. A hat-trick at Anfield against Manchester United. It doesn't get much better than that.

The Dutchman, the ball under his arm, shakes his opponents' hands. Always the sportsman, he gets those pleasantries out of the way. He takes a few pats on the back and then it happens. The crowd are up on their feet and a wall of sound goes around the ground as the fans applaud what they have seen. Is this it? Is this Kuyt's moment? He's been at the club for five years, he's had acclaim, he's taken plaudits after scoring vital goals but this sounds different. This is after a match-winning hat-trick against Manchester United.

He holds the ball, he looks toward the Kop and then it dawns on him, the din being made isn't for him. It is for Luis Suarez, the Uruguayan who brilliantly set up all three of his goals. Kuyt smiles, applauds the crowd, he applauds Suarez. He gets it. The glorious limelight has never chosen to shine brightly down on him, whatever his efforts. Maybe he likes it that way.

On this occasion, Sir Alex Ferguson's team had been torn apart by Suarez who showed all the attributes that would soon make him feared and adored in this country in equal measure. Chris Smalling and Wes Brown in the centre of United's defence were stretched and contorted by Liverpool's number seven like a bored kid pulling at his bubble gum. Kuyt and the team had benefited from Suarez's efforts and in total, the Dutchman's goals had been scored from around two feet out. He clutched the ball as the crowd applauded another, but he would have smiled. The goals and the ball were enough for him. They always had been.

Dirk Kuyt enjoyed six years at Liverpool. The incident after his hat-trick is a microcosm for his time there. He did great things, he scored goals and he helped win the biggest of games. He wasn't the type that wanted fireworks, chants and hyperbole. And anyway it never came. Fans, team-mates and managers talked of his energy levels and enthusiasm. Rafa Benitez, the man who brought him from The Netherlands to Merseyside, famously described him as the 'Duracell Bunny', a reference to his never stop attitude that belied normal lung capacity.

To some fans, he wasn't deemed quality. It was though a shortsighted attitude. He wasn't Fernando Torres in his pomp at Anfield and he wasn't Steven Gerrard. Without him and his commitment though, neither was he able to charm those fans in the way they did. Wasn't it Bill Shankly who once said, 'Football is like a piano. You need eight men to carry it and three who can play the damn thing.' Kuyt was no mere carrier but he was also not one for a concerto.

He divided opinion at times, but mainly when things were going badly for the team as a whole. Whenever his name popped up in a pub debate, no one could argue about his work-rate. Ah yes, his work-rate. The thing so used to justify his play when things went badly but also used by those who felt their team needed more.

The football fan, especially the modern football fan doesn't think that attributes such as work-rate and commitment to the cause are enough. They should be a prerequisite for multi-millionaire players who get to drive home in a supercar and sleep under Egyptian cotton sheets with a beautiful girlfriend. Night, night.

Fans can't sleep after games. If things go wrong, for some fans work-rate won't cut it. For some his efforts off the ball were used to belittle his work on it. With Torres and Gerrard flying as a twosome up front, Kuyt was asked to play wide right in a 4–3–2–1. Some thought Benitez was shoehorning him into the team but what the Spaniard knew is he had a very modern attacker in Kuyt, one able to adapt and be flexible.

Yes it helped the team but let's not get bogged down with this notion of Kuyt the selfless yes man. Kuyt was a player who understood the game implicitly, he understood a manager's wishes and tactics and he executed them. Brilliantly.

In 2009, Martin Samuel wrote in the *Daily Mail*, 'Kuyt will never have an FA Cup Final named after him like Gerrard or draw comparisons with Pele as [Wayne] Rooney did in Portugal but at the top of his game for Liverpool, pound for pound, he continues to punch his weight against the best of them. He knows what his manager wants and he delivers it without ego or introspection.'

Dirk (pronounced like Derek – a name much used among some fans) Kuyt comes from fishing stock, where egos are as pointless as paper nets. The youngster loved his football but every which way he turned, people doubted him. He played for an amateur team called Quick Boys in Katwijk aan Zee but with the big clubs – PSV Eindhoven, Feyenoord and Ajax – apparently not interested, the never workshy Kuyt began to think of a life on the North Sea, like his father.

It was his dad though who saw something in him and pushed him to keep his ambition about him. Kuyt loved to play, he loved to score and aged 17, a surprise move by professional club Utrecht saw him break into the pro ranks. His life would consist of nets but these were of the goal variety and 51 goals in 160 appearances at Utrecht ensured not only lifetime popularity at the club but the attentions of Feyenoord.

The doubts had always been there but Kuyt just ran, worked, played, scored and with that effort, each hurdle dropped in size. At Quick Boys, with no club coming in, coaches agreed that making their first team would be the best he could hope for. At Utrecht, his coach Mark Wotte agreed he was doing well but decreed that he would, 'Never play for one of the big clubs.'

Wotte wasn't being overly critical. Frans Adelaar, his assistant, first worked with Kuyt when he was only 16 and whilst impressed with the young man's devotion never envisaged a player who would one day score in a Champions League Final or win over 100 caps for Holland.

'He had incredible energy,' says Adelaar. 'The ball control and the technique weren't totally there and he wasn't the quickest but he had good game intelligence. Such was his ability to move around the pitch, he would often take defenders with him, creating space for others.

'At Utrecht we actually played him on the right side of the attack a lot and he was immediately adaptable. He was also very humble. He never talked of bigger and better ambitions. He just wanted to do well the following week. His ambitions were all short term. I think that came from his parents who were also extremely down to earth. They would support him all the time but never put any pressure on him.

'I always thought, he had enough about him to move up a level and one day play for one of Holland's big three clubs (PSV, Ajax or Feyenoord) but that would have been his limit. In my mind and most other coaches at the club. Had you said he would play all those games for Holland and excel at Liverpool, I wouldn't have believed it.

'It was his rate of progress that was deceptive. Dirk never suddenly switched into a player who took your breath away. His progress was slow and steady but it was continuous. Whilst some more gifted players stopped improving, Dirk didn't stop and that has been his secret.'

Feyenoord made their move in 2003. He would be captain two years later and their top scorer on three consecutive occasions. The coach, Bert van Marwijk (his future national team coach and always a huge fan) had argued with his technical director, who thought Kuyt wasn't up to it, and said there would be no chance of a sell-on as this was a young player who still, 'Wasn't good enough to play for one of the top European clubs.'

There was doubt. Every time. But then so were there goals; 71 in 101 games for Feyenoord. Kuyt had simply taken to each task with that customary verve. 'It was how I was brought up,' he said.

'Always to try and do your best and make the best of yourself. My dad started working at 14 and when I was young he would go to sea for a few weeks and only be back for a few days. It was tough but he did it so we could do the things we wanted to do. Play football, buy nice clothes.

'It gives you a good feeling when you work hard for something and you achieve it, and that is the attitude I have always had when it comes to football. Scoring the most goals doesn't worry me, because only if you work together, as a team, can you achieve anything.'

Whilst he was scoring at Feyenoord, Rafa Benitez, the manager at Valencia, had cast his eye toward Holland and liked what he saw. Benitez's Valencia were winning La Liga titles and would win the UEFA Cup and Kuyt was everything Benitez liked in a player. Fully committed to the cause, talented and most importantly willing and able to carry out meticulous instructions.

In August 2006, he would come to Liverpool. Benitez had once again looked to push the club on. He had won the Champions League and then the FA Cup in his first two seasons, but he wanted to push on once more. Cash wasn't as free-flowing as at other clubs, and so a manager had to work on his wits. Craig Bellamy had come in, Peter Crouch was there as was Robbie Fowler enjoying a second spell at the club but the manager wanted more. Benitez liked to talk of net spends and so £9m on a fisherman's son would more than do.

'We've been trying to find a top goalscorer in Europe,' the manager said having secured the signing. 'That's difficult, but we knew Kuyt was one such player. He's been playing well for a long time, and he's someone I'm sure will bring quality to the team. Sometimes you see a top class player who may find it hard to adapt to the Premiership, but in his case he has the work-rate, game intelligence and goalscoring ability to make him succeed in England.

'We needed someone who would be different to Bellamy and Robbie, but maybe similar in a way to Crouch. Kuyt can not only play as a target man, he can play as the second striker, on the right or on the left. For sure, he's not someone we'll use as a winger, but he can play alongside Bellamy, Fowler, Crouch and Luis [Garcia] and give us many options.'

'Not someone we'll use as a winger' might not have been too prophetic but he was right, he would score goals. Fourteen in the first season was a good return for Kuyt. Not the prolific rate seen in his homeland but this was the Premier League.

Kuyt's first goal for the club came in a 3–0 win over Newcastle at Anfield, a night that also saw Xabi Alonso score from his own half. What was it with Kuyt's team-mates? Like bridesmaids walking down the aisle in lingerie they were always upstaging the bride. Kuyt couldn't cut a break when it came to that limelight but he did quietly get on with scoring goals. A fine effort against Chelsea at Anfield in his first January increased the love from the stands, as did the decisive penalty against the same opposition at the same end to send the club to their second Champions League Final in three seasons.

Kuyt played a lot of games against Chelsea. Twenty times. He scored three but in the hugely tactical battles that happened between the two sides in the latter years of the 2000s, Kuyt was always a thorn in their side. If the Londoners arrived with a weakness at centre-half like they did in the league clash in January 2007, Kuyt would exploit doubt with his sheer weight of will. If they were strong in the centre of their defence, Chelsea liked to get their full-backs high up the pitch but rarely did

Ashley Cole enjoy a fruitful time when up against a Kuyt deployed on Liverpool's right.

At the end of his first season, Kuyt found himself starting a Champions League Final. It was a strange night in Athens. Liverpool were far more in control of the game than they had been in Istanbul. Again their opponents were AC Milan but the Italians were often pinned back and relied on two counter-punch goals to take a two-goal lead before Kuyt scored with his head from close range to set up a nervy finish for a team still haunted by events in Turkey's capital.

Kuyt had played as the team's focal point up front. It was a case though of right formation, wrong personnel. The 4–3–2–1 Benitez played was his ideal but Kuyt lacked the mobility and movement to stretch the wily old foxes in the Milan back four.

Benitez would have liked to have played Kuyt right in the forward three. There he could have faced the play, pestered Paolo Maldini at left-back and used that work ethic to support Gerrard and another striker. The manager came home a frustrated man. Liverpool had new owners in Tom Hicks and George Gillett, and Benitez, refusing to sit back and enjoy another experience in the final bemoaned the coffers and went public with what he saw as the necessities of buying big, especially up front. Fernando Torres was on his way.

It dawned on many fans that the free-scoring striker Liverpool had snatched from the Eredivisie was not going to be a fruitful centre-forward at Anfield; and such was the speed in which Torres hit the ground running, the Dutchman got lost in the Spaniard's blaze of glory.

Kuyt's second season at Anfield was to be a hard one. His dear father died from cancer. Dirk senior had been vital to Kuyt. He had pushed him, supported him and shared in each of those leaps he had made over his doubters.

When Kuyt made his debut for Liverpool, his dad had ensured vital surgery on his lungs was delayed by a few days so he could visit his son, and award him his Dutch Player of the Year award from the previous campaign.

The event was televised in Holland. Kuyt's father had a surgical tube in his nose. Kuyt was close to tears. They both were. It was a heartfelt moment, unstaged and very real. That seemed to sum up this most un-modern of footballers. He cared little for fads or for blingy fashions. There was something very human about Dirk Kuyt. It was a hard time. Kuyt played of course but it wasn't easy.

'Rafa was very supportive,' Kuyt said later. 'Even when I was having problems after my father died he told me he still believed in me. Everyone at the club was very supportive at that time. Everyone in the city too.' Benitez believed in him. Not many people, other than his dad, had said those words and now Kuyt was in a city that had taken to his eagerness to impress.

He only managed three Premier League goals though that season and whilst he scored big goals in the Champions League against Porto, Marseilles, Inter Milan (the winner in a tight game at Anfield), Arsenal and Chelsea, Kuyt's displays were more about graft than goals. He did though have a fine day at Goodison. Something that will always please those watching you draped in red and harbouring dreams of greatness.

Liverpool had gone in at half-time a goal down but in what was a fraught and angry second half, Kuyt equalised from the spot shortly before the hour mark. Everton's Tony Hibbert had been sent off for his part in that penalty and Kuyt himself might have been in the Goodison dressing rooms early after a two-footed challenge on Phil Neville. It's a great photo. Kuyt looks like a crazed eagle landing on a done-for rabbit but he stayed on and in the last minute, Liverpool won another penalty and once again he coolly knocked it in.

Gerrard had been substituted late on by Benitez, for what the Spaniard cited as, 'trying too hard'. What he meant was that he feared his skipper might get a red card himself but it was Kuyt, that player who could never try too hard who won the spoils.

Another fine moment for Kuyt came almost a year later at Manchester City. Liverpool had gone two goals down at half-time and when Torres pulled the team back with two efforts in the second period, it seemed the new hero had done enough to ensure a job well done. Kuyt added a late one again to change the mood from mediocrity to bedlam.

Kuyt grabbed the goal and went ballistic with the fans. His shock of blonde hair lost in a sea of arms, torsos and smiles. Kuyt did that a lot. When it mattered, he could unsettle defenders. By now he was very much the right-sided attacker in the 4–3–2–1 but with those instincts from his days at centre-forward still firing and the energy to move from touchline to infield, he was a potent threat.

Kuyt scored 15 goals during the 2008/09 season. Liverpool got as close as they had to winning the league in a very long time, playing the kind of exciting and flowing football that will put four past Real Madrid and then Manchester United in as many days.

'I'm proud to be part of a great team playing some great football,' Kuyt told the press at the time. 'Some strikers might not like to see someone like Fernando Torres coming in and scoring so many goals. But I'm proud to be playing alongside him, and proud to be playing with Stevie too. If I do have qualities, one of them is my ability to play in different positions and I am happy with the contribution I am making. Coaches used to tell me not to run so much. That if I saved myself I would have more power to score goals. But I want to win the game, and to win you have to work. I like to run and I like to play as much as I can. The more I play, the stronger I feel.' There were those shortcomings. Work alone wouldn't cut it. Fans would often – when a game was being lost – bemoan his touch. Too heavy at times, his touch could fail him and the team, but never did he then shirk from showing for it in games, whatever the unrest from the stands around him. The boo-boys at football are thought of as a modern trait. That is wrong.

Liverpool in the 1950s got plenty of stick. Jimmy Melia was called a 'cheeky bastard' for taking a penalty when Billy Liddell was on the field. Ray Kennedy, a three-time European Cup winner, suffered plenty of abuse from a Kemlyn Road individual who mistook his languid style for sheer, bloody bone-idleness. No, the modern footballer might have to put up with Twitter trolls but footballers have long had to deal with them face to face.

Kuyt had the opposite problem to Kennedy. Picky fans thought him too busy, too heads down. 'Can someone please explain to me exactly what Kuyt is supposed to bring to our side,' wrote one irate fan to the BBC football forum, 606. 'Is he really comparable to the likes of [Carlos] Tevez, [Robin] van Persie, [Salomon] Kalou who are all currently playing second fiddle to the respective other goal scorer at their clubs?'

It missed the point of course. Gerrard was second fiddle to Torres at the time; Kuyt was asked to do a shift, work for the team, stop attacks and start them. To criticise Kuyt for doing what he was asked to do was like having a go at a milkman as you sipped your tea.

During his first season, one fan wrote to the *Liverpool Echo* saying Kuyt might, 'One day be as good as Kenny Dalglish'. Wishful thinking maybe but for every boo-boy there were plenty of fans buoyed by what he did in red.

'Though it is true to say that he might not be as technically gifted as his illustrious countrymen and has the change of pace of Neil Ruddock in chain-mail underpants, unless you also acknowledge that he offers a prodigious work-rate, positional intelligence and the embodiment of the team ethos then your outlook is unfairly skewed,' wrote Neil Scott on the fan website, The Anfield Wrap.

'Kuyt's importance is only emphasised by his adaptability, his capacity for operating in a range of roles and systems. We have seen him effectively fill a number of positions, from lone front-man to nominal right winger to supporting attacker to compact midfielder, depending on the formation and tactics employed.

'Both on and off the pitch he conducts himself with a degree of humility, selflessness and professionalism that acts as a shining example to any aspiring young talent. In many ways he is the modern-day epitome of that sometimes overused cliché – "a real Shankly player."'

It is an interesting point. Bill Shankly loved flair, especially in his wide men. He grew up with Tom Finney, he quietly adored George Best and in Peter Thompson and then Steve Heighway he had left-wingers who were more trick than track-back. He would have liked Kuyt though. Like Ian Callaghan, Kuyt offered balance and industry. He didn't have Callaghan's pace or ability to beat a man but he did embody the socialism in life and football that the manager so cherished.

In the seasons post-Rafa Benitez, Kuyt arguably played his best football for Liverpool. It was as if he took on the club's woes during the Hicks/Gillett/Hodgson debacle and decided to work even harder for a beleaguered club's cause.

He scored 13 league goals in the 2010/11 season, his best return. Dalglish had replaced Roy Hodgson in the January and under the prodigal son, Kuyt played some great stuff, scoring in five consecutive Premier League games in the spring. His big moment though was at Wembley a year later.

Liverpool fans made their first visit to the stadium since 1996 but found a resolute Cardiff City put up a huge Welsh fight, taking the game to extra time. Kuyt came on as a substitute that day and like a vitamin shot, the Dutchman gave the team the energy they had so lacked on the big pitch.

Kuyt set about the Cardiff defence like a man possessed. A killer of giant-killers if you will. He scored a fine goal that looked to have made him the hero but once again, as ever, that limelight decided to ignore him when the Championship side equalised in the last two minutes. He did of course score his penalty and won his first and only trophy for the club.

Kuyt left that summer. Brendan Rodgers came in as manager and ushered in a new system and new players.

'I had a great time,' he said on leaving. 'I had great team-mates. The club was great, the people were great and the people from Liverpool – the text messages, the phone calls, the emails, all the tweets I had on my Twitter account – it's unbelievable how much respect they showed me and it's also a bit emotional.'

Those fans who got what Kuyt brought to their team would have been fairly emotional themselves when watching him perform for Holland at the 2014 World Cup in Brazil. In one game he played at right wing-back, right-back and centre-forward. He had once said to Benitez at Liverpool when an injury struck that he could happily play at right-back and of course he could. He has played over 100 times for Holland. You have to be good to do that.

Even Johan Cruyff, that keeper of the beautiful game's good name, has announced his love for Kuyt. You can imagine in football heaven that at the gates, judging those who wish to get in, is Cruyff. No matter, he is a fan. 'Someone like that is worth his weight in gold,' St Johan said recently.

Kuyt had gone to Turkey. Many fans won't have noticed his absence, especially in the heady, free-flowing days of Rodgers's poetry in motion. Some though with longer memories will think of Dirk Kuyt and they will smile. The big goals against the biggest of teams in the biggest of games is one thing, the passion and the commitment that would have seen him sell programmes had it have helped the team is another. Good old Derek.

Luis Suarez

2011–2014
Appearances: 133
Goals: 82

IT happened at an unglamorous location during an unglamorous moment in what turned out to be his penultimate match for Liverpool Football Club. Luis Suarez, playing in south-east London at Crystal Palace, it's the 55th minute. His back to goal, he receives the ball, he tries a dummy, it fails but he has already turned and the ricochet off his marker's shins lands perfectly at his toes and he's away.

He slips it to Raheem Sterling who repays the favour and with his left foot he knocks the ball past the Palace keeper. 3–0 to Liverpool. And then it happens. Liverpool fans, since his arrival at Anfield in January 2011, had had plenty of examples of what it was about this most mesmeric, bizarre, brilliant and bewitching of footballers they had fallen in love with. His actions on the ball were rich and varied, too many to choose. 'I just can't get enough,' they used to sing.

But then without a football at his feet, it happened. The reason why as a Liverpool fan, this man had captured your heart and your imagination. At 3–0 he didn't celebrate, he ran into the goal, picked the ball out of the net and ran back to the centre-circle. 3–0 to Liverpool and he wants more.

If anyone wonders how Luis Suarez – this candidate for all-time Liverpool greatness – can be a cult, the answer lays, not in some sort of siege mentality where fans wanted to rage against the machine that very audibly criticised Suarez during his time in Liverpool, but in this brazen display of crazed hunger for more.

Suarez played for Liverpool on the edge. Everything he did at Anfield, good or bad, was the product of his game walking on the thinnest of precipices. Two defenders offering you only the byline, doing their job, shepherding you seemingly into a cul-de-sac? Get your head down and aggressively and equally as purposefully as your markers, drive toward that line and use that tiny space to your advantage.

Mind and body are trying to work together and often they so beautifully do. Sometimes they don't. The game is going against you and a more than competent defender is shackling you with strength and guile? Get in close and bite his arm. Life on the edge. Genius, madness, fine lines and all that.

A fan can buy into that. Watching a player who week in and week out never fails to shock, surprise and beguile can be addictive. 'I just can't get enough'. Greatness is one thing but not everything. Fans of all generations at Anfield have seen greatness and fallen in love with it. There was a time when it was even taken for granted. Suarez brought something different. An edge and a desire that fascinated supporters because maybe, just maybe, it bettered even theirs.

'Even in the warm-up,' Suarez said during the 2013/14 season (his last), 'when I practise my shooting I can hear the fans going, "oof" if I score a good goal. It's a great feeling.' There's something about Suarez, something that makes a fan forget about the match, the points, the cup tie. It's a warm-up. 'Oof.' It's madness at times, but it's pure madness.

Neil Atkinson, the erudite presenter of fans' podcast, The Anfield Wrap recalls that moment at Crystal Palace and gasps. 'He got the ball out of the net. At 3–0. That for me is the greatest thing, the most astonishing thing anyone has ever done on a football pitch and defines Brendan Rodgers's football team. He scores, we go 3–0 up and there he is, getting the ball and acting like we're three down, like he's just pulled one back. Who does that?

'In 2012, Manchester United lost the Premier League title to Manchester City on goal difference. It was a tight affair. City won the league by a difference of around eight goals. Not once during the last few games did Sir Alex Ferguson – this most attacking and brave of managers apparently – ever address that and neither did his players, none of them went gung-ho. They were too sane. Suarez was mad, he wanted more; he wanted to address the goal difference thing. Suarez scored a third and believed – genuinely believed – we could score eight. No one in the history of football ever thinks that. He did. How can you not buy into that?

'Suarez is a cult, not because of how well he does things, but what he tries to do. Raheem Sterling, in my opinion, if he stays at the club a long time could easily be the greatest player we have ever had. He's that good. He will never be a cult though. Suarez is because he tries things and does things that defy logic. If a player did one of the things in his career at Liverpool that Suarez tries he might be a cult. Suarez has done eight or nine or ten. He is quintessentially astonishing.'

Getting the ball from the net at Palace takes fans back. Back to a summer's evening. You've been playing for hours with mates and you're losing 22–21. The sun is going down and the first faint call from a mum to come in; dinners are ready. You ignore it. It will go away. Your pace quickens, your actions more decisive. It's not pretty but you want more, you must score more. You can't go in having lost. Suarez is that young player ignoring a mother's call to dinner.

Because of it all, Atkinson suggests that Suarez is in fact the best player in the world to watch. He's not necessarily the best player in the world. Cristiano Ronaldo and Lionel Messi have a say there, but neither of them is better to watch than the Uruguayan. 'He's not at Messi's level,' says Atkinson. 'He's scruffier but I know who I'd rather watch. Suarez plays for ricochets. He plays for ricochets. What a maniac.'

Liverpool's most (in)famous maniac was born in Salto, Uruguay's second city, built on the banks of the River Uruguay on the border with Argentina. One of seven children, the Suarez clan moved to the capital, Montevideo where he started to play for a club called Urreta. 'A lot of people were talking about this club where there were a lot people with money so I took him there,' his mother has said. 'They were losing 2–0 so they put Luis on, he scored three to make it 3–2.'

Those in the Uruguayan know, knew about this bright young footballer but Suarez quit football as a boy after his father and mother split, being enticed back by the coaches at pro club Nacional. Rumours of his drinking habits and distractive desires to party were rife. At 15 he met a 13-year-old girl, Sofia. 'I found a girlfriend and that sorted my head out,' Suarez said recently. Today Sofia is his wife.

His focus returned but not for long. Sofia had to leave, ironically for Barcelona where her family had relocated. Once again he withdrew from football's clutches but once again – perhaps driven to one day get to Barcelona himself – he knuckled down. 'What matters is that I realised in time that I had to dedicate myself to this beautiful sport.' From there Suarez was the driven man who would so enthral a set of fans 7,000 miles away. In one game for Nacional, their opponents had been beaten 3–0. In the showers afterwards, Luis Suarez cried. He hadn't scored.

'He was very temperamental,' said Ricardo Perdomo, his manager at Nacional. 'Whenever things were not the way he wanted he used to cry, was embittered and suffered a lot. But this is something common in Uruguay and all Latin America; we are completely immersed in football and when something doesn't happen as we would wish, there's a lot of frustration. What I emphasise more about Luis is his appetite whenever he stepped onto the pitch. He didn't care about anything else. That's what I most remember of him: the way he lived for football.'

Ten goals in 27 games in Uruguay and Dutch club, Groningen, in the country scouting someone else, spotted the young man and spent £670,000 (more than this modest club had ever spent) to bring him home with them. It was 2006, Suarez was 19, but his career had started. Europe was the place to conquer. Sofia had made it, now he would too.

One season at Groningen was enough. The fans at the club still idolise him but Ajax had seen enough. He'd scored ten goals in 29 games and in 2007 was among the footballing hotbed that is Ajax of Amsterdam. He wasn't one to stand still and admire pictures on the wall though. There was, after all, a goal rate to get started on. 81 in 110 league games at the club had curtains twitching all over Europe. The 2010 World Cup in South Africa outlined his footballing ability and of course, the edge, the precipice on which he must play. A move to one of the bigger leagues in Europe was imminent.

Liverpool were going through hell at the time. Hicks and Gillett had brought their fire and brimstone and with Roy Hodgson as manager, the team were struggling, not only to win football matches but also to find their identity. Hodgson had been told about Suarez's availability and a tentative offer made. It wasn't enough. With new owners in place as well as a new (caretaker) manager in Kenny Dalglish, that offer was upped and Luis Suarez was a Liverpool footballer.

Not that there was a huge fanfare. Not for Suarez anyway. The last day of a transfer window in England and hyperbole reigns. The story on this occasion on 31 January was Fernando Torres. The Spaniard had been sold to Chelsea from Liverpool for a record, £50 million. Liverpool had acted swiftly to replace him, a move that shook the game in England. No, it wasn't the signing of Suarez; it was Newcastle's young forward, Andy Carroll. Liverpool invested £35 million of Roman

Abramovich's money on him, and that was whose face adorned 1 February's back pages.

Suarez, this most noticeable and heart-wrenchingly watchable of footballers, actually came to Anfield through the back door. The press men and the photographers who would one day sit and report, capture and judge every move he made, hardly flinched as he finalised his £22.8 million move to the Premier League.

Liverpool's players noticed him though. Jamie Carragher, along with Steven Gerrard, the faces in the dressing room at Melwood might have wondered about the last-minute revolving door but it took just one glance at Suarez undressing to know the right move had been made. 'I could tell he was a good player as soon as he walked in,' recalls Carragher. 'You could tell by just looking at his legs. Massive they were. He's got proper, big footballer's legs. The way he moves, the way he walks. Jesus listen to me. I'd be asking players to take their jeans off if I was a manager.'

That last half of the season and the fans also knew. Knew that this was someone special. He destroyed Manchester United at Anfield. He span their defenders around and he turned supporters' eyes seemingly inside out so that fans thought they were looking at their own dreams.

At Fulham he was part of a brilliant team performance, his world-class presence galvanising those around him in a 5–2 win. Soon that influence on young players around him would raise the bar to possible title-winning levels but for now, the entrée had been served. 'I just can't get enough.'

There were problems though. Big problems. That was maybe to be expected. Anyone who read the small print on the brochure when they bought Suarez could have predicted that. The Dutch FA had come down on him not long before his move for biting PSV Eindhoven's Otman Bakkal.

Liverpool weren't in the market for a saint though. The goalscoring record enticed them not the criminal one. For the first several months, Suarez proved himself tricky. Tricky to defend against and tricky to gauge. What might be his next move? Pundits talked of a street style of football that verged on the side of dangerous.

And then in October 2011, after a tense game against Manchester United, Patrick Evra accused the striker of racially abusing him during a 1–1 draw. The FA charged Suarez and a panel would find him guilty.

He would serve an eight-match ban. The fall-out from the whole affair was messy and at times downright ugly.

Those fighting racism in the game were of course appalled at what had happened at Anfield. The problem had not gone away, racism was still rife in football and those thinking that it was from an age-old time were wrong. Weeks later the former England captain John Terry was accused of a similar charge. Suarez was part of the problem.

He had rowed with Evra and words were exchanged. Then though, things got blurry. Liverpool fans who rallied against the FA's decision to find Suarez guilty and to ban him, were accused of merely standing by their star man, a simplistic accusation that mistook a mistrust of the system for footballing bias.

Sure there was some who just wanted the star striker to play, but many fans looked at the panel's report, read around the incident and felt uneasy about the outcome.

'My issue is, if there is reasonable doubt, he doesn't get convicted,' says Neil Atkinson. 'I completely understand why football wants to work in a tribunal sense and on the balance of probabilities, but when it can result in people being tarred as racists, then I have issues with that. It's too loose. It seemed to be one person's word against the other and you start to think that it was Manchester United who were much more organised and Liverpool went about it like it was a court of law, which was a profound mistake and a misreading of the situation.

'In an employment tribunal one of the main things you are trying to bring about is the idea that both parties can walk away and feel that the outcome was fair. Suarez clearly fucking didn't.

'He might have said it and he might have said it in a disparaging way and if he did then he's completely out of order. There has been a lot written about culture and race in South America that can explain it far better than I could and in all fairness to Evra, people had to take into account how difficult it had been to be a black Frenchman. What should have happened is, if Evra's offended then the club must immediately err on the side of the fact that the offence has been caused, and deal with it quickly.'

Liverpool Football Club were caught in the headlights. They went into defensive mode, they stood by their man, which is fine, but in hindsight the bunker routine – 'us against the world' – was a mistake. The PR blunders at the club stemmed from Kenny Dalglish up. 'It went on and on,' says Atkinson, alluding to the occasion when Liverpool went to Old Trafford for the return fixture and Suarez came face to face with Evra. A handshake was not forthcoming. Cue more public disgust. 'Suarez should never, ever have been asked to start that game at Old Trafford when the handshake incident happened.

'People use that to slaughter Suarez and say he did for Kenny, but it is much more complicated than that. Look at it back, it is not clear Evra was going to shake his hand, it could go either way. Evra has every right not to shake his hand but in my opinion, Suarez should not have been starting there. Just bring him on at half-time.

'The other side of that was when Evra was running around the pitch after a later win and is in Suarez's face and I think the Uruguayan's reaction to that, or lack of reaction spoke volumes. Then in 2014 when Suarez scores a third goal for Liverpool, there is no glorification, it wouldn't have occurred to him to, it had gone in his head. It's not about Suarez; it's about winning the football match. He could have got in Evra's or the fans' faces but he didn't.'

What was hard for many fans, whether they agreed with the ban or not, was the reaction. 'RACIST' was the back page splash in the *Daily Mirror*. The panel and Evra had both said they didn't believe Suarez to be a racist and he has passionately argued he isn't but there it was, the cast had been set and Suarez, well Suarez was the football's public enemy number one. 'Luis Suarez, you know what you are.'

Suarez was adamant about his involvement in the Evra case. He kept counsel but felt wronged. Evra did too of course and it is unclear exactly what happened that day but that lack of clarity wasn't taken into account when he was immediately labelled a racist. 'I was very calm with all the Evra stuff because a lot of things were written about me that I knew were false,' Suarez later said.

'I was accused of something without any evidence. I was suspended without evidence, too. I know I'm not, nor ever have been a racist and I said nothing racist to him or any other footballer. Ask anybody who I've ever played football with. My conscience is clear, and will be for the rest of my life. Anybody who knows me at all knows I'm no racist. That's the most important thing for me: that my family, friends and team-mates know who I am.'

And then came the bite. Suarez had enjoyed a great 2012/13 season, but at the end of it, something clicked, he fell from his precipice. Chelsea were the opponents at Anfield. Suarez was being tightly kept at bay by the Chelsea rearguard. Liverpool were losing, he gets in close with

Branislav Ivanovic who blocks his progress well and it happens. He has fallen from that cliff and once again the nation is disgusted and bans are served.

'I have no problem with the biting,' says Atkinson. Other fans would agree. Yes it's ugly, yes its primitive and yes the role-model question rears its head. Kids won't bite people if they see Suarez do it. Something has to already be there to make someone bite an opponent. Something primitive. Ask him and he couldn't tell you why but it seems related to the jaw-droppingly brilliant things he does. Something clicks, he nutmegs two defenders. Something clicks, he bites. 'Luis Suarez, you know what you are.'

But the fans' affection for Suarez doesn't stem from some sense of protecting their own. The nation's pantomime villain served his ban and came back to enthral that same nation. Pantomime villain? 'He's behind you!' He played with a style not seen before, a menace that would see him use his whole body, all his wits, every ounce of skill he could muster. Between two whistles – one starting and one finishing a football match – nothing else mattered. For those wondering how Liverpool fans could idolise the man, try watching that for 90 minutes, try seeing a player do that for your team.

'I think that every defender in England hates playing against him,' said Arsenal manager Arsene Wenger, keen to buy him in 2013 but not keen enough. 'He has a strong, provocative personality. From the information I gathered on him it appears that on a day-to-day level he is really easy to work with. Also that he's respectful, he loves training, he's an angel. He turns into a demon when he's on the pitch. We all dream about having players like that.'

Fans dream of supporting them. Suarez came up, seemingly on the spot, with new ways of beating defenders, of using their weaknesses against them. He had pick-pocketed Everton at Wembley in April 2012 in the FA Cup semi-final, anticipating Sylvain Distin's error before equalising with the outside of his right foot. 'He did that scarily well,' says Atkinson. 'It's not about taking a gamble. There is some piece of information he computes and he is off, knowing a player will make a mistake. He does that loads. He did it at Stoke in the 2013/14 season and he did it at Cardiff too. He did it against England in the 2014 World Cup for his second goal. He finds new ways to be better. He can implicitly trust his own touch and his ability so it is as if he needs to work out other ways to be better.

'It's like when he wins penalties. Winning penalties is a thing whatever people say and he found new ways to do just that. He did it at Manchester United and West Ham. He would get the ball in the box, a defender wouldn't want to stop him, so he could stand them up and then he could pop the ball up and give his marker options. Let him by with no foul and no penalty; they could handball it, or they could foul him. Who pops the ball up in the box? It's incredible. It's like Shane Warne looking for an lbw.'

'Luis Suarez, you know what you are.' It's not clear that he does. On the pitch anyway. This is a player who with his team 2–0 up away from home at Southampton and in the last 15 minutes, is fouled but seeks retribution by using his head to tackle the perpetrator. He is on the floor and bang; the head goes into a defender's knee. 'That was brilliant,' laughs Atkinson. 'That clip should be used as evidence whenever he does something wrong as mitigating evidence. "Yes your honour, he did bite someone again, but this is a guy who also trips people up with his head." He is astonishing.'

Having come back from the biting ban in the autumn of 2013, Suarez played the best football of his career. The best football (some would argue) the club has ever seen. Liverpool had started the season well, Daniel Sturridge was scoring, games were being won, but like the countdown at a rocket launch, the return of the team's number seven symbolised the ignition that sent Brendan Rodgers's plans to new unexplored heights.

That autumn was Suarez's zenith in red. He scored two on his league return at Sunderland, he got three against West Bromwich Albion (an incredible display of the striking arts with both foot and head), he got two against Fulham, another two against West Ham and he got four against Norwich. It says a lot when the least memorable goal is a wonderfully crafted free kick, but when others include a looping effort from 40 yards and a piece of skill that turns defenders into jelly followed by a sublime strike past an England goalkeeper, you know you are witnessing something special.

In the December, Liverpool went to Tottenham. Steven Gerrard was injured and so Suarez was given the armband. Something happened that day. Raheem Sterling became the world-beater fans believe he will be, Jordan Henderson the combative midfielder now so admired. Liverpool won 5–0. Suarez scored twice – brilliant both of them – but it seemed to be the day the team was galvanised by him. They hunted in packs behind him, they played off him but they didn't rely on him. Leaving North London they now believed that they were something special.

'I'd never imagined myself as Liverpool skipper,' Suarez later said. 'After everything that happened with me, to retain the support of the club, the coach and my team-mates showed me they were happy to forget and forgive. Being Liverpool captain is something that validates you and makes you feel appreciated, because there have been some fantastic leaders here.'

As the season wore on – whilst the boo-boys around the country would never fully extinguish their dislike for their tormentor in chief – attitudes mellowed.

There was no doubt that people had got themselves very much in a twist about Suarez. In January 2013, he scored a goal at Mansfield Town in the FA Cup. The ball had been blasted at him and his arm controlled the ball. The goal was given. Uproar. He's a cheat and a disgrace. He kissed his wrist in celebration. He's a smug cheat and a smug disgrace. How dare he kiss his hand, as if in mocking glee over the crime he had got away with. He in fact kissed his wrist after every goal for there you'll find a tattoo with his daughter's name on it. Things were slightly out of hand.

By the spring of 2014; personal awards – the PFA and the Football Writers' – were won and there was even sympathy in some quarters when he cried following the draw at Crystal Palace that all but ended the team's very real title hopes.

Liverpool fans didn't feel vindicated. The uproar and the hate would soon return after the World Cup when once again he bit an opponent and anyway, fans didn't want to take away too much of that bile against him for he thrived on it. The villain was part of who he was. When he was sent off in the 2010 World Cup for a blatant handball in the quarter-finals against Ghana, his face as the referee approached him brandishing the red card, was one of incredulity. 'Me?' his eyes screamed. 'He knew it was him, but there was a 0.1 per cent chance that the referee might not,' said his team-mate Diego Forlan. 'He took that chance. I realise not everyone agrees with that attitude, but to us in Uruguay, he's a hero.'

It is thought that in England a fan loves a trier. Foreign football fans might mock the public here for cheering perhaps even more heartily for a player who sprints 30 yards to make a sliding tackle than the player who waits and waits and then beats two men with a trick and gets his shot away. Luis Suarez mixed the two. He hated to lose, he only wanted to play. If there is football to be played and goals to be scored, he had to be there. Managers would substitute him if he had scored a hat-trick and the game was won as way of reward, so that he could milk the crowd's adulation. Suarez's face at such an act of treachery spoke of a man not interested. How long is left? Let me play. Again, it is the kid who ignores a mother's cries that dinner is ready and the game must end.

He works and works in training. People at Melwood tell stories of him keeping the goalkeeper out in the rain so he can go again and again at free kicks. It's a dedication to his art that has seen him able to – as one admirer has put it – 'nutmeg a mermaid'.

Ah yes, the nutmeg. From primal days on the playground, putting the ball through an opponent's legs has long been regarded as a footballing slap. For Suarez it is simply a way of better getting to where you need to be; in front of goal. '[Nutmegs] are nothing personal,' Suarez has said. 'It's all instinct. A lot of defenders know what I'm going to do now, so they try to protect themselves. But I do it anyway.' There it is. Not logical, but he does it anyway.

Suarez signed for Barcelona in the summer of 2014. Maybe the bite in Brazil made it impossible for him to return to a nation largely disgusted by his actions. Maybe La Liga was too big a draw for this fiercely Latin footballer. For Liverpool fans, sitting and discussing his moments, good and bad, there is only melancholy that he no longer lights up their matchgoing experience. He was there, now he isn't.

His daughter, born in Holland and named before he came to Liverpool is called Delfina, an anagram of Anfield. Coincidence of course, but it all adds to what is surely the most bonkers tenure a Liverpool player has ever given the club. Nutmegs, 40 yard goals, FA panels and that desire to just play more and score more.

It's hard which one to dwell on but let's go back to that mad night at Crystal Palace. Neil Atkinson puts it best when summing up Suarez's time at Liverpool. 'He got the fucking ball out of the net.'

Bibliography

Aughton, Peter. Liverpool: A People's History, 2008

Aldridge, John. John Aldridge: My Story, Hodder & Stoughton 1999

Benitez, Rafa. Champions League Dreams, Headline 2012

Carragher, Jamie. Carra: My Autobiography, Bantam 2008

Cormack, Peter. From The Cowshed To The Kop, Black & White 2012

Dalglish, Kenny. Dalglish: My Autobiography, 1996

Dalglish, Kenny. The Liverpool Year, Collins Willow 1988

Etherington, Peter. One Boy And His Kop, self-published 2001

Evans, Tony. I Don't Know What It Is But I Love It, Penguin/Viking 2014

Fagan, Andrew & Mark Platt. Joe Fagan: Reluctant Hero, Aurum 2011

Fowler, Robbie. Fowler: My Autobiography, Pan 2005

Gerrard, Steven. Gerrard: My Autobiography, Bantam 2007

Hamann, Dietmar. The Didi Man: A Love Affair With Liverpool, Headline 2012

Hansen, Alan. A Matter Of Opinion, Patridge 1999

Hughes, Simon. Red Machine: Liverpool FC In The 1980s. Mainstream 2013

Jones, Joey. Oh Joey Joey, John Blake 2001

Keith, John. Bob Paisley: Manager Of The Millennium, Robson 2001

Keith, John. Billy Liddell, The Legend Who Carried The Kop, Robson 2003

Lees, Dr Andrew & Ray Kennedy. Ray Of Hope: The Ray Kennedy Story, Penguin 1993

Lawson, Hedley. Elisha Scott's Diaries and Press Cuttings, His Life Story, self published 2012

BIBLIOGRAPHY

Platt, Mark & Shaw, Gary. At The End Of The Storm, self published 2009

Shankly, Bill. Shankly: My Story, Sport Media 2009 Edition

St John, Ian. The Saint, Hodder & Stoughton 2005

Thompson, Phil. Emlyn Hughes: A Tribute to Crazy Horse, Stadia 2006

Williams, John. Red Men, Mainstream 2011

Wilson, Jonathan. Inverting The Pyramid, Orion 2010

Wilson, Jonathan with Murray, Scott. The Anatomy of Liverpool, Orion 2013